STUDIES IN PUBLIC LAW AND THE RETAIL SECTOR

Studies in Public Law and the Retail Sector

ANN ROSEMARIE EVERTON
Department of the Built Environment,
University of Central Lancashire

DAVID HUGHES
Environmental Law Institute,
De Montfort University, Leicester

Routledge
Taylor & Francis Group
LONDON AND NEW YORK

First published 2000 by Dartmouth Publishing Company and Ashgate Publishing

Reissued 2018 by Routledge
2 Park Square, Milton Park, Abingdon, Oxon OX14 4RN
711 Third Avenue, New York, NY 10017, USA

Routledge is an imprint of the Taylor & Francis Group, an informa business

A Library of Congress record exists under LC control number: 99069525

ISBN 13: 978-1-138-70357-5 (hbk)
ISBN 13: 978-1-138-70353-7 (pbk)
ISBN 13: 978-1-315-20310-2 (ebk)

Contents

Acknowledgements

In the pursuit of this venture, we have received with appreciation helpful guidance and assistance from many, including Dr Martin Howe (formerly Director of Competition Policy, Office of Fair Trading); Dr Ross L. Davies (Director, Oxford Institute of Retail Management); Mr Malcolm Ross; Jean Monnet Senior Lecturer, Faculty of Law, Leicester University; Miss Tina Ranalescotos (a Pupil Barrister), and a number of friends in the food industry.

We are grateful, too, for the valuable contributions to the preparation of the work made by Mrs S. Smith, Librarian, Leicester University; Mr Maurice Everton; Mrs Barbara Goodman, and members of the staff of Ashgate.

Introduction

'History is from day to day, and nothing in our national life has been more daily than keeping shop and going shopping'.[1] That shopping is an integral part of life, and has been so for centuries, cannot be denied, whether we happily espouse the view of England taken by Smith as '...a nation of shopkeepers'[2] or, by contrast, join Chesterton in shunning '...the awful shop'.[3] More prosaically, it has been observed that '...the vast majority of the population is involved in some direct or indirect way with shopping activities...',[4] shopping being necessary to obtain the great majority of requisite goods and services, and the '...concept of shopping as an increasingly leisure based activity [having] gained widespread acceptance as an important element of popular culture'.[5]

During the early post-war decades changes in retailing appeared which increased in pace and scope until, in the '80s, they assumed such proportions as to attract the title 'retail revolution'. From the '50s, when the food retailers took their first steps along the supermarket path, the UK shopping scene became one of continuing and accelerating transformation.[6] Spectacular for their vigour, and under the spotlight of close media attention, supermarkets, superstores, hypermarkets, retail warehouses, megastores and out of town shopping centres began to emerge as citadels to a creative, commercial vision.[7] Whither the United States, so too the United Kingdom.

Conditions which led to and inspired the development of new shopping forms were many, varied and intertwined: legal, social, commercial, economic and environmental. Not only of course did they lead and inspire, they were in their turn consequent upon and inspired by the development in question. Further, if any of the groups of strands in the skein were taken in isolation they were in themselves multicoloured and complex. Very much was this the case with the legal strands. Amongst the legal strands, however, two predominated as determinants and governors of modern shopping development. These were, respectively, competition law and planning law.

Though fundamentally disassociated one from the other, in conjunction, the nature, pattern and, above all, guiding philosophy of these two areas of public law provided an atmosphere conducive to the emergence of new shopping forms. It was not, moreover, a matter merely of the character of two legal arenas providing an environment which was non-hostile to novel retail establishments. On the contrary, they were positively accommodating, to the extent indeed that they at once encouraged and promoted the development.

With the development of the new shopping forms in full spate, the present authors published *Public Law and the Retail Sector*.[8] The purpose of that volume was to explore, in turn, these two major contributors to the favourable legal climate, and its aim to show and explain the many ways in which they served to foster the so-called 'revolution'.

In the years following publication, consumers' enthusiasm for the new shopping forms has continued unabated, and vast, crowded car-parks have reflected the enthusiasm of a society 'voting with its wheels'. But this testimony of affection is only one aspect of what has proved for the sector a period of themes as multi-faceted as any of its predecessors. In its progress through the '90s, retailing has been shaped by divers issues and influences. To those, for instance, of a deep recession, the burgeoning of information technology, concerns for the environment, and a widespread urge to 'de-regulate', have been added shifts in public lifestyle, spending power and behaviour, even a shift in public opinion so great as to lead to a landslide Labour victory in May 1997. For many, the consequential pressures would be undue, but the retailer's hallmark lies in his ability to adapt to change, and many have not only survived but greatly prospered.

Now, with over a decade since our earlier publication having passed, the retail scene still vividly painted, and in particular, the vigour of the 'in or out of town' debate undiminished,[9] we thought it time to revisit the relationship between retailing and planning and competition policy. In so doing, we shall look again at that coincidental convergence of policies which helped to fuel the retail revolution. Here we shall discover that while competition law has continued to foster the ever-onward march of the large new retail format, planning control has faltered in its accommodating approach, and this because the two systems have been required to dance to different tunes, the former to the simple and unswerving air of 'pro-free competition', but the latter to a more complex melody embracing the needs of conservation, 'sustainable development' and urban regeneration.

In addition, however, to dealing with the direct interaction of planning and competition policy, we shall consider also matters arising in both arenas which, though lacking such direct interaction, nevertheless require our attention. Thus, to take but a couple of instances, the significant subject of 'planning gain' calls for treatment in the planning arena,[10] while in the competition sphere the problem of regulating 'vertical relationships' requires attention.[11] Accordingly, these studies will range over a wider area than did their predecessor, though they will still embrace the earlier theme.

So far as approach is concerned, the very width of our topic has naturally posed a problem, as has the intertwining of many of its elements, and, again, its inherently dynamic quality. As will become apparent, the relationship of retailing and regulatory policies is ever a subject of constant movement, its patterns forming and reforming in kaleidoscopic fashion. Given these difficulties, an orderly account, free of artificialities and overlap, is impossible to achieve. However, from a number of possible approaches, we have chosen one we believe to be comparatively straightforward. We begin with a written résumé of the shifting patterns of retailing. Then we follow this with discussions (from various aspects) of planning and competition policy.

Finally, the point must be made that, so far as planning is concerned, the focus of this work is on England and Wales. For historical reasons, English and Scots law are separate systems, and while it happens that competition law is the same north and south of the border, Scots planning law differs in many ways from its English counterpart.

Notes

1. *Shops and Shopping 1800-1914*, A. Adburgham, George Allen and Unwin Ltd (1964) p. *ix*.
2. *An Inquiry into the Nature and Causes of the Wealth of Nations*, vol. II, book IV, ch. 7.
3. 'The Song Against Grocers', G.K.Chesterton.
4. *Retail Change – Contemporary Issues*, R. Bromley and C. Thomas (eds), UCL Press (1993) pp. 2-3.
5. *Ibid.*
6. – with food retailing ever in the forefront.
7. A useful descriptive list of types of retail outlet, types of centre and types of location is provided in Annex A to Revised Planning Policy Guidance 6 (June 1996) – Department of the Environment, HMSO London. Very precise definitions do not exist.
8. 'Public Law and the Retail Sector, a Study in Planning and Competition Law', Longman, for the Oxford Institute of Retail Management.

   Justification for adding to the already abundant material on retailing was found *inter alia* in the fact that the new stores were viewed not in an active but a responsive rôle, inasmuch as whereas consideration was generally given to the impact of new shopping forms on society, here, by contrast, attention was focused upon those aspects of public law which had fostered their growth.

9. – a debate involving matters as widely varying as those including high street decay, urban regeneration, green field protection and traffic congestion, to name only some of the innumerable contributory elements.
10. – *i.e.* the practice of negotiating, when seeking planning permission, some separate but associated community benefit.
11. By 'vertical relationships' are meant relationships between firms at different levels of the distribution chain. Vertical relationships involving agreements containing provisions aimed at exclusivity and/or selectivity have been proving a focus of concern.

PART I

SHIFTING PATTERNS OF RETAILING:

A JOURNEY TO AND THROUGH THE 'GOLDEN AGE'

1 Highlights of the earlier history

For the purpose of the present study, the more distant chapters of the extensive history of retailing do not need a detailed account. They can be quite simply related. This is because, for a very long time, the evolution of shopping in this country proved a slow affair. It was only in the last century that movements appeared heralding the momentous changes which are central to our theme.

In a paper entitled 'Retailing, Past Present and Future', Lavery reviews the earlier history of the trade in this country. She begins:–

> The origins of modern retailing can be traced back to medieval times. Households then were self-sufficient and produced all their own food and clothing, buying any other items required from travelling fairs or 'festivals'. These fairs were usually held at a focal point in the town such as a church courtyard. Often the streets leading off this area would house specialist 'producer-retailers' who sold their goods from the front of their homes. However, by the beginning of the seventeenth century, fairs and markets were becoming less important and 'home producers' gave way in the eighteenth century to shops with closed fronts and window displays. At this time more than 50,000 families were either merchants, tradesmen or shopkeepers.[1]

Up until the late nineteenth century shop development was almost static, and independent shopkeepers predominated, but the scene changed with the growth of manufactured goods and with people becoming concentrated in large towns. Lavery explains:–

> In the Victorian era retailing became 'big business'. Shops and other industrial and commercial developments were erected on cleared residential sites. In the 1860s prices began to fall when imports and ways of mass producing and distributing food became cheaper. Multiple retailing increased as family shops were replaced by chains and large department stores...[2]

The earlier parts of this story are also told in a mid-'70s study by Elizabeth Mills on 'Recent Developments in Retailing and Urban Planning'.[3]

Beginning with the medieval trades congregating around traditional market places, she proceeds, *via* reference to the gradual establishment of permanent shops, thence to tell of the way in which, post industrial revolution, '...the demands of a rapidly increasing and more affluent population stimulated a number of changes'.[4] She speaks of the arrival of the co-operative societies and multiple food chains, '[catering] for a growing working class demand, ...and [pioneering] the sale of manufactured foods'.[5] They became increasingly important during the inter-war period, she explains, '...and by 1939 had become socially acceptable to the middle classes as well as the working classes...'.[6]

This author also makes reference to the introduction into this country of department stores from France. The early ones, catering largely for the affluent middle classes with increasing disposable income, were established in town centres, and then these '...were followed by variety 'bazaars' such as F.W.Woolworth'.[7] Again, in her survey, she notes the way in which, during the '30s, the town centres came under growing competitive pressure, because of the '...considerable migration of potential customers from inner residential areas to new suburbs and [the consequential encouragement of] the growth of parades and small groups of shops in outer areas...'.[8]

During the last war, the winds of change which had then been blowing so strongly naturally died down. The development of new shops practically came to a halt, other, that is, than in situations where damage occasioned the need for re-siting. With the return of peace, however, the winds began to blow with renewed vigour, until indeed, they eventually assumed such power as to achieve the gale conditions of a 'retail revolution'.

With the highlights of retailing's earlier history thus briefly chronicled, the issue must now be addressed of the impact upon them of the laws relating both to land use and competition.

Taking first the law relating to the regulation of land use, a distinction has to be drawn between the public law of planning and private land law. It was only towards the end of the era that the seeds of what is at present called 'planning control' were sown. The nineteenth century transformation of an agricultural into an industrial nation, together with enormous population growth, produced adverse social conditions which led, in their turn, to a tide of legislative activity in the areas of both public health and housing. But improvements in the more sophisticated matters of amenity and convenience were to come later, and the dawning of planning control arrived only with the passing of the Housing, Town Planning etc. Act 1909.[9] Moreover, it was not to be until after the Second World War, when the Town and Country Planning Act 1947 was enacted, that there would begin the system of planning which was to develop into the modern régime of today.

Although prior to 1947 only tentative steps were being taken in the direction of planning control, it was not the case that land use was unrestrained. The *public* control of land use such as is expressed in current planning legislation might not have existed, but certain aspects of *private* law (both land law and the law of torts) regulated a person's enjoyment of land, and, in so doing, might well constrain its use for the purposes of trade.

Thus, for instance, for centuries the law of property had provided that where a relationship of lessor and lessee[10] was created (by one person granting to another a lease of land in which he held the freehold) covenants which were entered controlling the use of the land leased would be legally enforceable, and further, might be legally enforceable not only as between the parties themselves but also their respective assignees. Somewhat similarly, (though only since the mid-nineteenth century) a principle of land law known as 'the doctrine of restrictive covenants' provided that where a person sold to another the freehold in part of his land and, in the course of the sale, covenants were entered into restricting the use of the part sold, those covenants might likewise be enforceable not only as between the original parties, but also, in certain conditions, their respective assignees. All these provisions were (and continue to be) forceful regulators of land use, albeit concerning the interests of private persons, and lacking, at least in concept, the public interest dimension.

In the context of covenants, reference must also be made to 'development schemes', for they afforded (and still afford) a particularly valuable application of the idea of a legally enforceable covenant as a 'tool' of land use control. A concept originating in the nineteenth century,[11] a 'development scheme' might arise where a common vendor or lessor laid out land in plots, sold or leased them to different purchasers or lessees, and, for the benefit of the whole area, took covenants from each that their plot would not be used in certain ways.[12] If the requisite conditions for the existence of a scheme were fulfilled, the covenants became reciprocally enforceable by and against the owner for the time being of any plot, the idea being that the covenants collectively formed a kind of local law for the estate.[13]

The private regulation of land was (and still is) also to be found in the tort of private nuisance. In developing the civil wrong of private nuisance, the common law was addressing the notion that there must be limits on a person's right to enjoy and exploit his land in order that adjoining owners of land might also have similar such rights of enjoyment and exploitation. So, if a person used his property in such a way that he interfered with another's use of his property to the extent that he either caused the latter sensible, personal discomfort or material injury to the property, the tort might be committed and an action for damages might lie,[14] a principle which is still with us.

In this brief outline of the mechanisms for the control of land use, developed respectively by the law of property and the law of tort, emphasis has been placed on the way in which they were (and still are) concerned with the regularisation of private matters. For such a purpose, they might have been satisfactory tools of control, and (in our context) might serve well as a means by which one individual could obtain protection from the adverse consequences of the trading activity of another. As society grew increasingly urban and industrial, however, their adequacy for dealing with consequential problems was thrown in doubt, and, with the emergence of a system of planning, the needs of the public interest began to be addressed.

Turning to competition law, we find a situation which cannot be simply described in terms of principles of private law in due course accompanied by, and overlaid with, a régime of public law. Its history has been a mixture of private and public law, their relative importance reflecting the endless shifting of the economic and political climate. Running throughout, however, has been a continuous principle, namely, that the maintenance of an unhindered competitive process is in the public interest.

For many years, and dating back at least to the thirteenth century, the law was concerned with the perceived social evils of monopolies. It sought to deal with them by statutes, which, by the end of the eighteenth century had been repealed. But by the fifteenth century, the horizon was extending to embrace lesser restraints on trade. At this time, the courts were just beginning to entertain cases in which the question arose as to whether, in the light of the value placed on free competition, a contractual promise given by one party to refrain from competing in the future with the other party was enforceable.[15]

It was to become apparent that a common set of circumstances in which such a question might arise would be where, upon the sale of a business (including a retail business), the buyer would take from the seller a promise by the latter that he would not, for a given number of years and within a given geographical area, set up in competition with him. The basic legal premise was that a simple promise not to compete was unenforceable unless justifiable. It was further thought though, that in circumstances such as these, *within certain limits*, such a promise might be justifiable and hence enforceable. Justification would lie, it was considered, in the protection of the buyer's legitimate interest in the goodwill which he had bought.[16]

The problem with which the judges were for centuries to labour was in the discernment of principles by reference to which the conditions for enforceability might be established. The troublesome issue was to what *extent*, in terms both of time and territory, a buyer might properly restrain the future trading activity of the seller and thereby safeguard what he had purchased. It was not until the end of the nineteenth century that the law was finally settled in the following way:– All restraints on trade, it was concluded, were *prima facie* void, but they would be held valid if they were reasonable, both in the interests of the parties and of the public.

Based on public policy, the 'restraint of trade doctrine' (as it has long been called) remains to this day an important feature of the law of contract.[17] In consequence, if, for example, upon the sale of a shoe shop, the purchaser should take from the vendor a covenant not to open a similar shop (say) within a 5 mile radius and over the next 5 years, and the covenant were then broken, the court might well be willing to enforce the covenant at the instance of the purchaser.

Though not as far reaching in terms of either scope or impact as the law of contract, the law of tort was also asked to enter upon issues of anti-competitive conduct. Attempts were made, for instance, by businessmen adversely affected by the activity of cartels (*i.e. collective* restraints on trade)[18] to make successful claims in damages by resort to the tort of conspiracy. The tort of conspiracy being directed towards collective activity resulting in injury to the legitimate interests of an outsider, it would have appeared *prima facie* to afford a promising route to compensation for a plaintiff whose business was damaged by the concerted endeavours of his competitors.[19] However, any such early promise became blighted when it emerged that, for a plaintiff to succeed in conspiracy, he had to prove that not only had he suffered harm, but also that the members of the trade combination in question actually intended to harm him.[20] So long as the acts of the defendants were not *in themselves* unlawful, if they could show their aim was to protect their own interests, they would have a sound defence.

In the context of the interaction of retailing and competition law, the most important part of the era under discussion was that which saw the acceleration of retail growth, *i.e.* the post 'industrial revolution' period. While it was a period which lacked any public based laws actually promotive of the competition process, equally the system was free from principles which might have proved unduly inhibitive. It is true, as has been seen, that the private law of contract contained principles allowing the enforcement of covenants restraining trade, but, again as has been seen, they constituted a limited exception to the basic premise that a simple promise not to compete was unenforceable.[21] The care which the judges of the time were taking to develop principles by which the boundaries of the restraint of trade doctrine might be properly limited testified to the great value placed on freedom of competition[22] and the untrammelled working of the market. And not only that, along with the reluctance to employ the tort of conspiracy, it was an illustration of a more widely prevalent philosophy of '*laissez-faire*'.

It was during these days of 'non-interventionism' that there developed a practice which was to prove of crucial significance in retail development and, in due course, to become a focal point of competition policy. This was 'resale price maintenance',[23] a process by which a manufacturer dictates and controls the prices at which his goods shall eventually reach the consumer. During the second half of the nineteenth century, with goods being packed and advertised on a rapidly increasing scale, and large firms expanding, unprecedented price competition led the small, traditional retailers to fear that their businesses would become engulfed by the new giants.[24] The device of r.p.m. being seen as a way of protecting the margins of small businesses and of curbing the onward march of the big firms, associations were formed which successfully pressed their claims on manufacturers for its introduction. Having thus 'sprouted', the practice of r.p.m., '...spread in several branches of the distribution of consumer goods', and, '...by the early 1930s was well established...'.[25]

To the basic question 'was such a practice void as an undue restraint of trade?', the court in the well known case of *Elliman v Carrington*,[26] concluded that it was not. As will emerge more fully in the next chapter of this part, the doctrine of privity of contract was to prove an obstacle to the enforcement of resale price systems, but this difficulty was overcome, and for many years the practice was to be a most powerful influence over the pattern of retail trade.

It was not only the specific practice of r.p.m. which came to flourish in the permissive climate of the end of the century. With the ancient statutes on monopolies having long since died away, with Parliament as well as the courts displaying an attitude of '*laissez-faire*', and with no public law for the advancement of competition,[27] commerce eventually became rife with cartels and monopolies in general. Somewhat strangely, perhaps, the unhindered flourishing of monopolies and cartels was to prove, in the early years of this century, a matter for acclaim rather than condemnation. In wartime conditions the economy underwent change, and structures and practices restrictive of competition which, in peacetime, might be thought detrimental to society, proved advantageous. When, however, peace returned after the two World Wars, those structures and practices became the focus of criticism, and a White Paper which was published in 1944 spoke of the potential harm to the public interest.[28] This lead, in its turn, to the passing of the Monopolies and Restrictive Practices (Inquiry and Control) Act 1948, the enactment of which was to mark the beginning of the modern competition régime.

By way of conclusion of the earlier period, it may be observed that the present century was entered with traders in a mood of expansion, and with an accommodating legal climate. With regard to the regulation of land use, where enforceable covenants existed such regulation would be forceful, but the overall impact was fragmented, and lacked the breadth of control which public law, operating alongside, would one day bring. Insofar as the regulation of trade was concerned, the minimalist approach of the law had indeed been inspired by and in turn inspired commercial growth, but it led also to the establishment and pursuit of inhibitive structures and conduct, the results of which new principles of public law were soon to be called to address.

Notes

1. *Shopping - a Housing and Planning Review Special*, vol. 42, no. 3, June 1987, p. 4. (There is a view which has been disputed, 'that it was not until the second half of the nineteenth century that markets declined and fixed shop retailing became general'. See 'The High Street of Tomorrow', Ian C. MacLaurin, Tesco Occasional Papers, No 15, 1986, – referring to *Retail Trading in Britain, 1850-1950*, J.B. Jeffreys 1954.)
2. *Shopping - a Housing and Planning Review Special*, *supra*, p. 4. (Whiteleys opened in the UK in 1863, and Wertheim in Germany in 1870. Macy's had opened in the USA in 1858, and, according to *Hutchinson's Encyclopaedia* (10th Edn. 1993) '...the world's first department store was the Bon Marché in Paris in 1852'.)
3. Planning Research Applications Group Technical Papers, TP3, 1974.
4. At p. 13.
5. *Ibid.*
6. *Ibid.*
7. *Ibid.*
8. *Ibid.*
9. Section 54 empowered local authorities to prepare schemes

    ...as respects any land which is in course of development or appears likely to be used for building purposes, with the general object of securing proper sanitary conditions, amenity and convenience in connection with the laying out and use of the land...
10. – or 'landlord and tenant', as it is more commonly called.

11. See *Whatman v Gibson* (1838) 9 Sim. 196.
12. – a commonly found covenant being one not to trade thereon.
13. – giving rise to '...an equity which is created by circumstances...'. *Lawrence v South County Freeholds Ltd* [1939] Ch. 656 at p. 682, per Simonds J.
14. 'Generally, the essence of a nuisance is a state of affairs that is either continuous or recurrent, a condition or activity which unduly interferes with the use or enjoyment of land'. *Winfield & Jolowicz on Tort*, 15th Edn. W.V.H. Rogers (Sweet & Maxwell) p. 494. A famous example from the turn of the century is *Adams v Ursell* [1913] 1 Ch. 269 where the plaintiff obtained an injunction to restrain the permeation of property with vapour and odour from a fried fish shop. The argument that an injunction would cause hardship to the poor persons who were customers failed.
15. See *Dyer's Case* (1414) YB 11 Hen 5 fo5 p. 126.
16. See *Elves v Crofts* (1850) 10 CB 241, (involving a five mile restraint in the meat trade).
17. See in particular *Nordenfelt v Maxim Nordenfelt Guns & Ammunition Co. Ltd* [1894] AC 535 (HL) and *Mason v Provident Clothing and Supply Co. Ltd* [1913] AC 724 (HL). The slowly developing principles had been worked out not only in the context of contracts involving vendors and purchasers of businesses, but also in cases concerning employers and employees, the courts being asked to consider the enforceability or otherwise of an undertaking made by an employee that, upon leaving his employer, he would refrain from competing with him for a given number of years and throughout a given area.
18. – such as, for example, a group 'boycott'.
19. As, for example, if their efforts excluded him from a particular market.
20. *Mogul SS Co. v McGregor Gow & Co.* (1892) AC 25 (HL).
21. Similarly, as principles facilitating the enforceability of covenants relating to land use developed, they were always hedged about with limiting conditions.
22. As important as freedom of competition is also, of course, freedom of contract. When a person makes a covenant which restrains trade, he is using his freedom of contract to limit his freedom to compete, and so the two 'freedoms' come into conflict.
23. hereinafter 'r.p.m.'.
24. See *Resale Price Maintenance*, B.S.Yamey, Weidenfeld and Nicholson (eds) (1966) p. 251.
25. *Ibid.* pp. 252-253.
26. *Elliman, Sons & Co. v Carrington & Sons Ltd* [1901] 2 Ch. 275. 'The courts saw no reason to adapt common law principles in order to prevent the practice, adhering instead to the view that contracts freely entered into should be enforced'. Whish, *Competition Law*, 3rd Edn. Butterworths (1993) p. 175. Indebtedness to this work throughout these studies is acknowledged.
27. It is worthy of note that a third person whose business was harmed on account of restrictive conduct exercised by a trade combination could not

generally rely on the restraint of trade doctrine to seek compensation. Indeed, while the doctrine was well developed in the context of business sales and employment, it was unclear whether it applied to harmful trade combinations.

28. – on Employment Policy, Cmd 6527 (1944).

2 The post-war decades ~ the '50s, '60s & '70s

It is to the immediate post-war years that what is called 'modern retailing' harks back. Despite two world wars, and a severely depressed inter-war period, Lavery explains that the expansion in retailing which began in the Victorian era continued.[1]

The period following the war witnessed many problems. Amongst them was one of shortage of staff. The shortage heralded a shift of emphasis from personal service to self service,[2] and was one of the key contributors to the introduction of a newcomer into the high street: the supermarket. Soon established, the '50s saw the breed flourish, and they developed in a razzmatazz atmosphere, epitomised by the early Tesco concept of 'pile 'em high and sell 'em cheap'.

The large scale, mass merchandising image of the supermarkets spawned shopping forms of yet larger dimensions. Still 'food-led', though involved too in the selling of other consumer goods, there emerged in the late '60s the superstore or hypermarket. Purpose built, their specific target was the car-borne shopper.

Some few years after there appeared another variety of free standing shopping development – the retail warehouse. In contrast with the primary food interest of the forms so far mentioned, the retail warehouse was at first concerned with bulky items, such as furniture and floor coverings, *i.e.* items not amenable to being sold in traditional surroundings. However, the range widened to include other goods such as clothing and car accessories, and there grew up the 'retail warehouse park' in which a number of such stores shared a single site.[3]

Notwithstanding the large scale design of these various developments, for size, the most spectacular and ambitious shopping concept of the late '60s and early '70s was the regional out of town shopping centre, (a form in which, for a while, interest was to wane but later revive). Combining shopping and leisure facilities and requiring very considerable space, such ventures sought to duplicate the functions of major town centres. Not surprisingly, proposals of this kind led to fears including those of harm to city centres and erosion of green belts, and it was not until 1976 that the first such centre (at Brent Cross) started to function. The fundamental shifts in the retail environment wrought in the '50s, '60s and '70s are summed up with particular clarity in *Retail Change – Contemporary Issues* (eds Bramley and Thomas), thus:–

> Until as recently as the mid-1960s the retail system of British cities had a traditional hierarchical structure. Characteristically, this focused on the central business district, which provided the largest concentration of the most specialized high-order goods and services for the surrounding urban region. This was complemented by a relatively small number of local town centres or district centres offering primarily a strong convenience-goods shopping function and a secondary range of comparison goods for specific sectors of the city. At the lowest level, a large number of small neighbourhood centres and corner shops provided a narrow range of convenience goods for the immediate residential population.
>
> Since the mid-1960s, however, suburbanization and counter-urbanisation, increasing affluence, rising levels of car ownership and increased female participation in formal employment...allowed and in some cases necessitated the development of new patterns of shopping behaviour. Combined with the demands of consumers for an increasingly specialized and sophisticated range of goods and services, and associated changes in the economic organisation of the retail industry, these changes...instigated a transformation in the character of the urban retail system.[4]

So, post-war retailing was being asked to dance to novel tunes, such as those called by greater mobility, increased wealth,[5] and working wives. Moreover, as the decades rolled, the beat of the music both quickened and became more insistent.

It was during these formative years that the modern régime of Town and Country Planning properly emerged and took shape. In 1947, the landmark Town and Country Planning Act of that year introduced a comprehensive system for the public regulation of land use.[6] By contrast with earlier legislative endeavours, it '...moved away from planning primarily in terms of amenity and convenience to planning on the basis of securing proper control over the use of land'.[7]

Relying on strong central and local government involvement, the system[8] featured two 'key' elements. First, '...each local planning authority was required under the Act...to carry out a survey of the whole of its area and to prepare a development plan based on the results of the survey...'.[9] The plan was to indicate '...the manner in which [the authority] proposed land in their area should be used, whether by development or otherwise, and the ways by which any such development should be carried out'.[10] Secondly,

> ...henceforth, no development was to take place without planning permission; normally this would require an application to the local planning authority who would then decide whether to grant planning permission, with or without conditions, having regard to the provisions of the development plan and any other material considerations.[11]

As the post-war years unfolded, planning law grew in scope and complexity, but the basic, pivotal components of the local formulation of a development plan[12] and the need for planning permission to carry out development remained at its heart, and, indeed, continues to do so.

Alongside this expression of society's desire to bring general order to land use, the vigour of the urge for growth displayed by the retail sector appeared to sit ill. What then, was to be the influence of one current on the other? It has been explained by Davies that, in the '60s, the traditional, hierarchical retail structure being thought capable of the efficient provision of services, the

> ...main objective of retail planning...was [to reinforce the structure and so]...maintain the *status quo*. [R]etail plans prepared at this time were still essentially zoning maps. There was little discussion of retail trends; the hierarchy of shopping centres was integrated into plans for housing and community development...[13]

In the '70s, he continues, attempts were made to sustain the restrictive stance.

> Supermarkets were by now being rapidly developed but guided to centres within the established hierarchy. Covered shopping centres had arrived, but, with certain exceptions, were built in existing town and city centre environments.[14]

Early in the decade, central guidance for all those involved in planning control had emerged in the shape of Development Control Policy Note 13 'Out of town shops and shopping centres'.[15] Although making reference to the deficiencies of many suburban shopping facilities and the problems of car-parking and congestion in town centres, this note was not favourable to development on isolated 'greenfield' sites,[16] and also attached importance to the meeting of the needs of those reliant upon public transport. Further, while it signalled appreciation of the fact that '...it [was] not the function of land-use planning to prevent competition between retailers...[or] to preserve existing commercial interests...', it sought to underscore the way in which '...[the] overprovision of shops on a large scale and the loss of trade by town and district centres...could change the character of these centres...and have serious economic, social, financial and other planning consequences'.[17] Some little while after the appearance of DCPN 13, in the course of comment on the treatment of retail development proposals, it was noted that '...the balance had weighed heavily against the out of town interest'.[18]

In the midst of increasing numbers of applications for large new stores, a revision of DCPN 13 appeared in 1977, DoE Circular 96/77. The stance which it took reflected still the needs of existing urban centres and of shoppers without cars. It was felt to be

> ...preferable for large new stores to be located where they can serve not only those able to travel by car but also customers travelling on foot and by public transport. This can best be achieved where the new store can be accommodated within the existing urban area, particularly within an expanding or redeveloping town centre or where it acts as a nucleus for a district centre where the commercial and social activities usually associated with a shopping centre can be provided.

Thus, the received wisdom as enshrined in central policy was adverse to out of town retail development. In spite, however, of the strength of this official presumption, the power of the supermarkets was growing throughout the '70s, '...central government [was] intermittently [relaxing] the planning control of retail development',[19] and, towards the end of the decade these companies '...were beginning to break through the planning restrictions of many local authorities to build large stores out of town'.[20]

If it might be said that new shopping forms were growing despite the approach of planning law, it could be noted by contrast that their development was a consequence of the thrust of competition law.

Just as the immediate post-war decades witnessed the gradual establishment of a sophisticated planning system, so too it saw the development of an equally intricate competition régime. They shared a similar growth path of successive statutes, and the same philosophical base of the promotion of the public interest. Beginning immediately after the Second World War, with the passing of the Monopolies and Restrictive Practices (Inquiry & Control) Act 1948, competition law advanced through a series of enactments to challenge a broad spectrum of inhibitive market structures and conduct. Doing so in the name of the pursuit of 'free competition', it made use of, and relied upon, a mixture of administrative and judicial mechanisms and authorities.

Although concerned to deal with a range of potentially anti-competitive situations and activity, it was its treatment of r.p.m. which is of particular significance in the context of this particular period. As explained in the first chapter of this part, this practice had been successfully advocated by associations of small traders as a device for the protection of their margins from the onward march of the large firms, and, further, had become well established by the early '30s. By 1938, it has been observed, '...between 27 per cent and 35 per cent of all consumer goods sold to the private domestic consumer in the United Kingdom were sold at prices fixed or recommended by the producers'.[21] Moreover, the point has also been made that '...the practice of r.p.m. was not limited to consumer goods...[but] flourished also in the distribution of such goods as office equipment, dental supplies and building materials...'.[22]

A legal problem which might considerably have hindered its progress was found in the shape of the doctrine of privity of contract, *i.e.* the doctrine which states that only the parties to a contract may sue or be sued upon it. Under a resale price system, the producer of goods takes from the wholesaler to whom he sells them a promise not to resell them below a price stipulated by the producer, and a further promise to extract from retailers to whom he in his turn sells the goods that they will not, in their turn, resell them below a price stipulated by the producer. Often, it would be the case that a retailer would resell below the established figure, and the producer would wish to restrain him. Any claim made by the producer against the retailer for a restraining injunction would, however, be blocked by the privity doctrine: the producer's contract was with the wholesaler, not with the price cutting retailer.[23] Meeting such failure, the producers in due course found ways of circumventing the obstacle posed by privity, with the consequence that resale price systems flourished.

The ways which the manufacturers found of by-passing the privity doctrine and bringing price-cutting retailers to heel were various, including not only refusals to supply but also the institution of private tribunals to 'try and then fine offenders'. Such conduct could obviously not escape attention, and in due course became the subject of particular criticism in the Report of the Committee on Resale Price Maintenance.[24]

Legal regulation of the practice in the nineteen fifties and sixties reflects the fact that it was being pursued in a climate of increasing hostility, with public opinion turning against it. To appreciate the regulation which was gradually effected, an understanding is needed of the distinction commonly drawn between 'vertical' and 'horizontal' r.p.m. The former title is given to the situation in which an individual producer puts a resale price system in place by extracting from his wholesalers promises of the kinds mentioned above. And the latter title is given to the more complex situation in which a group of manufacturers agree with each other that they will each operate a vertical system. Moreover, in a horizontal r.p.m. agreement there may appear enforcement provisions, such as, for instance, if the parties agree that they will collectively refuse to deal with price cutting retailers.

The Restrictive Trade Practices Act 1956 contained provisions which brought horizontal r.p.m. agreements under control, but which, by contrast, actually fostered the pursuit of simple vertical agreements. This it did by enabling a producer successfully to sue a price cutting retailer even though he was not in a contractual relationship with him,[25] so long as the latter took the goods with notice that a resale price condition was attached to them. The Resale Prices Act 1964, however, brought about a *volte face* in the legal treatment of simple vertical agreements. It made them unlawful, though making provision for the exemption from the prohibition of particular classes of goods if a case could be made out on one of a number of specified public interest grounds.

A quarter of a century after the enactment of the Resale Prices Act the Monopolies and Mergers Commission observed simply that '...the abolition of resale price maintenance by the explicit action of Parliament has been a major factor in the creation of today's competitive retail market'.[26] But this terse summation reveals nothing of the charged atmosphere in which the legal change was wrought. In 1960, consumer goods greatly affected by the practice were widespread, including

> ...cigarettes and tobacco, chocolates and confectionery, motor cars and cycles, radio and television sets, electrical goods, gramophones and records, books, magazines and newspapers, chemists' goods, photographic equipment and supplies...tyres and motor accessories...beer, wines and spirits.[27]

With the practice so extensive, and the future of so many small retailers perceived to be in jeopardy, it was scarcely to be wondered that the law reformers should have encountered deep hostility. Tracing the history to and through the Resale Prices Bill, Professor B.S.Yamey comments on the stormy passage through Parliament which the Bill sustained. And, he continues,

> [p]ublished in late January, the bill received a generally favourable public response, but thousands of small shopkeepers, egged on by the *Daily Express*, protested vehemently; and Mr Heath had to contend with a Tory back-bench rebellion which rumbled on from January through April. The rebellion reached its climax on 11 March 1964, when 21 Conservatives voted against the government and at least 17 others abstained; on a later division the Government's majority fell to one.[28]

Small shopkeepers of all kinds lobbied with tremendous vigour,[29] but it was to no avail. Aspiring to increase efficiency in distribution, encourage competition in the economy, and benefit consumers, the Bill passed into the law.

As mentioned above, the Resale Prices Act 1964 made provision for the exemption from the prohibition on price maintenance of classes of goods, if it could be shown that their protection from price competition would be in the public interest. Any hopes, however, that this provision might prove a harbour for the continuance of the practice were soon to be checked. The lengthy and unsuccessful efforts of the confectionery manufacturers signalled to business the nigh impossibility of satisfying the court that consumers or users of a particular class of goods would suffer greater detriment from the absence of a resale prices system than from its continuance.[30] Other than in respect of books and medicaments, direct and enforceable individual r.p.m. had been largely brought to an end.[31]

With the virtual ending of the long reign of r.p.m. the way was opened up for an eventual fundamental shift of power in supplier-distributor relationships, and more specifically, it was opened up for an equally basic change in pricing practice. The demise of r.p.m. led, in the '70s, to the development of a particular practice which was to command considerable attention. This was 'price discrimination', *i.e.* the practice of selling similar goods to customers of similar standing at different prices, where the difference does not directly correspond with any difference in the cost of supplying them. It is a practice which can be pursued in a myriad ways and the impulse for which can come either from the seller or the buyer. As the next chapter of this part will describe, it was a practice which assumed such proportions as to become one of the key features of the retail revolution.

If, to conclude the present part of the journey, we draw together the threads of this post-war review, we find we are once more leaving a period whose climate was eager for growth and change. New shopping forms were emerging, planning control was proving unable to contain retailers' zeal for innovation, and r.p.m. was all but abolished. Writing in the mid-'60s,

Yamey had concluded his telling of the r.p.m. story in this country, with a warning:–

> ...the implementation of central and local government controls over the establishment and the extension of shopping centres and sites may temper somewhat the intensity of price competition and the pace of structural change in some branches of distribution after the abandonment of r.p.m. Official controls over the expansion and adaption of retailing facilities may well prove to be the most serious remaining constraint on competition and innovation in the distributive trades after the scope and extent of r.p.m. have been reduced.[32]

As circumstances developed, his fears were to prove groundless – at least in the relatively short term. The next two decades would witness an intensity of price competition and speed of structural change which was without precedent.

Notes

1. *Shopping - a Housing and Planning Review Special*, vol. 42, no. 3, June 1987, p. 4. She points out that '...in the "never had it so good" era of the 1950s there was an increase in household ownership of consumer durables like refrigerators, TV sets and washing machines – largely aided by the use of credit'.
2. In 'Marketing Myopia', *Harvard Business Review*, vol. 38, no. 4, (1960) Israel Sieff speaks of self selection and self service, and the organisation of the emporium to that purpose, as being amongst the most important principles of mid-twentieth century retail distribution.
3. Either grouped together on industrial estates, or sited along main roads.
4. UCL Press (1993) at p. 6.
5. A noticeable feature was credit growth.
6. It was greatly guided by the recommendations of two reports. The 'Barlow Report' (the Report of the Royal Commission on the Distribution of Industrial Population – Cmd 6153) recommended that industry be dispersed from congested urban areas, and, where necessary, that those areas should be redeveloped. The 'Scott Report' (the Report of a Committee on Land Utilisation in Rural Areas – Cmd 6378) recommended *inter alia* the regulation of sporadic building in the countryside.
7. *Planning Law and Procedure*, A.E.Telling & R.M.C. Duxbury, 10th Edn. Butterworths (1996) pp. 8-9.
8. – which '...made a completely new start with effect from July 1st. 1948'. *Ibid.* p. 8.

9. *Ibid.* The plan had to be reviewed every five years from the date of its being approved.
10. *A Practical Approach to Planning Law*, Victor Moore, 6th Edn. Blackstone (1997) p. 4.
11. *Planning Law & Procedure, supra*, p. 9. A right of appeal was given to an applicant aggrieved by the local planning authority's decision.
12. Development plans formulated under the provisions of the 1947 Act were based on detailed maps, accompanied by a written statement. Under the Town and Country Planning Act 1968, however, there was brought in a 'two tier' system of development plans – broad, strategic 'structure plans' and 'local plans', both being in the nature of policy documents, with illustrative maps.
13. *Retail Planning Policies in Western Europe*, Ross L. Davies (ed), Routledge (1995) p. *xi*. According to Mills in 'Recent Developments in Retailing and Urban Planning' PRAG Technical Papers TP3:

    the early Development Plans made little specific mention of retailing activity. They did, however, provide for the reconstruction and redevelopment of war damaged town centres, which of course involved the provision of new shops in central areas.
14. *Retail Planning Policies in Western Europe, supra*, p. *xvi*.
15. (1972) The object of such notes ('DCPNs') was to indicate current ministerial policy and to guide planning control. This particular DCPN had, as its background, an influential report of the Economic Development Committee for the Distributive Trades. This report, 'The Future Pattern of Shopping', urged the publication of guidelines by central government to intimate the circumstances in which new shopping locations would be acceptable.
16. It rehearsed (at para. 9) a list of objections to proposals for such development.
17. *Ibid.* para. 6.
18. 'Municipal Review Supplement', February 1974, p. 342.
19. *Retail Change - Contemporary Issues*, R.Bromley and C.Thomas (eds), UCL Press (1993) p. 8.
20. *Retail Planning Policies in Western Europe, supra*, p. *xvi*.
21. *The Distribution of Consumer Goods*, James B. Jefferys *et al*, Cambridge (1950) p. 112.
22. *Resale Price Maintenance*, B.S.Yamey, Weidenfeld and Nicolson (eds) (1966) p. 254.
23. – the retailer is a third party and outside the producer-wholesaler contract. See, for instance, the famous case of *Dunlop Pneumatic Tyre Co. Ltd v Selfridge and Co. Ltd* [1915] AC 847 in which a manufacturer's attempt to restrain a third party retailer from selling in breach of a resale price system failed.
24. Cmd 7696 (1949).
25. – thus enabling him, *via* the statute, to surmount the privity obstacle.

26. *Black and Decker* Cm 805 (1989).
27. *Resale Price Maintenance*, *supra*, p. 276. The point it made, however, (at p. 275) that difficulties attended the measurement of its extent. 'Effectiveness of enforcement varies from trade to trade; and the degree of enforcement tends to fluctuate with economic conditions in the trade'.
28. Quoting *The British General Election of 1964*, D.E. Butler and Anthony King, p. 23.
29. See *Anatomy of Britain*, A.Sampson (revised edition, 1965) pp. 46-7.
30. See *Re Chocolate and Sugar Confectionery Resale Price Reference* [1967] LR 6 RP 338, RPC.
31. It may be added that the Act did not prohibit the *recommendation* by the seller of a price at which the goods might be re-sold.
32. *Resale Price Maintenance*, *supra*, p. 298.

3 The 'Retail Revolution' of the '80s ~ the creation of the 'Golden Age'

Introduction

While the immediate post-war years began to see the most considerable changes in the retail scene of Britain, it was in the '80s, in the Thatcher years of enterprise culture and with a retail 'boom',[1] that its geography became so radically transformed. Moreover, both the speed and scale of that transformation were unprecedented, and together involved such a fervour of activity as to gain the appellation of a 'revolution'.

Under the glare of the spotlight of public debate and scrutiny, the features of the retail revolution were well chronicled. For instance in May 1987, the Unit for Retail Planning Information reported the opening of 31 superstores and 3 hypermarkets during 1986,[2] observing this to be '...the largest number of new stores ever to open in any one year'.[3] As to the number of hypermarkets and superstores with planning permission but not yet open and trading, the report went on to advise that '...the number of stores with planning permission has been generally increasing, resulting in 87 hypermarkets and superstores with planning permission at January 1987, the highest number on record'.[4] A little later, Lee Donaldson Associates reported in their '*Superstore Appeals Review 1988*' that '...by the end of 1986 there were at least 389 superstores trading in England and Wales with some 15.1mn sq.ft sales floor space... The number of superstores in England and Wales...more than doubled during the '80s'.[5] And alongside the 'mushrooming' of superstores[6] were proposals for out of town shopping centres. Such proposals, according to Lee Donaldson's '*Shopping Centres Appeals Review 1986*', rose '...to an unprecedented pitch',[7] while in a mid-'80s study commissioned by Tesco and conducted at the Oxford Institute of Retail Management, reference is made to applications outstanding around the country for forty out of town centres of varying sizes.[8] The excitement generated by the pace and scope of such activity was intense, the atmosphere of the time being well caught in an article in *The Times* entitled 'Queuing up for the retail revolution', concerning the battle of some developers to build five megacentres next to the M25.[9] And it still echoes down the years. Very recently, Davies wrote of the way in which, in just a few years

> ...the retail geography of the entire country had been radically transformed. Free-standing superstores and retail warehouses grew by the hundreds; the new concept of the retail park became a feature of every sizeable town; four major outlying regional shopping centres were opened, matching in size the biggest of those to be found in North America; new, outlying regional centres were built; and the catering services developed a new generation of drive to/drive through facilities.[10]

With the abundance of development and proposals for development, and suggestions of the prospect of a North American type retail environment, it was scarcely surprising that the subject became a cynosure. Here indeed was media material, a revolution composed of major wars and minor skirmishes, of richly assorted victors and vanquished, unwitting participants and innocent bystanders.

To give an orderly account of the situation is a task beset with difficulty. To begin with, *everyone* was involved. To list as 'key' sectors the retailers, property developers, financial institutions, architects, planners and councillors would be to omit the most important sector, namely, the consumers. And each sector had its own interests and needs, were it, at one end of the scale, the developer seeking a suitable 'greenfield' site, or, at the other, the rural dweller, reliant on patchy public transport and in need of a few basic commodities.

The issues involved spread across the communal board: social, environmental, economic, commercial, legal and political, and they were not only intertwined but each multi-faceted. Again, the debate comprised, according to context and purpose, an endless mixture of arguments, spreading across a spectrum of enormous breadth. On the one hand, it might be a small independent trader seeking the protection of his livelihood from the threat of the opening of a superstore virtually on his doorstep, and on the other, it might be a planning 'silk' seeking, on the grounds of shopping need, the development in the 'green belt' of a new regional centre.[11]

Given such circumstances an effective summary is defied, and a sense of the situation is perhaps best gained *via* a very brief review of certain of the principal issues which were at stake. For ease of presentation and no more, they may be approached as a series of issues perceived as problematic, and considered under a series of headings, *viz*:– environment, social, planning control, and economic.

Environment issues

The issue of location was seen as amongst the major problems of large store development. Such development, it was claimed, involved too much sacrifice of the countryside, and resulted also in the decay of town centres. The point was raised in *The Sunday Times* early in 1986, Hugh Pearman writing:– 'A boom in shopping centre developments is threatening the character of a number of British towns and cities, according to conservationists and a growing number of architects'. Referring to the claim that '...the development of out of town shopping centres is threatening to kill town centre trade and eat away at green field sites', he explained that conservation lobby groups were urging '...local authorities [to] allow new developments to prevent the stagnation of old city centres, while still protecting the environment, both in town and on the outskirts'.[12]

On the same point but a year or so later, Derek Harris, the industrial editor of *The Times* wrote in different vein. Under the headline 'New routes to the retail revolution', he observed:– 'The move to edge of town sites for retailing, from modest district centres to those of regional scale, will reach an unstoppable pace in direct proportion to the disinclination of local authorities to do something radical and effective about convenient, as well as sufficient, car parking in town centres...'. It is '...only a matter of time before a critical mass of local authorities emerges which will see the light and accommodate our taste for wheels with everything'.[13]

Set against the rising tide of out of town shopping development, questions inevitably arose of potential saturation,[14] and whether town centres could revive. In a paper entitled 'Out of Town Shopping: Will the City Centre bounce back?', reference was made to a much publicised campaign launched by Southampton City Council when faced with proposals for 3.5mn sq.ft of out of town retailing,[15] and it was observed that '...the populist approach reflects a very real concern that out of town shopping is being forced through on the crest of the retail wave'.[16] The campaign to 'Keep Shopping in Southampton', was soon to be supported (according to the food trade press) by some twenty-seven councils spread across the country.[17]

The view that large retail development brought about the twin evils of countryside erosion and stagnating town centres was one which was never to fade. On the contrary, in the next decade it was set to become one of a range of high profile environmental concerns. Such concerns, however, were for the future, and, while the consumer was 'king', new shopping forms were set to proliferate.

Social issues

The surge of out of town retail development brought in its train the view that it had created a number of social problems. Prominent amongst them, and as much a social as an environmental matter, was the adverse impact of retailing decentralisation on the state of urban areas. Inner city decline and the need for regeneration became a focal point of communal attention, and one, moreover, which would attract increasing debate and concern. In parallel, there was a further problem of access to shopping facilities. The move to out of town sites, geared as it was to the car-borne shopper, led to serious difficulty for the disadvantaged, less mobile members of society, a matter which often came under scrutiny. A typical example of allusion to the issue was a short report in *The Grocer* of a plea made to the government by Janet Graham, the then vice-chairman of the National Consumer Council. Made shortly before the 1987 General Election it highlighted the difficulties of '...hundreds of thousands of consumers...the low income families, the single parent families, the elderly, the disabled and the non-car owners...who have to rely on wherever they can walk to or on public transport'. Pleading for consideration of their needs, she expressed the belief that 'society could no longer afford to adopt a piecemeal random approach to retail development'.[18] To growing fears that the community was becoming increasingly 'polarised' between rich and poor, the out of town movement was claimed by many to be a contributory factor.

A further feature which caused concern was the matter of employment. On this, battle was joined by the multiple retailers on the one hand and the small, independent traders on the other. According to the former, the increase in large modern stores brought with it an increase in jobs, their employment creativity being widely proclaimed. Thus, to take one of innumerable references, an article in *The Times* in May 1987 was headed, '18,000 new jobs planned by Safeway store chain'.[19] In opposition, the small independent trader took the view that rather than the creation of new employment, new large stores tended to 'suck' employment already established elsewhere. The point, often made, was for instance afforded prominence in *Convenience Store* with the terse headlines 'Superstores destroy jobs, says Purkiss'.[20]

Planning control issues

While, in this study, the impact of planning law and policy on new retail development is a matter in its own right, and addressed as such, the severe difficulties faced in the actual day to day operation of the system in coping with the spate of development proposals is also discussed here, as being one of the key, problematic issues of the 'revolution'.

A major difficulty was the pressure brought to bear on planners by the sheer volume of the workload which the intensity of interest in large retail development produced. For example, in the context of planning proposals for regional shopping centres, Bryan Johnston, editor of *Planning*, spoke of the burdens cast on 'luckless local authorities' by the appearance of '...a multiplicity of huge schemes designed to test out the water'. He referred to them as a 'merry go round' which 'starkly illustrates the complete absence of any national policy or guidance on how retailing on this scale can be properly accommodated'. And he pointed out at the same time that proposals for megacentres '...represent only a small proportion of shopping schemes in the pipeline at any one time'.[21]

Apart from the general matter of *volume*, a further issue concerned 'multiple applications', *i.e.* a number of different operators seeking to establish retail premises in a particular area. The resultant multiple inquiry or inquiries presented difficulties both in terms of substance and procedure.

From the aspect of substance, the Lee Donaldson *Review of Superstore Appeals* made reference to the complexity of the problems of analysis. Having noted that the multiple inquiry had become commonplace, these consultants observed that:–

> The principal effect of a multiple inquiry is to heighten the relative rather than the absolute merits or problems of each project under consideration for a particular location. The determinant factors become relative rather than absolute. A problem, for example, of some nuisance to nearby residential areas which might be considered as acceptable or remediable when considered in isolation, becomes a determinant reason for refusal if the same inquiry considers other schemes where this problem is absent.[22]

In terms of procedure, multiple applications led to difficulty in the sense of the great importance assumed of the need to treat applications 'fairly'. If, from a planning point of view, all the proposals were equally worthy of going ahead, theoretically it could be argued that all the applicants should be granted planning permission and the market then left to sort it out. As, however, the number of large shopping developments which a particular area could sustain was limited, in practice it might be that to grant one particular application resulted in the refusal of another, hence the underscoring of the need for 'fairness' of treatment.[23]

An economic issue

In contrast with what appeared the more heady environment issues was one of a less emotive type, but which, nevertheless, went to the roots of the revolution. This was the issue of concentration, *i.e.* the continuing disappearance of the small, independent trader from the market place, and the concentration of trade into ever fewer, and, hence, more powerful, hands. In a ranking of the top 500 retailers compiled by the Corporate Intelligence Group, the leading 100 companies were reported (in November 1987) to account for more than 60 per cent of total British retail sales. Moreover, the top 10 groups were reported to enjoy 31 per cent of the overall market.[24]

It was, perhaps, in the food sector of the retail trade that the trend to the concentration of economic power in the hands of a few was most sharply etched, although it was a phenomenon by no means restricted to that sphere. Between 1976 and 1984 the number of single outlet grocery retailers fell by 25,000.[25] From 20 per cent of the market in 1950, grocery chains increased their enjoyment to 70 per cent in 1986.[26] In 1987 it was estimated that out of 50,000 grocery outlets in the UK, 25 per cent of grocery sales were effected by some 450 superstores.[27] In the Office of Fair Trading's Report on Competition and Retailing (1985) a table was provided (using data from Audits of Great Britain) showing region by region, and over the period 1980 to 1984, the share of trade of the packaged groceries market enjoyed by the various kinds of retail enterprise: the climb of the multiple retailers was both continuous and steady.[28]

Again, the extent of the strong position of the multiples was portrayed in an article in *The Grocer* in March 1988 dealing with the annual report on the grocery trade from 'Verdict Research'.[29] A 'league table' of market shares showed Tesco with 14 per cent, Sainsbury with 13.5 per cent, Dee with 11.1 per cent, Argyll with 9.6 per cent, Asda with 7.4 per cent, other multiples with 16.1 per cent, the Co-op with 12.1 per cent, and the independents with 16.2 per cent. According to the Verdict study, although the multiples had only 9 per cent of all grocery sites, they represented 54 per cent of sales space, Co-operative stores with 8 per cent of outlets had 18 per cent of selling area, while independents with 83 per cent of units had just 28 per cent of space.[30] Looking to the future, a highly controversial prediction made in the mid-'80s by the management consultancy, Management Horizons, was of a grocery market in the mid-'90s dominated as to 80 per cent by three chains, Sainsbury, Tesco and one other. It was a prediction which quickly evoked criticism.[31]

Given the advantages afforded by organisational methods and by sheer 'size', the ascendance of the multiples in food retailing, as elsewhere, appeared inevitable. A few of their many advantages included their ability to deal in volume, their capacity for innovation, their exercise of buying power, and their ready potential for cost savings. Against these and other expressions of superior market strength, the small, traditional independent trader could truly not compete: he was unable to match them either in price, choice, variety, scale of presentation or shopping 'ambience'.

That the issue of concentration lacked the emotive quality of the environmental issues stems, it is suggested, from the fact that for a time the decline of the small independent trader was perceived as a purely local matter. Viewed as isolated instances rather than for its overall impact, it was not, despite its continuance, and its arguably adverse economic and social consequences, to grip the imagination of the public at large. That said, the subject of concentration was to remain, indeed yet remains, one of very real concern for the community. Trade falling into ever fewer hands is a multi-faceted matter, only one aspect of which is the marginalising of small business. It raises questions of whether, should the hands into which trade falls become too few, they may come to possess excessive power, and to use that power to reap so called 'oligopoly profits', to pursue anti-competitive practices, and to wield an undue degree of influence in their relationships with both their suppliers and their customers.

Although the concentration process was not particular to the food sector, Neil Wrigley, writing a few years ago on the phenomenon, refers to the fact that in the '80s grocery retailing underwent '...a massive and sustained concentration of capital...'.[32] He explains that while the

> ...trend towards concentration had been present for the previous twenty years...the 1980s were characterised...by the emergence of a small group of retail corporations whose turnover, employment levels, profitability and sheer market and political power came to rival the largest industrial corporations in any sector of the UK economy.[33]

He then points out that in '...the early 1980s the top three firms – Sainsbury, Tesco and Asda – held a combined market share of around 20 per cent of national grocery sales',[34] and were in due course joined by the rapidly growing Argyll group and Dee Corporation (later Gateway). The dominance of this 'big five' increasing greatly between 1982 and 1988, '...their combined market share reached approximately 43 per cent by 1984, and 58 per cent by the end of 1988'.[35]

While, of course, many factors contributed to the growth of concentration, two factors tended to stand out. The first was price discrimination, a practice which has already been described in simple terms as the supplying of goods of like grade and quality to customers of similar standing at different prices, where the difference in price does not correspond with differences in the supplier's costs. Practised for years in such mass markets as home furnishing, TV and radio, it had become rife in the food trade. Again, as earlier noted, it can be initiated by either a powerful supplier or a powerful customer, and further, when initiated by the latter, it is a particular instance of an exercise of 'buying power'.[36] Regardless of the source of its initiation, it can have as one of its consequences the driving of the small trader from his business. Put continuously at a price disadvantage too great to be compensable by any advantages which he, as an independent can uniquely offer, he may find it too hard to remain in the market place.[37]

A second, notable contributory factor was the merger. The period under consideration saw a wave of mergers and takeovers of such magnitude as amply to justify its description as a bout of 'merger mania'. The year 1986 witnessed around £13.5bn worth of take-over activity, with more than 400 acquisitions in each of the third and fourth quarters of the year.[38] Numerous mergers took place in the retailing sphere. Colourful deals involving household names abounded. Furthermore, not only were mergers amongst the prime contributors to concentration in retailing, their contribution to both its pace and proportions was considerable.[39]

The overshadowing concern

Of the various issues immediately raised by the 'revolution', it was not, however, the economic which predominated, neither was it the social. What caught and held the attention was the spate of large new store development, and where that development should take place. The principal and overshadowing concern was thus geographical and environmental. The fact that location was a prime focus of controversy raised, moreover, a further and vital point. While dispute attended the question of *where* the new shopping forms should be sited, it did not appear to extend to the more basic question of *whether*, in fact, they were *per se* desirable. Quite rightly, they were perceived as bestowing many benefits, inasmuch as they were designed *inter alia* to hold down prices, to provide variety and choice, to offer pleasant shopping conditions, to promote the interests of the car-borne shopper, to afford associated public amenities and (eventually and in some instances) to add a leisure and entertainment dimension. It seemed that these advantages were held in such high regard as to render the increase of their conferment a matter scarcely to be a subject of query. Of such treasure houses, the unspoken argument seemed to run, society could only want more. It is true that fears for the long term future were raised, and the question put as to what would happen when the forces energising the revolution died down. It was wondered by some whether there would be a glut of empty stores and warehouses, and, paying attention to the long term, there were those who urged the introduction of a national strategy.[40] The raising of anxieties was, however, only occasional, and in no way detracted from the buoyancy which infused the mood of the day.

With a subject like the retail revolution, where numerous associated issues would crowd and jostle for attention, it is not easy to provide even an impressionist picture. But the selection made will, it is hoped, serve to convey at least something of the hectic quality of this colourful chapter in the history of shopping. So dramatic were the events of the period that they made profound changes in the retail scene. Not only that, for the major actors on the stage, they also created what came to be regarded as a 'Golden Age' of UK retailing.

Planning and Competition: accommodating régimes

In the introduction it was noted that various intertwined conditions led to and inspired the explosion of development which characterised the '80s, each intrinsically complex. It was explained that this was very much the case with the legal strands in the skein, but that amongst them, the planning and competition régimes predominated as determinants of the modern shopping scene. In conjunction, it was said, the nature, guiding pattern and philosophy of these two systems provided an atmosphere in which new shopping forms might emerge and flourish. Moreover, not only was it the case that the two legal arenas afforded a non-hostile environment, on the contrary, they were positively accommodating.

Let us take first planning control. As the period in question dawned, the centrally expressed policy seemed somewhat unpromising. The applicable policy, enshrined in DoE Circular 96/77, was, it will be recalled, in a sense adverse to out of town retail development. It was thought preferable for large new stores to be sited where they could serve not only the car-borne shopper, and there was a desire to direct their location into existing urban areas. However, increasing numbers of successful appeals from refusals of planning permission for new stores testified to increasing readiness to accommodate the surge of retail power.[41] Against a background of mounting pressure for out of town shopping, and in answer to a parliamentary question, the Secretary of State in 1985 emphasised that the planning system should not inhibit competition, neither should it seek to preserve existing commercial interests, (although he did also say that, in exceptional circumstances, it would be necessary to take into account recent or proposed large scale retail developments, and to consider whether they were such that they could seriously affect the vitality and viability of a nearby town centre as a whole). His advice proved influential, and was reproduced in 1988 in a Planning Policy Guidance on Major Retail Developments (PPG 6).

It should be added that factors other than a PPG which to a certain extent emitted favourable signals were involved in the gradual 'warming' of planning to retail innovations. One was the fact that at the very heart of the planning régime there existed (and indeed, though somewhat modified, still does exist) a presumption in favour of granting planning permission. It had long been policy that permission should always be granted, unless there were important countervailing reasons. The other was the fact (as is well illustrated by the famous case of *Great Portland Estates plc v Westminster City Council*),[42] that the planning system did not (and still does not) strictly regard 'competition' as a planning consideration. Taken together, the (albeit partial) favourable tilting of inclination in central policy, the basic 'pro-developer' presumption, and the strict exclusion of 'competition' from planning considerations, all combined to provide an atmosphere conducive to the blossoming of new stores. And the combination was to prove yet more influential when, in its turn, its approach was combined with that of competition law.

Moving to competition law, we find that its fostering of the retail revolution lay in the way in which, after its virtual outlawing of r.p.m.,[43] it dealt with price discrimination and mergers. In both instances, though in different ways, it was the benign quality of its treatment which was the significant feature.

With regard first to price discrimination, there appeared in the statutes which followed the enactment of the Monopolies and Restrictive Practices (Inquiry and Control) Act 1948, provisions under which the practice might be confronted. Thus, under the Fair Trading Act 1973, references could be made to the Monopolies and Mergers Commission enabling investigations to be carried out into either the granting or inducing of discriminatory preference by a firm or firms in a monopoly position; and under the Competition Act 1980, investigations could be carried out by the Director General of Fair Trading, and if necessary, the Monopolies and Mergers Commission, into price discrimination as an instance of an 'anti-competitive practice'. However, unlike some systems, and notably that in the USA, the domestic competition law of the UK contained no specific prohibition of the practice, and the two enactments just mentioned were, as will emerge later, of limited impact.

Further, if there were explored the EEC as distinct from the domestic provisions of this country's competition régime, the position was taken no further. Article 85 of the Treaty of Rome outlawed anti-competitive agreements, and Article 86 the abuse of dominant position, and both expressly included within their sphere of influence the infliction of competitive disadvantage *via* discrimination, but, for either provision to bite, trade *between* member states had to be affected,[44] and the conduct in question impinged principally in the domestic market.

With regard to mergers, the key factor was the weakness of the control which the law exerted. The Fair Trading Act 1973, made provision for the referral of mergers meeting certain criteria to the Monopolies and Mergers Commission for investigation in the light of the public interest, and, if found to be in conflict therewith, for remedial action. However, only a tiny percentage of mergers were actually referred, and not only that, for a merger to be sustained there was no need to show any apparent derivative positive advantage, and there was also a presumption that a merger would not conflict with the public interest unless it was actually shown to do so.[45]

As with price discrimination, the market upon which the impact of mergers fell to be assessed was the domestic market. Even so, had the EEC provisions arisen for consideration little would have been added, for the control over mergers at this time might best be described as sparse. There was no specific Community-wide mergers régime, efforts in that direction having proved lengthy and controversial. Article 85 of the Treaty of Rome was considered rather inappropriate as a tool of merger control, and the utility of Article 86 was restricted.

In conjunction, the tolerance of discrimination and the diffidence towards mergers facilitated the remarkable growth of the major retail concerns. When added to the eventual (if guarded) 'acceptance' by planning policy of new shopping forms, the climate for the revolution was complete. If the one régime encouraged the runners, then the other smoothed the course, and together they provided an unprecedented opportunity. It was an opportunity which the major firms seized, and, having seized it, they ran the race with the most spectacular success.[46]

Indeed, it could be said that the success of these firms in meeting the fast-growing needs of an increasingly mobile and acquisitive society was the undoubted cynosure of retailing in the '80s. This truly was their 'Golden Age'.

Notes

1. In 'Retailing, Past , Present and Future', Lavery concludes her history of retailing with reference to the '80s retailing 'boom', noting that 'figures for April [1987] show a record level of spending...' *Shopping - a Housing and Planning Review Special*, vol. 42, no. 3, June 1987, p. 4.
2. p. 1.
3. *Ibid.*
4. *Ibid.*
5. at p. 1.
6. A vivid illustration is provided in an article on Tesco's £500mn development programme, in *Supermarketing*, 21st August 1987.
7. at p. 3.
8. – 'Help for the High Street: Some new approaches to revitalisation', April 1987. The mid-eighties arrival of the MetroCentre in Gateshead and Merryhill in Dudley attracted enormous attention.
9. 13th January 1987.
10. *Retail Planning Policies in Western Europe*, Ross L. Davies (ed), Routledge (1995) p. *xvii*.
11. Moreover, it was not necessarily a case of raising argument, the subject became the focus of the expression also of myriad opinions and views.
12. 28th January 1986.
13. 15th August 1987.
14. 'Retail Saturation (Part I)' Jeremy Smither, Equity Partner, Hillier, Parker, May & Rowden; 'Retail Saturation (Part II)' Peter Howitt, Director, Argyll Stores Ltd; IGD Convention 'New Perspective' 1987.
15. – more than twice that in its city centre.
16. Nigel Pitt (Principal Planner, Plymouth City Council) in *Shopping - a Housing and Planning Review Special, supra*, pp. 14 and 26. Leaflets, carrier bags and badges carried the message 'Southampton needs out of town shopping like a duck needs a rubber ring'.

17. *The Independent Grocer*, 19th June 1987.
18. *The Grocer*, 11th July 1987, 'Remember needs of urban shoppers'.
19. 27th May 1987.
20. 15th May 1987.
21. 'Megacentre Madness', *Shopping - a Housing and Planning Review Special, supra*, p. 7.
22. p. 2. It was pointed out that an inquiry into a single superstore proposal had become a rarity.
23. The point is illustrated by the case of *Solihull M.B.C. v The Secretary of State for the Environment and Tesco Stores Ltd* [1987] JPL 208. In this case, planning applications relating to a superstore and a town centre redevelopment scheme having been 'called-in' and made the subject of planning inquiries, the Secretary of State followed recommendations of the Inspectors and granted the former application but refused the latter. The Council sought to challenge the decisions by appealing to the High Court. The challenge was made on the ground that the Secretary of State had failed to produce a co-ordinated determination of the relative claims of applicants for sites in the area in question. On the contrary, he had pre-determined the Council's proposal by his determination of Tesco's proposal. The challenge did not succeed. McNeill J. could discern no basis '...for a finding [of]...pre-emption or prejudgement...there was nothing to suggest that the [council] lost because [Tesco's] had succeeded'.

    It may be added that where multiple applications are concerned, the inquiries themselves also raise difficulty.
24. *The Times*, 25th November 1987.
25. Statistics in *Hansard*, 24th July 1987, col. 552.
26. From the report of the speech to the 32nd annual congress of Spar UK by John Irish, the chief executive, reported in *The Grocer*, 30th May 1987.
27. *Ibid.*
28. Table 10.
29. *The Grocer*, 5th March 1988.
30. 'Verdict on Grocers and Supermarkets', *Verdict Research*, London.
31. See *Supermarketing*, 18th September 1987.
32. 'Retail concentration and the internationalisation of British Grocery Retailing', *Retail Change - Contemporary Issues*, R.Bromley and C.Thomas (eds), UCL Press (1993) p. 41.
33. *Ibid.*
34. *Ibid.* p. 43.
35. *Ibid.*
36. – a phenomenon to which we return.
37. Price discrimination both promotes and is, in turn, promoted by, the ascent of the large trader. There is a 'spiral' effect.
38. *The Times*, 13th August 1987.
39. Illustrative instances included Sears Holdings-Foster Menswear, Burton Group-Debenhams, Argyll-Safeway, Tesco-Hillards.

40. See, for instance, 'Trade Winds - the changing face of retailing and retail employment in the south east', Dr. John Montgomery (published by South East Economic Development Strategy), and, for instance, *The Grocer*, 9th May 1987, 'Moves to curb growth of out of town shopping centres'.
41. Reference was made in the previous chapter of this part to comment on the way in which earlier years had already seen relaxations of central government control, as also to the overcoming of local planning regulation by retailers.
42. [1985] AC 661. In this case the House of Lords were of the view that the bases on which plans are made should not include one of directly protecting individual traders. However, the continuation of certain industrial uses of land which were important to the character and functions of an area *was* a genuine planning purpose, and it did not matter that the result of its inclusion would be the protection of certain individual businesses, for this would merely be a *consequence*, not a *purpose*, of the plan.
43. – *via*, as noted earlier, the passing of the Resale Prices Act 1964.
44. – *i.e.* the law was *international* in nature.
45. All of which characteristics of the régime, as we shall see, remain with us still.
46. By the end of the decade the value of retail spending had risen by more than 40 per cent in real terms. 'The fastest growing areas were DIY and furniture and furnishings, though food sales also grew faster than retailing as a whole'. 'Trouble in Store? UK Retailing in the 1990s', Terry Burke and J.R. Shackleton, IEA Hobart Paper 130, 1996 p. 17.

4 The early and middle '90s ~ less certain times ...and a 'watershed'

Powerful influences and retail response

For retailing as for many other sectors of activity the years from the close of the '80s to the middle '90s were marked by some uncertainty, and this uncertainty culminated, in the Spring of 1997, in a watershed. They were times in which retailing was still shaped by numerous, powerful forces. Consumers themselves were changing, as, too, were their locations, shopping demands and behaviour, their spending power, lifestyles and values.[1] Furthermore, it was a period witnessing an incredibly rapid development of information technology, swiftly growing concern for the needs of the environment,[2] a passage of the major economies of Europe through recession, and an on-going tension between the need for continuing controls and the widespread desire for de-regulation. Such influences present considerable challenges to any sector, but the strength of the retail sector has always lain in its particular capacity to cope with change and changing needs, and even if the mid-'80s sense of excitement had begun to pale, the actual dynamism of the market would remain undiminished.[3]

An illustration of the sector's capacity for swift response appeared in the recession induced growth of discounting, and spread widely through food, DIY, clothing, shoes, household goods and bedding. In the food trade, mainland European discounters such as Aldi and Netto came to these shores showing an early understanding of the position. Between them, these two entrants registered sales of £473mn in 1994, and, together with Lidl, were reported in the food trade press in the late summer of 1996 as having achieved in the year 1995-6 a turnover of £1.2bn.[4] Other retail innovations which sprang from the price sensitive climate were warehouse clubs[5] and factory outlet malls. The former, located out of town, in simple style and having large car parking facilities, specialise in bulk sales of goods of quality but at reduced prices. The latter, also situated away from town centres, are comprised of groups of shops which specialise in seconds and end-of-line goods, usually under the manufacturers' names.[6] But instances of the sector's ability to move with the times would not all take the shape of 'price conscious' formats. Reflecting not only shifts in consumer habits, but also the underlying trends of increased affluence and consumption growth,[7] there emerged the highly successful development of 'convenience shopping', a shopping form in which 'price' is not, by definition, the predominant factor. While, as Corporate Intelligence Retailing (CIR) observed, the number of retail businesses had been falling continuously through the '80s and into the '90s, the CTNs[8] and convenience stores held up well.[9] In fact, more recent years would see a very rapid expansion of convenience shops, in particular those located on the forecourts of petrol stations,[10] and despite the intensity of the competition emanating from the multiples, this section of the market began to host players of real strength.[11]

If the retail race is viewed from the standpoint of successful development where price was not the governing determinant, the prize still, however, went to the grocery multiples – and it was surely a prize thoroughly earned. Their provision of choice, quality and variety, and the ease of access and pleasant ambience which they afforded, combined to bestow numerous and clear advantages upon the consumer.

During what was a critical period in British retailing, CIR observed that '...one of the most fundamental features [was] the exceptional expansion of the major grocery chains'.[12] Referring to the multiples' 'relentless development of one-stop shopping' and their irresistible encroachment into the domain of the small grocers and specialist food retailers, the group adverted to the fact that '...the multiple grocers raised their share of total retail sales from 23.8 per cent in 1980 to 32.4 per cent in 1994, while that of small grocery and specialist food retailers halved from 16.7 per cent to 8.2 per cent'.[13] Noting that '...the degree of penetration of the national retail fabric by just a handful [was] most advanced in food retailing',[14] CIR's research found that, from an existing high level of concentration,[15] there was a '...continuing trend towards even greater concentration in general, if not in all sub-sectors'.[16] In 1993 the top five retailers[17] accounted for 25 per cent of all retail sales, while the top ten[18] made up 33.9 per cent.[19]

Key aspects of the continuing development of the grocery multiples constituted the theme of a series of major contributions to the subject made at the turn of the decade by Neil Wrigley. In certain illuminating explorations of their growth path, he referred, for example, to the way in which the critical areas of competition between them shifted from price competition to new store development, and thence to a battle fought in terms of differential access to capital.[20] Drawing attention to the way in which the tolerant approach of the domestic competition law of the UK facilitated the multiples' ascent, he noted the shift in power away from the manufacturers, and the '...immense oligopsonistic buying power which conditions all retailer-supplier relations'.[21] Asking whether the multiples' 'golden age' could continue, he concluded 'yes', in terms of simple impact on the built environment, but perhaps 'no' in the sense that a different political climate might '...witness a tightened regulatory environment'.[22] Later, he was then to observe that, the spatial switching of retail capital on an intra-urban scale having produced a new urban landscape, it was the switching on an international scale which would prove a pivotal feature '...in any analysis of the future trajectory of corporate growth in British food retailing'.[23]

In contrast with the vigour evidenced by the emergence of new shopping forms, and more especially with the seemingly unassailable advance of the multiple retailers, a significant characteristic of the overall retail profile remained the continuing decline of the independent. Allusions to that decline are generally instanced by that of the small grocer, perhaps because it is a concomitant of the striking success of the superstores. Along with the inexorable rise of the latter, the arrival of Sunday trading and the growing number of discounters, a heavy toll was taken of independent retailers.[24] But the precariousness of independence was by no means particular to food retailing. To take another example, there was enacted in 1988 a statutory provision prohibiting resort to any condition which required that spectacles should be bought from the person conducting the eye test,[25] and supervening years saw the gradual vacating of the High Street by the independent optician.

Somewhat similarly, small carpet retailers and independent petrol dealers also found themselves in a fragile position. The retreat of the former came in the wake of the advance of out of town retailing, but the dwindling of the latter emerged from a more dramatic backdrop. For some thirty years independent petrol dealers had been fading, but their decline accelerated when superstores began a serious, successful drive into petrol retailing,[26] and their challenge was met by Esso with a high profile, price cutting exercise called 'Pricewatch'.[27] A fierce price war followed, as a result of which numbers of independents fell by the way.[28] When enquiries into the general state of the market were made by the Commons Trade and Industry Select Committee no deep seated fears were raised,[29] though there were expressions of anxiety regarding potential loss of garages in rural areas[30] and concerning the possible creation in such areas of local monopolies.[31]

To this saga of the uncertain state of so many independents,[32] there came also a contribution from certain challenges made to the still legally continuing resale price maintenance of medicaments.

For a quarter of a century, under the umbrella of an Order granted to protect small dispensing chemists,[33] resale price maintenance had been allowed on 'ethical medicines'[34] and 'proprietary medicines'.[35] In a vigorous and high profile campaign Asda launched an attack on that legality,[36] and alongside that move the competition authorities took interest in the continuing appropriateness or otherwise of the protective exemption. Anxious to learn whether the exemption should be retained, the Director General of Fair Trading initiated a review of resale price maintenance on medicaments and in due course launched a Consultation Paper to seek views.[37] The Paper brought together pointers which tended to suggest changes in circumstances such as *prima facie* to cast doubt upon the wisdom of any retention.

From the insights gained from his enquiries, the Director General reached the conclusion that over the years the position of community pharmacies had greatly altered. Contrary to the strenuous arguments of the Community Pharmacy Action Group that supermarkets would cut prices and lead to the departure of large numbers of community pharmacies, he believed that such businesses were '...now protected from local competition by Department of Health rules and on average 60 per cent of their gross margins [were] guaranteed by NHS prescription business'.[38]

Under the Resale Prices Act 1976, the Director General could apply to the Restrictive Practices Court for the discharge of an exempting Order, but needed the leave of the Court to make such an application, and the Court would grant it only if there were *prima facie* evidence of a material change in the relevant circumstances. In the Autumn of 1996, being of the belief that there was such a change (with, in his view, small pharmacies more secure than formerly) the Director General announced his intention of asking for leave to apply for a discharge of the exempting Order. To this situation we shall return,[39] it being sufficient now to say that at the end of the period presently under discussion the issue remained unresolved.[40]

With the emergence of new retail forms, the decline of the small, and the unremitting trend to concentration, it is notable that the *focii* of the '80s did not fade. Similarly the issue of the *siting* of retail premises remained pivotal. And while these highlights of the shopping scenario might be viewed simply as part of a natural evolution of retailing, it is impossible to ignore the controversy which they all continued to generate.

Continuing controversy

In a Paper entitled 'Trouble in Store – UK Retailing in the 1990s',[41] Burke and Shackleton addressed what might be regarded as 'key' issues for UK retailing in the final decade of the century, including high retail rents, the liberalisation of shopping hours, and environment matters such as waste generation and the industrialisation of horticulture.[42] Amongst them, there naturally featured the difficult questions of economic concentration and geographical location. Regarding the former, the authors noted its increase but also the persistence of competition,[43] and took the view that, in its present degree, the public was unharmed. Regarding the latter, they acknowledged the importance of environmental considerations, but believed that tighter control of out of town and edge of town retail development might of itself have undesirable consequences, such as protection from competition, the frustration of consumer preference and increased congestion in town centres.

From their wide ranging scrutiny the conclusion was drawn that here was an industry which was at once innovative and greatly important to the economy, the costs of interfering with the development of which or of trying to reverse it were, they suggested, '...likely considerably to exceed the benefits'.[44] However, in a discussion paper entitled 'The Public Policy Implications of Increasing Retailer Power' by Paul Dobson and Michael Waterson,[45] a different view of retail developments was taken. Rather than being necessarily promotive of consumer welfare and efficiency, these authors thought that increased concentration might involve higher profit levels for established retailers and plausibly prove to reduce consumer welfare.[46]

Although they considered that many advantages had arisen from changes in retailing, they regarded as questionable the view held by the Monopolies and Mergers Commission and the Office of Fair Trading that the exercise of buying power was advantageous because benefits extracted would be passed on to consumers. They proffered the thought that greater concentration could afford an increase not only in buying but also in selling power, and that while the effect of the former might be to reduce intermediate prices, the effect of the latter might be to permit increased price-cost margins, '...effectively increasing the total surplus available to firms'.[47] Then, if the second effect sufficiently dominated, concentration might actually permit increased intermediate prices and this, '...combined with increased retail margins, might lead to distinctly higher final prices'.[48]

In marked contrast with any 'anti-further regulation' argument was the burden of a publication entitled 'Off our Trolleys' – though this Paper was confined to food retailing and the hypermarket economy.[49] The authors of this contribution to the debate conducted a broad survey of many facets of food retail power, and took the line that food retailing *via* superstores involved subsidy, on account of costs to both the environment and to those groups of society who are at a disadvantage. Thus, they noted that the benefits which such outlets might provide for certain consumers were '...at the expense of others without access to supermarkets – typically the old, the car-less and the poor'.[50] They contended that from a social viewpoint the market was not 'appropriately structured', while from the 'land use' aspect, retail development might cause damage to sites of ecological value, and edge or out of town stores undermine town centre shopping.[51]

Being of the view that growing retail concentration and its consequences were matters of priority for public debate, they concluded their report with numerous recommendations. So, for instance, in the context of competition policy, they recommended *inter alia* the introduction of a policy of restricting price discrimination, an enquiry by the House of Commons Select Committee on Trade and Industry into the implications of concentration, and the bringing in of a Green Paper on the future of food retailing, as part of a review of the whole food economy.[52]

In the context of the controversy surrounding retailing, reference may lastly be made to a survey which, like 'Off our Trolleys' concerned *food* retailing, but which was very brief. 'Food for Thought' was a report by *Which?* in March 1996 which set out succinctly the various 'fors' and 'againsts' of the 'multiple dominated' retail pattern. Speaking on the one hand of the freshness of the product, the vastness of choice, the ease of parking and the long opening hours offered by the multiples, and, on the other, of allegations of damage done by such formats to town centre shopping as, too, of their disadvantaging of the poor, it emphasised the need for local authorities dealing with development proposals '...to strike a balance between the needs of the community – including non-car users – and retailers, the local economy and the environment'.

While these Papers varied in thrust, they all bore witness to the continuous vibrancy of the sector. If, however, from the multi-coloured skein of relevant issues we confine our attention to those of location and concentration, what, in the first half of the decade, was the picture? There were out of town centres with at least 25 per cent of all retail sales,[53] innumerable projects blessed with planning consent, and many retailers having yet a strategic commitment to moving out of town.[54] Again, there was a stirring in merger activity after the recession induced halt,[55] and an unabated exercise of buying power, as manifested in *inter alia* the negotiation of discriminatory discounts.

Legal influences over 'key' issues

It being the case that the exercise of buying power and the interest in out of centre development remained amongst the 'key' factors in the shaping of modern retailing, it is necessary to explore the continuing impact upon them of competition and planning policy respectively. Earlier it was pointed out that the benign character of the domestic competition law of the UK, the lack of involvement of EC competition law, and the eventual (albeit guarded) 'acceptance' by planning control of new shopping forms, all served greatly to fuel the revolutionary fire of the '80s. Further, it was explained that the coinciding of these tendencies facilitated the spectacular developments of the time. However, while it was the case that, in the '80s and for a while beyond, the direction of competition policy and retail planning policy converged, as the present decade progressed their paths parted. The reason was simple: the aim of competition policy remained constant, while the goal of retail planning moved.

If we take first domestic competition law and its influence over the extraction of discriminatory benefits we find no change. It will be recalled that there was no specific prohibition of the practice, and the statutes which provided for investigation of such conduct were of limited impact. More particularly, the period now under consideration witnessed no introduction of any specific control of discrimination, because, perhaps, of the recognised difficulties associated with its regulation. Further, in the EC as distinct from the domestic component of the competition régime, there was no shift in the position already recounted. As earlier noted, Articles 85 and 86 of the Treaty of Rome both sought to challenge the infliction of competitive disadvantage *via* discrimination, but theirs was an inter-state jurisdiction, and the matter would remain a primarily domestic one.

Turning to mergers, it is again necessary briefly to advert to both the domestic and the EC components of the control régime. So far as the former component was concerned, it remained inherently benign. Only a tiny proportion of mergers were referred for inquiry, and the system remained overall favourably inclined towards them.[56] In the case, however, of the European component, the law greatly developed at the turn of the decade, on account of the adoption and operation of the EC Merger Regulation,[57] a Regulation specifically designed to regulate 'concentrations with a

Community dimension'.[58] It provided for the investigation of such 'concentrations' by the Commission. The investigation was to be carried out to test compatibility with the aims of the Community, and, where a concentration was found incompatible, provision was made for its blocking or reversal.

Despite the law's enhancement in the period under examination, however, EC merger control had as yet greatly to weigh upon the UK retail scene, and for the following reasons:– As earlier observed, the retail market was primarily a domestic one. Not only that, the Merger Regulation would not catch large numbers of concentrations. The criteria by reference to which it was to bring within its embrace only those concentrations with 'a Community dimension' set very high quantitative thresholds, and, furthermore, excluded those involving undertakings each of which achieved more than two thirds of its aggregate Community-wide turnover within one and the same Member State.[59]

With the promotion of free competition remaining a major plank of UK competition policy, the lightness of touch shown in its approach to both the exercise of buying power and mergers comes as no surprise, for, according to context, such conduct can be as much pro- as anti-competitive. Furthermore, it chimed naturally with the high profile 'de-regulation' philosophy which came to permeate the national fabric. While this de-regulatory thrust enjoyed both a high profile and widespread impact, it was its expression in the loosening of control over shop hours that is of direct relevance to competition in retailing. Given the immediacy of its impact, the legislative development in question must (albeit briefly) detain us. Two Acts are involved, the Sunday Trading Act 1994, and the De-Regulation and Contracting Out Act of the same year.

It was a prolonged and bitterly fought battle which culminated in the enactment of the former. Many thought the previous law, as enshrined in the Shops Act 1950, had too many anomalies to be sustainable. There were traders who opened on Sundays regardless of the law, law enforcement was patchy[60] and numerous efforts were made directed to law reform. In 1993, after years of controversy, the Government issued a White Paper in which three options were put forward. Between concepts of total de-regulation on the one hand and detailed regulation on the other, there was a notion of partial de-regulation in which smaller stores would be able to open at will on Sundays, but larger stores would be confined to opening for six hours only. Eventually, it was this mid-way option which found favour. Under the Act, shops with a floor area not exceeding 280 sq. metres may open on Sundays for as long as is desired, but, subject to certain excepted shops, larger retail premises may not open unless *inter alia* they give notice to the local authority. Further, they may open only for six hours between 10.00 *a.m.* and 6.00 *p.m.*[61]

In the De-Regulation and Contracting Out Act 1994 there are provisions for the removal of other earlier restrictions on shops' hours of opening and closing. Since the bringing into force of ss 22 to 24 of this Act obligations regarding the time of closing in an evening are removed, and the rules relating to early closing are also removed.[62]

While in the period under discussion the de-regulation of shop hours had only a short history, it was influential. The opening up of Sunday in particular appeared to accentuate the trend to out of town shopping and the drift away from the town centre.[63] Moreover, it was regarded as a contributory factor to the continuing heavy toll of the independent.[64]

Even if by 1994 the notion of market forces as a panacea for all social and economic ills was beginning slightly to fade, a spirit of freedom was coursing as vividly through shop hours reforms as through competition policy, and the strength of their parallel sense of purpose was patent. This being so, it becomes all the more interesting to observe the distance which was growing between the path trodden by these two régimes on the one hand, and by retail planning on the other. It was a crucial distancing, to which we now turn.

As has been mentioned, the reason for the growing gap was not to be found with any change of direction on the part of competition law. This system, together with the de-regulation régime, would remain true to the lodestar of free enterprise: the gap came from a shift in retail planning policy – the earlier, to some extent 'accommodation' of large out of town development giving way to a less favourable stance.[65]

The gradual route by which the shift would take place can be traced by reference to certain landmarks. We begin with the 1988 Planning Policy Guidance note which, it will be recalled, reproduced the advice of the Secretary of State that, whereas planning should neither inhibit competition nor preserve existing commercial interests, it was, *in exceptional circumstances*, necessary to take account of the effects of large-scale retail development in the locality, and consider whether they could seriously affect the vitality and viability of a nearby town centre as a whole.[66]

A few years later, following mounting anxieties over adverse impacts upon the environment,[67] and deepening concern for the equality of social opportunities,[68] a revised edition of retail Planning Policy Guidance (PPG 6) emerged.[69] Extended so as to cover shopping policies across the spectrum of shopping,[70] and also the rôle of town centres for a whole range of purposes,[71] this important revision did not try dramatically to alter earlier policies,[72] but nevertheless signalled more clearly the Government's desire to ensure both the vitality and viability of town centres and the *general* availability of a broad range of shopping facilities. As to the former, it envisaged the refusal of permission for out of centre development where there was clear evidence of an undermining of a centre's vitality and viability, and as to the latter, it exhorted the siting of retail development where it was likely to be accessible by a choice of means of transport.

To the tilting of the balance against out of town locations effected by the revised PPG 6 greater emphasis was soon to be added by a further pronouncement of central policy. This came a year later in the shape of Planning Policy Guidance 13 on Transport. Embracing the location of a variety of forms of development and transport policies associated with them, this PPG aimed at ensuring local planning authorities pursue land-use policies and transport programmes in a way which furthers the *desiderata* of environment protection. To this end it sought *inter alia* to reduce reliance on the car and encouraged alternative means of travel, and, in the context of retail development, furthered these objectives via a range of exhortations. It urged, for instance, the maintenance and revitalisation of existing centres, the encouragement of convenience shopping, a search for edge of centre sites for large stores where central locations are not available, and the avoidance of sporadic siting of comparison goods units along road corridors.[73]

Regardless of the strength of the signal emitted by these expressions of policy, the clearest message was even so still to come. It appeared in 1996, and took the form of yet a further revision of PPG 6. In this version of guidance on 'Town Centres and Retail Developments' the increasing chill of the official climate to out of town development was made plain for all to see.

With the objectives of reducing reliance on cars, maximising opportunities to use other means of transport, and sustaining and enhancing the viability of town centres, it exhorts local planning authorities to adopt planning policies designed *inter alia* to locate major generators of travel in existing centres, and to safeguard and strengthen local centres. In keeping with these objectives, the Guidance seeks the pursuit of the so called 'sequential approach' in the selection of sites for new retail development. This approach requires local planning authorities and developers, when choosing sites, to be able to '...demonstrate that all potential town centre options have been thoroughly assessed before less central sites are considered for key town centre uses...'.[74] If such a sequential approach to preferred sites is taken,[75] then, the Guidance continues, this '...means that first preference should be for town centre sites...followed by edge of centre sites, district and local centres, and only then out of centre sites in locations that are accessible by a choice of means of transport'.[76] Here, it will be noted, is an approach characterised by an aura of restraint, an aura which similarly permeates that part of the Guidance which sets out considerations for the assessment of out of centre retail development, (considerations including accessibility by a variety of modes of transport, and impact on nearby centres, their quality, character and physical condition).[77]

So it was that in the space of only a few years, and *via* a continuous re-shading of emphasis rather than any abrupt change of direction, an atmosphere of fairly ready acceptance of new retail forms came to yield to a sense of more cautious accommodation. The measure of the change of direction sought by the revision was implicitly highlighted in an account given of the unveiling in Summer 1996 of the foundation stone of the vast Bluewater out of town shopping centre in Kent. Under the headline 'Huge out of town shopping and leisure centre beats policy switch', there was described the commencement of a £700mn development which was '...the largest and possibly last of the out of town shopping centres that have changed the face of many communities...'. Had they applied later, the developers admitted, such a scheme would have been unlikely to gain approval; this was one of the last to be granted planning permission before the rules were tightened.[78]

It was of course realised that undoubted advantages may attend such development. They include the regeneration of earlier used industrial land, the bringing in to an area of thousands of new jobs, the attraction of inward investment, and the creation of a shopping environment simultaneously safe but 'fun'.[79] But these benefits constitute simply one side of the coin. On the other are the deep concerns sought to be addressed by the revised PPG – the part played by out of town shopping to the running down of city centres, and the pollution caused by the encouragement of car-borne shoppers. In seeking to address these concerns, the revision might be said, moreover, to have a double benefit: in addition to its intrinsic domestic worth, there was its contribution to the UK's commitment to the international, environment protection goal of 'sustainable development'.[80]

Although in theory the revised PPG might appear a really cogent planning 'tool', the important question would be as to the attainability of its objectives. Was it not arguable that in truth it could be no more than an attempt to latch the stable door after the horse had bolted, in that, by the time of its inception, the great surge of out of town development was, to an extent, already spent? Likewise, might it not be contended that the public were so wedded to the motor car that any effort to break that bond would be resisted, and would furthermore require not simply the appearance of a revised PPG but a fundamental shift in attitude?

In March 1997 there was published a report of the House of Commons Environment Committee on Shopping Centres.[81] In the course of it, the Committee referred to the general expectation that the sequential test contained in the revision would '...lead to a significant improvement in the overall picture, with retail development increasingly likely to take place in or on the edge of town centres and less likely to take place on out of town sites'.[82] That expectation, they observed, had been largely fulfilled.

Even so, the Committee explained that certain concerns remained, and amongst those which they chose to highlight were an increase in development pressure from the leisure industry, and what was seen as a continuing threat to small and market towns. Regarding the former, they noted that while the main focus of concern had been non-traditional forms of retail development, the more recent growth area was large-scale leisure development, in particular multi-screen cinemas. And regarding the latter, they noted the way in which, the large towns and cities having been catered for, developers of the non-traditional retail forms were turning their attention to the smaller towns, '...in their quest to maintain market share and competitive edge'.[83] It was a trend, the Committee opined, which had given rise to concern.

Amongst the concerns which the Committee considered was also the significant one of existing planning permissions. They observed that '[M]any of the developments which are still taking place on out of town sites...were approved before the introduction of the sequential approach',[84] and, further, recorded their understanding that a '...number of [the] 'existing permissions' [remained] to be developed, in some cases years after permission was first granted'.[85]

Relevant recommendations of the Committee reflected the desire for a tough approach to applications for large scale leisure applications,[86] for full impact studies to accompany applications for significant retail development particularly in or around small towns,[87] and for the considering afresh, with the sequential approach, of applications for renewal of lapsed permissions.[88] Such aspiration testified amply to the strength of the desire for environmental protection, but a doubt would surely linger as to the long term capacity of a planning régime to constrain the forces of the market.[89]

If the revised PPG evidenced the implicit tension between environment protection and market trends, so, likewise, it also revealed the considerable nature of the distance between the régimes of planning and competition policy, a distance which certain parallel activity confirmed.

Shortly after the revised PPG appeared, the Department of Trade and

Industry launched draft legislation for the reform of certain aspects of competition law. A document enshrining a Bill and inviting comment on the implementation of reform proposals was issued in the late Summer of 1996, as the latest stage in a reform exercise of many years' standing. Briefly, the desire was to replace the Restrictive Trade Practices Act 1976, with a prohibition of anti-competitive agreements, and to strengthen the power of the Director General of Fair Trading to deal with abuse of market power under the Fair Trading Act 1973, and the Competition Act 1980.[90] Inasmuch as mergers lay outside its embrace, and the treatment of price discrimination under its aegis would probably not have significantly differed, the proposed reforms appeared to lack immediate significance for those particular elements of commercial activity which had driven the retail revolution, but the proposals demand attention for two reasons:– First, their objective was the pursuit of the yet more effective promotion of free competition, and so served to emphasise the gap which had grown between the two régimes under consideration. Secondly, they were to prove a forerunner of more far reaching proposals yet to come.

As the days of 1996 gradually shortened, there was no lessening in importance of the retail issues on which we have focused: there was no sudden, neat solution to the continuing 'in or out of centre' debate, neither was there any reversal of the concentration process or of the powerful rôle of the major retailers.[91] All such matters and indeed others at the heart of the sector, such as, for instance, the growth of internationalisation,[92] the increase of diversification,[93] the value of customer loyalty[94] and the problem of crime[95] still bubbled in the retail cauldron. But along with other innumerable economic and social issues, they were to become for a while eclipsed by an issue of increasing and overarching importance: the office of the then current Government would soon terminate, a General Election was due.

Eventually, it was called for 1st May 1997, and there followed an exceptionally long campaign.[96] Throughout, the view was widely held that there would be a change of Government, but the extent in the shift of public mood had, perhaps, not been anticipated. On a flood tide of excitement, 'New Labour', personified in Tony Blair, a deeply committed and vigorous leader, swept to power with an unprecedented majority. In a state of public euphoria, a 'new dawn' was heralded, and a chapter of eighteen years' duration closed.

Only time would tell whether any long term changes following so dramatic an election would share the intensity of the occasion, and whether they would do so either in the context of our particular subject or in the far broader context of the national fabric, but the happenings of that historic May night provided of themselves an ending to this stage of our retail saga. They did so because they testified to an urge for a change of direction. The retail revolution and its shopping legacy were the product of an era which had cherished to the point of devotion the free market ethic. Now, it seemed, there might be a wish to dilute that espousal with the recognition and pursuit of other equally desirable goals. Yet, it had to be asked, would the altered mood be translated into new and different policies? Or, by contrast, would it still be (and in particular for our purposes) 'business as usual'? We could continue our progress by considering these questions in the light of the experience of the efforts to date of the Blair administration, but it is thought that at this point the study is aided by turning to a closer consideration of the two areas of law in issue. We move on accordingly to Part II, which contains a review of the law and policy of planning and its impact on retailing. The following part then deals with competition control and retail matters. We shall find that there emerge in the course of these explorations both the recent and current issues of moment, and the approaches being taken to them.

Notes

1. See further 'Retail Change in the European Community', John A. Dawson, ch. 1 in *Retail Planning Policies in Western Europe*, Ross L. Davies (ed), p. 1. The chapter contains a useful summary in tabular form of major changes in food retailing in Europe between 1970 and 1994.
2. An intriguing, if somewhat particular, instance of environmental concern emerged in the development of Hampton, a new town for Peterborough. According to a feature entitled 'Space for newt tenants in new town' (*The Times*, 31st January 1996), one of the greatest conflicts concerned the future of what was claimed to be the largest colony of great crested newts in Europe. The answer was to relocate them in a specially created wildlife reserve.
3. In their report entitled 'Retailing in Europe – United Kingdom 1995', Corporate Intelligence Retailing (CIR) noted (at p. 29) that total retail sales reflected '...almost frantic growth during the 1980s, equally rapid retrenchment to 1992, and a return to a more even keel in 1993 and 4'.
4. – according to CIR (See *The Grocer*, 24th August 1996).
5. – though not with any great success; (See *The Times*, 18th March 1996 – 'Shoppers shun American-style retail hypermarkets').
6. Both these shopping forms are rooted in the USA. Shopping as a leisure activity is emphasised in the latter form, the shopping village of Street in

Somerset, for instance, providing a notable visitor 'attraction'. (See, with regard to the popularity of such shopping formats as a destination for a British 'day out', a feature entitled 'A whole new retail experience', the *Sunday Times*, 28th July 1996.)

7. In his chapter 'Retail Change in the European Community' *supra*, Dawson notes that '...alongside...evolving demographic changes is [a] steady, long-term increase in affluence [in] the European population. Inevitably there are short-term fluctuations with business cycles but the long-term trend is of growth', (at p. 18). In 'Retailing in Europe 1995', CIR pointed out (at p. 3) that the British economy was now in its third year of recovery, and that the outlook remained positive for 1996. Further, *The Grocer* for 23rd March 1996 noted that (at p. 10) according to figures released by the Institute of Grocery Distribution '...from 1990 to mid-1995 the grocery retailing market in the UK rose 30.1 per cent from £58.2bn to £75.8bn'.
8. *i.e.* retailers of confectionery, tobacco and newspapers.
9. 'Retailing in Europe - United Kingdom' 1995, p. 36.
10. *The Grocer* for 14th September 1996 speaks of '...another multiple [jumping] into bed with a petrol giant and a bouncing forecourt baby [being] conceived...'.
11. An interesting short article on a perception of the great potential of the convenience sector as a high quality complement to the multiples is given in *Convenience Store*, 25th August 1995. In *The Grocer* on 10th August 1996 it is noted that around '...75 per cent of households visit forecourt and convenience stores every four weeks and annual sales are estimated at over £1.9bn a year and growing'.
12. *Supra*, p. 31.
13. *Ibid.*
14. *Ibid.* p. 22.
15. In this Report it was calculated that in 1992 a mere 0.1 per cent of all retail business accounted for 59.4 per cent of total retail sales; (see p. 22). It was noted (*ibid.*) that in clothing and footwear the leading ten multiples accounted for virtually half of all sales, and in other non food sectors about 30 to 40 per cent.
16. *Ibid.*
17. *i.e.* Sainsbury, Tesco, Argyll (now Safeway), Marks and Spencer and Asda.
18. *i.e.* adding in Kingfisher, Boots, Isoscelles, Kwik Save and the John Lewis Partnership.
19. *Ibid.*
20. 'Is the "golden age" of British grocery retailing at a watershed?' *Environment & Planning A*, 1991, vol. 23, p. 1537.
21. In 'Antitrust regulation and restructuring of grocery retailing in Britain and the USA', *Environment and Planning A*, 1992, vol. 24, p. 727, he underscored the benign ethos of the UK law by contrasting it with the more rigorous approach which for a while dominated the American experience. Providing a sketch of the exercise of buying power in the UK, he pointed out

(at p. 730) how the multiples, controlling the allocation of selling space, could impose ever more stringent conditions of supply, and demand ever larger discriminatory discounts. (See, further, his chapter on 'Retail concentration and the internationalisation of British grocery retailing' in *Retail Change - contemporary issues*, R. Bromley and C. Thomas (eds), UCL Press (1993). In this chapter (at pp. 45-6) he drew together the principal features of the way in which power shifted through the '60s, '70s and '80s from manufacturers to retailers, referring to aspects including not only the latters' buying capacity but also their highly efficient distribution systems, low operating costs and typical negative working-capital cycles).

22. 'Is the 'golden age' of British grocery retailing at a watershed?', *Environment and Planning A*, 1991, vol. 23, pp. 1542-3.
23. 'Retail concentration and the internationalisation of British Grocery retailing', in *Retail Change - contemporary issues, supra*, at p. 42.
24. (See, on this subject, an article in the *Sunday Times* 8th September 1996 dealing with Booker's bid for Nurdin & Peacock.) Similarly, in *Convenience Store*, 5th April 1996, the editor, Tony Hurren, highlighted the way in which, since 1960, great numbers of small food retailers had been driven out of business, '...and, although perhaps not entirely to blame, the pricing policies of major multiples [had] been a contributory factor'. One of the ways in which they remain able to overcome the disadvantageous position in which they are placed is via entry into buying groups, and CIR in their 1995 Report explained that '[M]any small grocers have joined symbol buying groups as a means of defence against the encroachment of the multiples'. *Supra*, see pp. 42 and ff, (on the grocery sector). Again, in 1994, in the European Commission Commerce and Distribution Series, it was observed that while in the UK there was no specific government encouragement of co-operation between firms, '...small retailers have been encouraged to form buying groups and to join voluntary chains by the growth of multiple retailers who have the ability to obtain better terms from manufacturers when buying goods'. (See 'Measures in the field of Commerce in the EU', vol. 2 Commerce and Competition, p. 19.) According to *The Grocer*, 25th May 1996, the independent sector slipped from a 15 per cent share of the market some eight years previously to 9.5 per cent, and a month previously a feature in *The Times* (30th April 1996) spoke of the pressure being brought upon the Government by independent bakers who were 'under threat from supermarkets' and sought help.
25. The Health and Medicines Act 1988, s 14. As a Bill, this enactment was regarded as a 'flagship' of the 'de-regulation' movement.
26. According to *The Times*, 12th March 1996, the superstores had more than 2.0 per cent of the annual £15bn retail petrol market.
27. –a campaign designed to match the lowest cost fuel in each area.
28. See *The Times*, 27th June 1996.
29. 6th Report. Petrol Retailing (Session 1995-6, HC 527).
30. Because garages often had associated facilities such as a shop, post office,

taxi service, *etc.*, it was found that communities could lose an important amenity. A brief but critical appraisal of the report appeared in *Forecourt News*, September 1996 Issue 52, where it was opined that '...the Government and the OFT [had] washed their hands...'.

31. An angle from which the Committee viewed the decline of the independents was that of its impact upon their value as providers of effective competition for the oil companies, and hence as inhibitors of any abuse of market power by the latter. The members thought (along with the Office of Fair Trading) that where they operated, the superstores had taken on this mantle (see p. *xiv*).
32. Though consider, by contrast, as noted in *The Times*, 12th March 1996, the arrival of 'family business' dry cleaners, and the way in which they were responsible for the disappearance of Sketchley from the high streets. Such businesses had the ability to offer a level of service which economies of scale could not match.
33. The Order provided exemption from the basic statutory prohibition of resale price maintenance under the resale prices legislation.
34. *i.e.* broadly speaking, branded prescription-only medicines.
35. *i.e.* broadly speaking, branded over-the-counter medicines.
36. See, *e.g.* 'ASDA ready for new offensive in drug price war', *The Times*, 12th June 1996.
37. 'Medicaments RPM Exemption Review', Office of Fair Trading, July 1996.
38. Office of Fair Trading News Release No 43/96, 18th October 1996, p. 2.
39. The other remaining bastion of r.p.m. was , of course, in the arena of books. The Publishers' Association formally announced the NBA's demise in the Autumn of 1995, and in due course the Restrictive Practices Court was to come to the view that resale price maintenance for books could no longer be upheld. (See *In re Net Book Agreement* 1957 (No 4) [1998] ICR 753.) In social terms, Tom Astill, Director of the National Pharmaceutical Association, impliedly highlighted the obvious contrast between books and medicines when he simply opined that '...it would be short-sighted to risk losing a valuable local pharmacy service, just to save 10p on a bottle of vitamins'. (*The Times*, 17th October 1995).
40. In the report of the Monopolies and Mergers Commission on the proposed mergers between *Unichem plc / Lloyds Chemists plc* and *GEHE AG / Lloyds Chemists plc*, a long-term trend towards increased concentration in pharmacy ownership was noted, as, too, an increase in pharmacies being located in supermarkets (whether directly managed or functioning under franchise or concession arrangements), Cm 3344 (1996) at p. 17.
41. Hobart Paper No 130, Institute of Economic Affairs, 1996. (As with all Institute Papers, the conclusions drawn are those of the authors.)
42. Regarding the industrialisation of horticulture, the authors referred to the claims being made that the exercise of buying power by superstores has led to the squeezing out of small producers. Again, they referred to the way in which (it had been alleged) the move of the large retailers into selling fresh

fruit and vegetables led to the pursuit of harmful, intensive methods of farming. (*Ibid.* p. 82)

43. They believed anxieties concerning the structure of the market to be exaggerated; 'although there is a fairly small number of big players with large market shares, there is a high degree of competition from both traditional and new forms of retailing' (*Ibid.* p. 88).
44. *Ibid.* p. 90.
45. A discussion paper from the University of Nottingham School of Management & Finance, 1996.
46. They suggested that the view of retailing as a highly competitive activity might be misplaced, and that competition authorities might have to give more serious consideration to the increasing power of the retail sector.
47. See p. 19.
48. *Ibid.*
49. – by Hugh Rowen and Tim Lang with Caroline Dumonteil – a publication of the Institute for Public Policy Research, '...intended to open a debate about what type of food economy the UK needs for the 21st century'. (The Report reflected the views of its owners not the collective view of the Institute.)
50. *Ibid.* p. 1.
51. *Ibid.* pp. 25-6.
52. *Ibid.* See pp. 51-2. On the 'downside' of multiple retailing in terms of social costs, see, too, a feature entitled 'True cost of aubergines all year round', *The Guardian*, 31st October 1995.
53. See CIR's 'Retailing in Europe - United Kingdom 1995', p. 19. This is noted in the context of the official attitude to retail planning.
54. The CIR Report *supra* commented that '...at the core of the matter is the fact that a majority of shoppers are wedded to their cars'. (p. 19).
55. At pp. 23-4, the CIR Report *supra* plotted the exceptional mergers and acquisitions activity of the '80s, its cease in 1990, its very low level in 1990-3, and its gradual stirring in 1993. The years 1994 and 1995 saw acquisitions such as Tesco's of Wm. Low and Sainsbury's of Texas Homecare, and, likewise the building up of the FACIA fashions and retail conglomerate.
56. Though, at the start of the decade, a significant 'retail sector' merger was viewed unfavourably by the Commission. Kingfisher plc, a large, diversified retailing group, wished to purchase Dixons Group plc, whose main activity was the retail distribution of electrical appliances and photographic equipment. This desire brought under scrutiny the retail market for electrical appliances. There was, the Commission noted, exceptionally keen competition in this sphere between the 'Comet' subsidiary of Kingfisher and the principal outlets of Dixons – these competitors being the largest 'players' in the UK. Inasmuch as this rivalry would cease, and would lead to higher prices without compensatory benefits, the Commission concluded (with one dissent) that the proposed merger would be against the public interest.

57. Regulation 4064/89, OJ [1989] L395/1, [1990] 4 CMLR 286.
58. The Regulation uses the word 'concentration', while in the UK it is more usual to speak of a 'merger'.
59. See Article 1(2) of the Regulation.
60. There were high profile legal battles in which the Treaty of Rome was involved.
61. A most interesting account of the circumstances leading up to the enactment of the Act is provided in the Current Law annotations, by W.H.Thomas, Solicitor, editor of the *Encyclopaedia of Consumer Law*. (Again, on the question when, for the purposes of Sunday trading a shop is a 'large shop', attention is drawn to *Haskins Garden Centres Ltd v East Dorset District Council* (*The Times*, 7th May 1998) where it was held that the '...court should take an extended rather than a snapshot view'.)
62. See The Deregulation and Contracting Out Act 1994 (Commencement No 1) Order 1994 (SI 1994 No 3037). In a feature on the 'brave new world of the nocturnal supermarket', Tesco and Safeway were reported to have '...confounded the sceptics and given a thumbs-up verdict to their first 24-hour shopping experiment outside the Christmas period'. (See 'People of the Night', *The Grocer*, 8th March 1997.)
63. In *The Grocer*, 7th September 1996, reference was made to a call by property consultants Healey and Baker for greater commitment to Sunday trading in the town centre. From research conducted, they believed that if such an effort were not made, there was the risk of loss of '...even more turnover to out of town stores'.
64. In the earlier noted article on the Booker bid for Nurdin & Peacock (*Sunday Times*, 8th September 1996), reference was made to an appreciation of the way in which the introduction of Sunday trading (along with the increasing number of discounters and the inexorable rise of supermarkets) was contributing to the decline of independents.
65. A most interesting account of policy change is given in 'Retail Planning Policy in the UK' by Elizabeth Howard, chapter 12 in *Retail Planning Policies in Western Europe*, Ross L. Davies (ed), Routledge (1995).
66. PPG 6 'Major Retail Developments', reproducing the answer given in 1985 by the Secretary of State to a parliamentary question.
67. How quickly environment protection was to become one of the most pressing problems of the current decade hardly needs saying. Major matters such as global warming and deforestation inevitably catch and keep the headlines, but the subject embraces issues ranging '...from the street corner to the stratosphere', (as noted in the famous White Paper on the environment, 'This Common Inheritance' (Cm. 1200, 1990). And its concern for the particular as much as the general is reflected in the earlier mentioned feature on the provision of sanctuary for the great crested newts.
68. In this context, perceived inequalities were in the form of access to shopping, *i.e.* whether or not the shopper was car-borne, or reliant on public transport.
69. 'Town Centres and Retail Developments' (July 1993).

70. – *i.e.* not only major new retail developments often located out of town centres.
71. – *i.e.* not just shopping purposes.
72. See further the Memorandum by the Department of the Environment in the minutes of evidence taken before the Environment Committee during the inquiry conducted into 'Shopping Centres and their Future'. (House of Commons 1993/4 4th Report, vol. II.).
73. Concerns over congestion and pollution have caused the link between shopping and access to shopping to become a matter of increasing significance.
74. Revised PPG 6 (June 1996) para. 1.10.
75. The Government recognised (*ibid.*, para. 1.12) that '...the approach requires flexibility and realism from local planning authorities, developers and retailers'.
76. *Ibid.* para. 1.11.
77. *Ibid.* see para. 4.3 and following.
78. *The Times*, 18th July 1996.
79. For a 'toast to Britain's temples of consumerism', see *The Guardian*, 8th October 1996 – a lengthy feature by Paul Barker on the social value and popularity of the shopping mall.
80. 'Sustainable development' is development of a kind which meets the needs of the present generation without foreclosing the ability of later generations to meet theirs. It embodies international aspirations for the reconciliation of the objectives of economic growth and environment protection – one hundred and fifty states committing themselves to the concept at the UN Conference on 'Environment and Development' in 1992, (the so called 'Earth Summit', held at Rio). Espousal by the UK of the principle is reflected in *inter alia* 'Sustainable Development: The UK Strategy', (1994 Cm 2426), which sets out this country's proposals for the attainment of the goal. In so doing, it addresses a broad range of subjects raising environmental considerations, including land use and transport planning.
81. House of Commons 1996-7 4th Report.
82. *Ibid.* at p. *vii*.
83. *Ibid.* at p. *ix*.
84. *Ibid.* at p. *xi*. In *The Guardian*'s feature toasting Britain's temples of consumerism (*supra*) reference is made to certain large scale permissions already granted, including the Trafford Centre (1mn sq.ft), Gibbs Causeway (702,000), Braehead (696,000), and White Rose Centre (650,000).
85. House of Commons Environment Committee Report at p. *xi*.
86. *Ibid.* at p. *ix*.
87. *Ibid.* at p. *x*.
88. *Ibid.* at pp. *xi-xii*.
89. Though in an interview for *The Grocer* (26th April 1997), David Webster, the new Chairman for Safeway, referred to the restriction on growth wrought by tighter planning constraints, and the fact that '...the huge development of

the '80s and early '90s [were] largely behind us'.

90. See 'Tackling Cartels and the Abuse of Market Power: A Draft Bill', (August 1996).
91. According to the Institute of Grocery Distribution, the leading ten firms increased their share of the grocery market from 1990 to mid-1996 by 15.7 per cent to 59.6 per cent (See *The Grocer*, 1st February 1997).
92. The opening of stores abroad by UK retailers was not something new, but towards the end of the period under consideration there was an increased tendency to venture across the channel. As was noted in a feature in *The Times*, 24th September 1996, on the rekindling of the Empire spirit, Marks & Spencer, Sainsbury, Tesco and MFI had all been expanding overseas.
93. Banking, dry cleaning, flowers, and compact discs featured among the areas into which supermarkets came to diversify.
94. Loyalty card schemes were to prove particularly popular with the public, involving basically the collection of points or stamps which may then be 'traded'. A means of capturing and retaining customer 'loyalty', such schemes were to be launched by innumerable retailers, varying, not surprisingly, in the detail of their operation.
95. The scale and persistence of the crime problem for long made it (and still make it) a priority issue for retailers. A subject sadly never far from the pages of the trade press, the opinion column in *The Grocer* of 5th October 1996, for instance, referred to Home Office research which revealed that 1.7mn of 2mn store crimes annually were cases of shoplifting, and staff in smaller shops were up to five times more likely to suffer assaults and threats.
96. – an energetic campaign, beginning and ending for the then Prime Minister, John Major, in a shopping centre.

PART II

PLANNING CONTROL AND RETAIL DEVELOPMENTS

5 The policy

New retail developments normally require planning permission as 'building' operations within s 55(1) of the Town and Country Planning Act 1990.[1] No special procedures are specifically designed to limit or control retail developments, but decisions on applications for planning permission take place against a background of a wide range of central and local policies on development. However, it is not only at the stage of application that planning becomes relevant to the retail process; it has a bearing on the development of retailing outlets at a number of points. It is necessary to consider planning's rôle under a number of headings: overall national policy, local policies, development control and appeals, and planning agreements. This chapter will be concerned with the first of these issues.

Overall national policy

The use of the word 'policy' may here be misleading. The United Kingdom does not have a national land use policy in a single documentary form. It is certainly 'policy' that land should not be developed in an utterly haphazard fashion, and that has certainly been the case since the '40s following the work of the Barlow Report of the Royal Commission on the Distribution of the Industrial Population,[2] the Uthwatt Report of the Expert Committee on Compensation and Betterment[3] and the Scott Report of the Committee on Land Utilisation in Rural Areas.[4] These established a broad notion of 'planning policy' under which an end was to be made to the haphazard distribution of industry and the working population, together with unchecked urban sprawl. Alongside this was to be the creation of healthy new planned communities and the revival of older ones. To a broadly recognisable extent this is still the basis of current planning policy, even though it is now overlain by wider environmental concerns, such as the need to secure development that is 'sustainable'.

But apart from this notion of planning policy one would look in vain for a 'national plan' for land. Policy on land planning instead 'emerges' from a complex pattern of documents of various sorts. Only rarely do these take a legislative form. Insofar as a nationally uniform framework of procedures for taking planning decisions is concerned, and uniform definitions of what constitutes development, *etc*, are needed, the Town and Country Planning Act 1990, as amended, provides the necessary infrastructure, supplemented by a host of statutory instruments containing detailed regulations. But anyone who simply read the legislation would gain a most imperfect idea of what planning is and how it operates. The policy of planning is to be found only by looking at a range of materials which include centrally issue guidance from ministers, ministerial decisions on individual planning application appeals, and the various plans made under the legislation by local planning authorities.

Even these categories can be further subdivided. Central guidance can take the formal published form of either a Planning Policy Guidance Note (PPG) or a Circular from the Department of the Environment, Transport and the Regions (DETR) formerly the Department of the Environment (DoE). The rough distinction between these forms is that PPGs are concerned with laying down broad general policy issues, while Circulars should be confined to containing more particular advice and to clarifying the interpretation of particular legal decisions and provisions in legislation. In fact, however, that distinction is not always adhered to and, for example, Circulars may still be encountered which give advice on broad policy issues. Furthermore Ministers may give policy advice in other forms such as statements in the House of Commons, or as press releases designed to accompany appearances at major conferences. The basic understanding is that these will have a policy guidance status if (a) the Minister intended them as such and (b) they are generally publicly available. The planning appeal decisions of Ministers assume a policy significance when it is clear that there is a definite trend in them which is hardening into a general understanding of and approach to a problem over a period of time. The various plans referred to above are not just the statutory plans of the various authorities, *i.e.* the metropolitan district councils, London borough councils, shire county councils, shire district councils, unitary authorities, and in Wales, county borough councils and county councils, but also include emerging statutory plans which may be relevant in the planning decision making process, and various forms of non-statutory planning policies adopted by local planning authorities – and indeed on occasions by central government, the best example being the South East Regional Plan (SERPLAN). Local planning will be examined in the next chapter.

Surrounding all the foregoing, sometimes doing no more than clarifying the wording of legislation, but sometimes elaborating upon, criticising, upholding, or quashing particular practices of local planning authorities and ministers are the decisions of the superior courts, *i.e.* the High Court, Court of Appeal and House of Lords. Sometimes these cases arise out of the statutory mode of challenge to a planning decision under the 1990 legislation, while on other occasions they will be the product of judicial review of planning decisions. However, the significance of these judicial decisions cannot be underestimated. For just as ministerial guidance may make it clear to local authorities what are the limits of legitimacy for what they can do, so do the decisions of the courts lay down the limits of legality. This again will be examined in the next chapter.

Planning policy has both national and local aspects and though there are general matters applying nation-wide there may be particular local variations. To know what 'policy' may be in relation to an individual given issue one may have to study a whole range of diverse documents.

There are, however, certain external political, economic and social constraints that policy cannot escape. In a free society which accepts the principles of a market driven economy, it is unacceptable for all decisions on land use to be made by bureaucrats and simply imposed on land holders. Planning policy must contain a strong consensual element in which those who own land or who wish to develop it co-operate with planning authorities. Similarly as new products and services and new activities and ways of living are developed and old ones superseded, there will inevitably be a process of change affecting society and how it uses land. Planning policy must then also co-exist with the seeming inevitability of change, and to a very real extent cannot do more than to seek the orderly management of change. On the other hand policy cannot be, nor should it be, swept hither and thither by external forces but must seek a certain continuity and stability – at the very least to ensure a degree of fair and equal treatment for all sections of society. This again leads to a need for a consensual element in both policy formulation and its application. The pressures outlined above cannot always be mutually compatible, and therefore some elements of compromise for some and disappointment for others must be accepted. What may, however, be questioned is whether the overall planning system has sufficient internal strength, clarity and coherence to achieve the best possible results which lead to the most effective and economic uses of land with the least number of disbenefits, not just to society as a whole but also to those sections of it least able to fend for themselves.

The overall institutional weakness of planning policy

In 1986 The Nuffield report 'Town and Country Planning'[5] pointed out long standing internal problems within the planning system. These included a prevalent and somewhat simplistic belief on the part of government that planning is a neutral system of values which does not reflect, and is not affected by political (in the widest sense) issues, such as to what uses land should be put – and how. The report concluded that what was needed was a planning system and policy to:

- monitor and control the environmental impact of land use, both current and future;
- anticipate and prevent nuisances arising from land use;
- create a consistently coherent framework within which the land market for development can operate;
- reconcile conflicting land use demands;
- assist the promotion of those developments considered desirable by public authorities whether the initiative comes from the public or the private sector (ten years on by 1996 it was clear the overwhelming majority of initiatives would come from the private sector);
- provide whatever information is needed for the discharge of the foregoing functions;
- ensure comprehensive coverage of the activities of *every* body whose activities have significant land use implications;
- create requirements so that every such body should be required to inform all other relevant bodies of their proposals for land use and the implications thereof;
- provide a system wherein the foregoing information is collected together by local planning authorities who would thus be able to identify connections and conflicts at an early stage;
- be so structured that central government concentrates only on articulating clearly national strategic policies leaving a great measure of discretion to local government;
- be open and accessible to the general public at both the plan making and planning decision making stages;
- accept that a degree of uncertainty in land use matters is inevitable and that it is not possible to set land uses 'in concrete' forever.

It was, however, accepted that planning must constantly adapt to new and changing circumstances, while to promote close connections between physical land use planning and social economic planning greater emphasis should be laid, the report argued, on local authorities being aware of the resources available for development proposals to be implemented. It has to be commented that as fewer and fewer public resources are available to fund development projects, and more and more emphasis has been put on private finance and private development initiatives by government, the foregoing recommendation has an increasingly hollow ring. Planning authorities in many cases must be quite dependent on the private sector for the achievement of certain development policies, and sometimes the involvement of the private sector can have considerable implications leading to major changes in what actually results on the ground as opposed to the initial plan proposals.[6]

In order to achieve the proposals outlined above, the report proposed a radical new 'shape' for planning policy and law.

At the apex of the system there would be 'National Policy Guidelines' having the force of directives and being central government's primary influence over planning. These guidelines would *inter alia*:

- identify and define those types of development which could raise national planning issues;
- lay down national land use issues to be considered by local government when drawing up development plans;
- lay down criteria for determining whether a particular planning proposal should be notified to the Secretary of State for the purpose of being called in for central decision;
- be cast in simple language and be subject to legally required consultation between central and local government;
- be coherent and consistent.

The guidelines would be supplemented by an annual white paper on land and the environment to give guidance to local authorities in the preparation of plans and the process of plan revision.

By the end of the '90s, however, what has been implanted into the planning system as a result of the Nuffield report is minimal. There is an annual white paper on the environment, but this does not take the form of the land and environment document called for by the report. There is a national system of planning guidance in the form of the PPGs, but they are not directives. Regional planning insofar as it takes place continues to do so on a basically informal and non-statutory basis.

What is, however, perhaps even more important is that in economic terms planning as a system – and that inevitably means planning policy also, for policy 'emerges' from the system – has become more and more reactive to private sector development pressures. As the public sector has shrunk throughout the '80s and '90s with the privatisation of so many industries once classified as 'statutory undertakers', and as more and more restrictions have been placed, from 1980 onwards, on the ability of local authorities to raise and spend money, the proactive rôle in planning has inevitably passed to the private sector – with the overall encouragement of central government let it be said. Moreover, the changing nature of that private sector cannot be ignored. No nation in western Europe has shed industrial capacity so rapidly and drastically as the United Kingdom in the last fifteen to twenty years or so. Industries already in decline before 1980, such as textiles in the face of cheap overseas competition, have continued to contract, as have coal and steel and other metal industries. Indeed in the mid-'80s one could well have been forgiven for believing that it was government policy that manufacturing industry did not really matter at all, and that what was of overwhelming importance was the service and financial services sectors – including, of course, retailing. There was, of course, a realisation after 1991 under the Major Government, and its successor, that of Tony Blair, that manufacturing industry is of great importance, and increasing efforts have been made to attract inward investment into the nation to shore up and recreate our industrial base. But in many ways and in many places the damage has been done. Land that could have been devoted to industrial use has been devoted to service industries and retailing in particular. This has occurred both on cleared urban 'brownfield' sites and on 'greenfield' sites at urban edges and in rural areas. A primarily reactive planning system has been unable to resist, or at least channel, the powerful forces unleashed by central economic policies. Perhaps, however, this is inescapable with a planning system that has been historically concerned largely to preserve amenity and prevent urban sprawl by being essentially regulatory in form and negative in tone (*i.e.* development may not take place without permission) rather than being a rather more positive system whereby financial, economic and land use planning issues are brought together.

Retail development ~ the control issue

It is against this overall background that the particular issue of retail development control has to be set. As has been stated above, however, planning policy is by no means fixed in the United Kingdom and actually consists of a number of 'layers' – central and local – which are articulated in a number of ways, sometimes as rules of law, more usually as policy documents, quite often as ministerial appeal decisions. The result is that, overall, policy is flexible – indeed even fluid – while on occasions there car appear to be internal contradictions between central and local policies.

This phenomenon has been examined and usefully summarised by Clifford Guy in *The Retail Development Process*.[7] Following a period of very considerable town centre redevelopment in the '50s and '60s, planning authorities adopted generally restrictive attitudes to retail developments 'off-centre' in the '70s, and tried to ensure that large new stores should only be developed in existing centres. However, many refusals of planning permission were overturned on appeal and it was clear that central government advice to inspectors at such appeals was to be more liberal than local planners in recommending that permission should be given. Even though the policy documents issued by the DoE (Development Policy Control Notes of 1972 and 1977) stated the case both for and against development outside existing centres, nevertheless they were much less restrictive in tone than many local authority plans. This liberality continued throughout the '80s under the Thatcher governments, and is evidenced to some extent by the numbers of appeals made against refusals of planning permission for developments classed as 'major retail'. Thus in 1984 there were 124 such appeals rising to 297 in the year ending March 1987. Guy argues that this increase 'probably reflected increasing pressure for retail development rather than changes of attitudes of local authorities'[8] but equally it could reflect increasing awareness by developers of the chances of succeeding on appeal, for as Guy also points out the numbers of appeals allowed rose from 35 per cent in 1984 to some 50 per cent from 1986/87 onwards.

This summary, however, needs a little expansion for it is clear that planning policy's flexibility (indeed variability) is influenced by a whole range of factors.

A range of determinants of policy

As Guy[9] makes clear the majority of developed retail space in the UK still exists as a result of the 'unplanned' development of towns before the advent of town and country planning, even though much of it may now be the consequences of redevelopment consented under legislation. Where that space exists its constituent units, however, may be of an inconvenient size – *i.e.* too small for the desires of modern retailers – or of the wrong tenure, *i.e.* available only on a short leasehold basis. To overcome these deficiencies, amongst others, local planning authorities have tended to favour town centre redevelopment schemes.

The influence of location

Initially, as Guy indicates,[10] such town centre redevelopment concentrated on reuse of areas damaged by Second World War bombing. This was followed by a wave of development of (frequently enclosed) central shopping centres, usually by specialist developers with local authority encouragement in the '60s and '70s, with some 300 town shopping schemes of 50,000 sq.ft or more being completed between 1965 and 1970. The Haymarket scheme in Leicester is an example of such a development, though not completed until the early '70s. Town centre development recommenced in the late '80s, often characterised by attempts to create consciously 'up-market' developments, with the Shires scheme, again in Leicester, being an example of this. At the same time the older developments of the '60s and '70s are also being refurbished and renewed. Planning policy is not averse to such developments – as with the sale of houses, therefore 'location, location, location' can be a major determinant in deciding policy stances on particular forms of development at both national and local levels.

Location has also been a major factor when off-centre development has been under consideration. There have been perceptions of particular types of trading moving out of established centres in waves or phases – first of all food, followed in the '70s and '80s by household and home improvement goods, 'white' and other electrical goods, furnishings and motor accessories, and more recently in the '80s and '90s by 'comparison' trades such as toy sellers, expensive specialist furniture retailers and retailers such as Marks and Spencer. By the late '70s the major grocery retailers clearly preferred to develop at edge of centre locations, a development particularly attributed to Lord MacLaurin (of Tesco) who saw the potential for the new form of retailing, though Sainsbury also have claimed to have been forced to develop such sites as a result of planning and other town centre restrictions.[11] Sainsbury's first such store opened in Cambridge in 1974, followed rapidly by one in Bedford, though the company also sought to redevelop inner urban sites where these were available. Even so it was not long before Sainsbury also developed a hypermarket of over 50,000 sq.ft, following the lead of Carrefour which had begun in 1972. Sainsbury's first 'Savacentre', owned jointly with British Home Stores, opened in 1977.

By the early '80s what are now recognised as retail parks had emerged - often, as Guy demonstrates,[12] by the coincidental development of a number of retail warehouses on industrial estates or in other locations where local policy was favourable. Such developments cannot be fitted into a scheme of town centre redevelopment where the largest sites may only offer 10,000 sq.ft of space. They need land for the stores, car parks and access roads, and to be connected with main road networks. They will frequently occupy land initially targeted for industrial development. Planning policy was not in general averse to their growth because they were not perceived as threats to existing centres. Where such parks catered for home improvement or gardening needs they would not, it was thought, impact too heavily on existing centres where such goods are not often sold. Where, however, there were proposals to include 'comparison' shopping units such as furniture, clothing or toy outlets, local policy in particular tended to be opposed to development, and a number of such developments only proceeded after planning appeals in the '80s because it was then central policy not to try to rein in this form of economic activity. Thus policy has been swayed not just by the question of 'where' but also that of 'what is to be sold'.

The influence of finance

Though financial issues are in general beyond the scope of this work, and the interested reader must be referred to Guy's excellent study for an in depth analysis of the topic, nevertheless it is impossible to ignore the matter altogether. This is because our system of land use planning is essentially reactive. The initiative to develop land normally comes from the private sector – though the assistance of the public sector may be needed to assemble a suitable site for redevelopment – and the desire and ability of the private sector to develop land will depend upon the overall condition of the economy, and the willingness of major financial institutions to become involved in the process. The major food store developers have historically been largely driven by a need to increase their individual 'shares' in a food market whose size has not noticeably increased. The preferred location for food superstores has become a free standing, edge of town site,[13] and as the number of stores operated by the great multiple food retailers has increased so has there been a decline in stores operated by independent retailers. The capital needed to build, and improve, stores, introduce new computerised sales systems and to invest in distribution networks can only be easily raised by the multiple retailers.[14] Asda and Tesco, for example have been prepared to invest in stores of 40,000 sq.ft or more costing over £20mn each. The major food retailers compete, however, in their search for new food store sites not just with independent traders but with one another; always seeking to 'capture' a significant share of food shopping within the area of a new store, which is the perceived way to increase market share overall, and thus to justify investor confidence in the companies concerned. As major food retailers have sought to become national concerns, moving north and west (for example Tesco and Sainsbury) or south and east (for example Asda and, to a lesser extent Morrisons) their moves into new areas during the '70s and '80s were largely not in conflict with one another. That is now changing rapidly, and a proposal to develop a new food store by one chain may produce a counter proposal from another, which can result in the local planning authority – and maybe the Secretary of State – having to determine the application not just on the basis of the desirability or otherwise of building a major food superstore, but also by having to behave even-handedly between conflicting applicants – an issue returned to in the subsequent chapter. This is well illustrated by the example of the City of Leicester. From an initial medium sized town centre store in the '60s Sainsbury went on to develop, by 1997, a medium size store in Wigston, an 'edge of the historic core' site (former railway land in Leicester), a greenfield site just over the City boundary adjacent to the Fosse Park retail park, and a site in Oadby (the former site of the Alliance and Leicester Building Society headquarters). These last three were all much larger than their predecessors. At the same time Tesco was unable to obtain planning permission for more than one major food store developed on a 'district centre' basis (Beaumont Leys) and failed to obtain permission to develop two pieces of land (one just in Leicester's boundaries and one in Oadby) owned by the University of Leicester. In the last mentioned instance both companies were vying for retail trade in Oadby.[15] Their applications to develop were clearly 'rivals'. To fund such expansion the food retailers rely on their own cash receipts, supplemented increasingly by new share rights issues, taking loans from banks, and by sale and leaseback schemes whereby the freeholds of sites have been sold to property companies. Whether and how the expansion of the multiple chains will continue remains an open question, and one to be returned to later, though it appears unlikely that large financial institutions will increase their involvement in this sector.[16]

So far as non-food store development is concerned evidence is lacking of either rights issues or sale and leaseback financing. Guy argues that the

> ...normal mode of development appears to have been...development of freehold stores by the firm itself, financed by cash resources... Premises in retail parks are, however, usually leased on standard institutional terms from the company owning the retail park.[17]

In some cases retailers of both food and non-food goods may join in financing a development – usually of the large shopping centre variety – along with a property company. In such cases the food retailer may fund the development of its own unit within the total complex as an 'anchor store' which attracts other traders to the development.

Wider economic issues

However, it is clear that, whether the finance comes from a retailer's own sources, or from a property company, or, less usually, a financial institution, the overall state of the economy is a major determinant of store development activity. This is well illustrated by the development of regional shopping centres, *i.e.* a free-standing centre with some 500,000 sq.ft of gross retail space developed away from existing urban centres.[18] The first of these in the UK was Brent Cross in the '70s, a property company development of some 760,000 sq.ft. This was paralleled by new regional centres in Runcorn, Telford and Washington. These were designed to be the commercial hearts of new settlements and so constitute a somewhat special case, as is the regional centre of Milton Keynes of 1979 funded by the Post Office Staff Superannuation Fund, though this is extremely large in relation to the community it serves and is clearly designed to draw in trade from a wider region. The economic euphoria of the early and mid-'80s led, however, to proposals for a whole raft of regional shopping centres – frequently quite close together – in a 'bandwagon' pattern. By 1987 there were proposals for no less than 43 of these, and a further seven proposals emerged by 1991. This movement was driven by a perception of a major new need for out of town comparison shopping, and central government attachment to an 'enterprise' culture in which new employment opportunities were seen to be generated by commerce and financial services while the importance of manufacturing industry declined. In some cases Enterprise Zones designated under planning legislation also specifically provided grants of automatic planning permission for retail development. This was the case in Dudley where the Merryhill development (see further the subsequent chapter) was to arise and Gateshead, home of the MetroCentre. The effect of such centres will be examined in detail later, but generally adverse reaction from local government, and a change in central government policy in 1988, coupled with a major downturn in the economy, led to only a few of the many proposals for regional centres being built. As Guy states 'the anticipated boom in regional shopping centre development has not taken place',[19] but that it could have been contemplated at all is evidence of the economic euphoria of the time, and shows how planning is subject to powerful economic forces.

For the future, however, it would appear that most institutional investment will concentrate on traditional town centre retail units. Major financial institutions have become wary of proposals for regional shopping centres, and are more likely to invest in those developments which are clearly favoured by local and central planning policies.[20] As an instance of this one may cite the late '90s proposal by Legal and General's property division to fund a £400mn shopping and leisure redevelopment in the centre of Bracknell. This was to cover 1.25mn sq.ft and create some 4,000 permanent jobs as well as 2,000 building jobs over five years. The new development had the support of the local planning authority, which could use its compulsory purchase powers to help assemble the site. It was hoped that planning permission would be granted in 1998 with site clearance in 1999, and opening in 2002.[21] Policy can, it seems, resist economic pressures – but perhaps only when both central and local policies coincide, and when the economy is not allowed to produce a condition of economic euphoria.

The influence of planners' attitudes

A word needs to be added on the attitude of planners themselves towards retail developments. There is an element of opportunism in planning practice, and not all planners have been opposed to off-centre retail development. Planners were not averse to the development of food stores because these were not always perceived as threats to existing town centres. Indeed local policies often encouraged the development of food stores as the 'anchors' for 'district centres' where a grocery superstore is supplemented by other smaller retail units to serve residential areas. In addition planners were not always averse to regional centre shopping development – the Meadowhall scheme in Sheffield had active local authority promotion.[22] However, it should be remembered that the incremental effect of decisions taken by individual planning authorities to allow off-centre retail development (whether willingly or not) has, in the space of a generation, transformed the urban landscape, bringing in its train a range of other social and environmental problems.

An interim summation

No matter what central and planning policies may in general be, their application in any given case may well be affected by a range of other factors such as: the location of the site for the proposed development; what is proposed for sale there; how the development is to be financed; what the current state of economy is both locally and nationally. Planning policy has to exist in a diverse world.

One point that needs to be reinforced is that while at the local level planning policy has from time to time been averse to major retail developments in off-centre locations, at a national level there was no such degree of aversion until the latter part of the '80s. Developers were able to exploit that dislocation between the 'layers' of policy. That such a dislocation should exist should not actually be surprising, for while, historically, specific central government criteria for retail development planning did not exist, what was most clear was the central presumption in favour of granting permission to develop land.

The presumption in favour of development

It was for long central policy that there should be a general presumption in favour of allowing proposals to develop land.[23] This was in 1988 ministerially reiterated:

> In 1980 we issued a circular emphasising the importance of getting planning applications agreed and reminding authorities that they must always grant permission unless there are important reasons against... There is [a presumption in favour of development]. That is the basis of the system. The British system is that people can do what they like with their property so long as an important interest is not damaged thereby.[24]

The planning system was thus on the side of the developer, with it being the exception, rather than the rule, to refuse planning permission. A refusal has only been considered justified where the proposed development would be clearly detrimental to some established interest.

The presumption in favour of development continues under the current law though it has been somewhat modified by s 54A of the Town and Country Planning Act 1990 whose detailed impact will be considered in the subsequent chapter, but which, in the words of PPG 1 (March 1992 para. 25) certainly 'introduces a presumption in favour of development proposals which are in accordance with the development plan'. However, the PPG makes it clear even before then that:

> The planning system...fails in its function whenever it prevents inhibits or delays development which should reasonably have been permitted. It should operate on the basis that applications for development should be allowed, having regard to the development plan and all material considerations, unless the proposed development would cause demonstrable harm to interests of acknowledged importance. (Para. 5).

A very strong presumption in favour of allowing a development proposal to proceed continues to exist, and where that proposal is in accordance with the terms of the relevant development plan it is virtually certain to be granted permission.

Policy on retail developments

As stated earlier there is no general national plan specifically related to retail development. However, with regard to such developments, government has periodically issued particular guidance. In 1972 guidance was issued pointing out the advantages and disadvantages of large new retail developments, and asking planning authorities to inform the Secretary of State of out of centre applications for developments of 50,000 sq.ft or more so that 'calling-in' of the application (for a decision to be made centrally under what was then s 35 of the Town and Country Planning Act 1971, see now s 77 of the Town and Country Planning Act 1990) could be considered.[25] This was revised in 1977 with the floor space limit raised to 100,000 sq.ft.[26] Guidance on wholesale and cash-and-carry warehouses was given in 1974.[27] Further policy guidance was given on major retail developments in December 1986.[28]

In January 1988 guidance was given in a new form: PPG 6 'Major Retail Development' largely replaced previous guidance. It retained, however, The Town and Country Planning (Shopping Development) (England and Wales) Direction, 1986,[29] directing local planning authorities to consult with the Secretary of State before granting planning permission for any development comprising or including gross shopping floor space of 250,000 sq.ft, or more, measured externally. It will be noted that central decision-making using 'call-in' powers concerned itself increasingly with only the largest proposed developments, and it was policy that an application would only be 'called-in' where it raised issues of more than local importance. This is still the policy stance of the DETR.

In its first version PPG 6 reiterated arguments that retailing is a dynamic sector of the economy, and changes which extend consumer choice promote efficiency and create a more pleasant 'shopping experience' were to be welcomed. Changes in the pattern of retailing with trends towards off-centre locations and ever larger trading units were simply noted,[30] as was the growth of 'customer mobility', though the needs of those without access to cars, such as the elderly, the infirm and the disabled, those on low incomes, and mothers with young children, were also noted. PPG 6 stated merely: 'Where possible, large new stores, especially those selling convenience goods, should be located where they can serve not only car-borne shoppers but also those who rely on other forms of transport'.[31]

In its 1988 form PPG 6 repeated a ministerial statement of 5th July 1985, (itself largely taken from Development Policy Control Note No 13) that the planning system exists to ensure that there is a wide range of shopping facilities, but not 'to inhibit competition among retailers or among methods of retailing, nor to preserve existing commercial interests as such'.[32] Planning Authorities were counselled to bear this in mind in drawing up their plans, and in deciding individual planning applications; certainly it was the policy applied in deciding individual planning applications, and it was the policy applied in deciding any planning application 'called-in' for central decision.[33] It remained central policy that modernisation and refurbishment of existing town centres was welcomed, especially where this could contribute to urban renewal and the re-use of derelict or unused land. It was, moreover, accepted that renewal of existing centres might require better access and parking facilities.

The guidance was, however, explicit in its condemnation of policies adopted by some local authorities which were based on estimates of future retail floorspace needs, and which then tried to allocate such retail growth between particular areas – even though that had been an approach at one time favoured by central government. The 1988 guidance, while indicating that planning authorities should, in plan making, take into account forecasts of retail expenditure and their implications for the location of relevant developments, specifically added:

> However, policies should not attempt to prescribe rigid floorspace limits for new retail development, either overall or in specified localities since this would impair the ability of retailers and the planning authority to respond to changing market conditions and the demands of customers.[34]

The presumption in favour of development was implicit in the guidance given in relation to 'large stores', *i.e.* those up to 100,000 sq.ft selling food and convenience goods and catering for car-borne weekly shoppers: 'the planning system has been able to cater for them'.[35] Retail warehouses were also commended: 'a successful way of catering for major household goods'.[36] The advantages of relieving central congestion by diverting trade in bulky goods to outlying locations was also pointed out. The guidance stressed stores and warehouses could be appropriate development for derelict urban land. Retailing was also identified as suitable for some land designated for industrial use provided there was a good supply of land otherwise available for industry in an area.

The favouring of retail development was, however, reversed in certain situations. In relation to land *recently* designated for industrial development, situated where such land was scarce and industrial demand high, there was a presumption the land should not be used for retail developments. The guidance was also clear that proposals for major developments on an out of town basis with a floorspace of over 100,000 sq.ft were totally out of place in green belts and hardly less acceptable in open country areas.[37] Rather more acceptable were out of town proposals depending on reclamations of otherwise derelict land which would have little effect on existing centres, or where an existing centre had no good facilities and could not easily be modernised.

However, between free standing urban stores, and retail warehouses on the one hand (where the presumption favoured development) and sites in green belts and open countryside on the other (where the presumption was adverse) there lay a 'grey area' where central policy was unclear. This was the area of the off-centre scheme lying within, or at the edge of, an existing urban area, but which would not impinge on a green belt or other open countryside. Government here largely left planning authorities to work out their own salvation *via* structure and local plan policies, and by careful consideration of development proposals in the light of all circumstances, including the environmental effects of a development and its road traffic implications. However, the guidance was explicit in pointing out that considerations of competition were *not* to be taken into account by planning authorities, though the cumulative effects of recent and proposed retail developments *might* be considered where they were such as to:

> ...seriously affect the vitality and viability of a nearby town centre as a whole – for example where they seem likely to result in a significant increase in

vacant properties, or a marked reduction in the range of services the town centre supplies.[38]

The 1993 and 1996 revisions of policy

The revision of PPG 6 in 1993 brought with it certain changes in the guidance on retail development planning. Though it was still the view of central policy that development should take place according to what the market determined to be shopping needs in any given location, with planning control existing primarily to ensure that proposals which would cause harm to interests of acknowledged importance were rejected, nevertheless there were certain changes of emphasis. Thus the guidance counselled authorities that their plans should make 'adequate provision for retail developments including a choice of sites for different types of retail development'.[39] What was new, however, was more specific guidance on protecting existing town centres against harmful off-centre developments. There had been widespread criticism of the 1988 version of PPG 6 as not being sufficiently restrictive of such new developments with regard to their impact on existing centres.[40] Accordingly the revised guidance, in attempts to meet arguments that previous guidance had been (a) vague and (b) too favourable to developers, advised authorities to take into account significant impacts on town centres of an economic, social and environmental nature, for example:

- likely adverse effects on private investment in town centres;
- the risk posed to a development plan's town centre strategy by the proposed competing development;
- any changes to the 'quality', attractiveness and character of an existing centre and its economic and social rôle in community life;
- changes in the ranges of services a town centre provides;
- likely increase in the number of properties vacant within a 'primary retail area'.

Even so the revised guidance indicated that permission for development should only be refused where there was 'clear evidence to suggest that the result would be to undermine the vitality and viability of that centre which would otherwise continue to serve the community well'. In addition, however, authorities were advised that retail development ought to be 'sited where it is likely to be accessible by a choice of means of transport, and to encourage economy in fuel consumption'.[41]

So far as 'major' retail proposals were concerned (*i.e.* in the new metric era those with more than 20,000 sq. metres gross floor area) the DoE indicated that developers should submit a statement of likely impact of their proposed development on existing retail locations.[42]

Within three years, however, the 1993 version of PPG 6 was superseded by yet another revision in June 1996.

While this continued to declare that it is not the task of planning to 'restrict competition, preserve existing commercial interests or prevent innovation',[43] it nevertheless declared that the government wished to sustain and enhance the viability of existing town centres, and to focus development in places where competition can flourish to the benefit of all consumers and where there is the maximum opportunity to use non-car means of transport. This was declared to be one means of seeking 'sustainable development', *i.e.* a form of development which meets today's needs without compromising the interests of tomorrow by, for example, restraining the needless use of resources consequent on over-use of private cars.

These objectives were further elaborated as the need for authorities to have policies: locating major generators of travel in existing centres; enabling town, district and local centres to meet their residents' needs; safeguarding and strengthening existing local centres which offer a range of everyday community shopping and employment opportunities; maintaining and enhancing a choice of non-car modes of transport to work; ensuring an appropriate supply of attractive, convenient and safe parking for shopping.[44]

To achieve these objects the guidance advises authorities to adopt a plan led approach, with development plans themselves being used where appropriate to designate existing centres as areas where shopping, leisure, entertainment, education, health or employment opportunities are to be retained or enhanced. Interestingly the guidance also indicates that regional planning guidance (RPG), which is issued on a non-statutory basis by the DETR, should also set out a development strategy for a region including, where appropriate, the scope for any additional regional shopping centres. This recognises, of course, that a major regional shopping centre can have a major effect in transferring trade and creating travel way beyond the borders of the district, or even the county, in which it is situated.

The sequential test approach

The guidance stresses the importance also of positive public and private sector co-operation in seeking and identifying new sites for retail development, and for including such sites at an early opportunity in relevant plans, (or where such plans are not yet revised, to include such details by other methods which should then be incorporated in plans at the earliest opportunity) for example by means of a highly detailed town centre 'planning brief'. The guidance states that where such a brief does not yet exist 'if a developer is proposing an out of centre development the onus will be on the developer to demonstrate that he has thoroughly assessed all potential town centre options'.[45] A similar approach is counselled in relation to the drawing up of relevant plans themselves – all potential town centre sites for new retail development should be assessed before less central locations are considered. This creates a hierarchy of sites for development – town centres first, then edge of centre sites, followed by district and local centres, and only finally out of centre sites – and even these must be accessible by a choice of modes of transport. Thus arises the so-called 'sequential test' to apply to all developments falling generically within the concept of 'off-centre'. It is further added that where no need or capacity for further development exists, no additional sites in a town need be shown in plans. Unfortunately the terms 'centre', 'edge of centre' and 'out of centre' are not defined and hence, in any given situation, their application may vary according to local conditions, though case law now gives some guidance which will be examined in the subsequent chapter.

Particular guidance[46] is given on planning for retail developments. It is now accepted centrally that regional shopping centres with more than 50,000 sq. metres gross floor spaces have substantial effects and can cause severe harm to nearby town centres. Central policy is now averse to the development of any more such centres save where:

- there is otherwise a deficiency of higher order shopping centres;
- the development is unlikely to jeopardise the continuation of private sector investment in nearby centres;
- greenbelt land, important open spaces, or habitats or the best grades of versatile agricultural land will not be lost;
- public transport will be able to serve a wide population adequately;
- there will be no more than an acceptable effect on the road network and on overall car use.

Clearly very few new regional centres would be able to meet the foregoing criteria.

In addition it is clear from the guidance that both planning authorities and developers need to be flexible in their co-operative approach to new shopping developments, for example with regard to format, design, scale and the provision of parking spaces. These need to fit local circumstances. Authorities also need to maintain consultation with developers to identify suitable sites for their proposals which are both viable and reasonably quickly available – again a matter to be returned to in the subsequent chapter.

So far as other newer forms of retailing, such as retail warehouse parks, warehouse clubs and factory outlets are concerned, a rather more case by case approach is adopted by the guidance. Retail warehouse parks, for example, may have an impact on existing town centres, while the guidance is clearly rather more averse to factory outlets (*i.e.* groups of shops selling seconds and 'end-of-line' goods at a discount) because these are likely to 'draw customers from a wide catchment area, predominantly by car, and as a result are unlikely to be consistent with the criteria in this guidance...'.[47] The same 'case by case' approach is also applied to discount stores selling limited ranges of goods at reduced prices – again they should be assessed according to their impact on the vitality and viability of existing centres.

The guidance is not, however, generally averse to large foodstores and supermarkets where these can be sited at 'edge of centre' locations. What constitutes an 'edge of centre' location is not, as already stated, precisely defined but the information is given, on an easy walking distance basis, that shoppers are unwilling to walk more than 200-300 metres, especially when carrying shopping, so some indication exists on how far out from an existing centre a site would be considered to be 'edge of centre'.[48] Even so this guideline is not to be treated as an inflexible rule with 300 metres as a 'magic number'. Where a town centre is attractive shoppers may be prepared to walk further into and through it, hence its 'edge' will be correspondingly further out.[49]

The guidance is also not opposed to the development of district and local centres of retailing, just the opposite in fact. The development of such centres offering a wide range of facilities is commended as it reduces needs to travel. Appropriately sized supermarkets may be included in such developments.[50] However, the guidance is opposed in general to the granting of permission for retail development on land designated for other uses by approved development plans. Neither does the guidance approve of using retail development simply as a mechanism for bringing derelict or vacant sites into use, save where this supports the vitality and viability of existing centres. Furthermore authorities are warned that job opportunities created by retail development may in fact be off-set by job losses elsewhere in an area as a result of the diversion of trade.[51]

In all these points the 1996 Guidance represents a major *volte face* from the actuality of planning policy at the central level in the '80s.

It is, however, in Part 4 of the guidance that the changes in central policy become most apparent. This sets out a number of key tests to be applied where a retail store is proposed outside an existing centre. If such a development is proposed for a location outside the preferred locations to be specified in development plans it will have to be assessed against the overall development plan strategy and should be refused if it undermines that strategy. Similarly where an application is made for a development which would have an impact on a nearby town, district or local centre planning authorities are counselled to consider:

- how far the strategy for the existing town centre would be put at risk, taking into account how that is progressing, particularly as a result of public investment;
- likely effects on future private investment which is needed to maintain the vitality and viability of existing centres;
- changes to the quality, attractiveness and character of an existing centre and its socio-economic rôle in community life;
- physical changes in the existing centre;
- changes in the range of services the centre will continue to provide;
- likely increases in the void property rate in the primary retail area;
- the likely effects on nearby centres if the proposed investment in the development is not made.

All of these matters should be assessed on a long term basis.

The guidance next articulates a presumption for new retail development in or next to town centres, or in other locations well served by public transport, or easily accessible on foot or by bicycle. Where an off-centre development is proposed, however, it should be appraised in terms of its accessibility by a choice of modes of transport. In particular there is a clear indication that sizeable numbers of staff and customers should be able to reach the new development otherwise than by car. Thus adequate public transport facilities to a new retail development from a wide area are a major factor in determining the proposal's acceptability. Furthermore as part of the overall policy of reducing levels of car travel, as enunciated in PPG 13, 'Transport', authorities are reminded that one of the advantages they should be looking for in new developments is whether they enable 'linked journeys' so as to reduce overall the number of journeys made. Such linked journeys, the guidance states, are more 'likely to happen on trips made to existing centres'.[52]

While authorities are expected to be particularly proactive in laying down policies for retail developments in their various plans, the guidance imposes a new requirement on developers which builds on the changes introduced in the 1993 version. All applications for retail developments over

2,500 sq. metres gross floorspace are now required to be supported by evidence:

- that the applicant adopted a 'sequential approach' to site selection, *i.e.* did the applicant consider sites in the order of town centre, edge of centre, district or local centre and, only finally, out of centre;
- as to the likely economic impact on existing centres and villages, including the cumulative effects of recently completed developments and outstanding permissions;
- that the development will be accessible by a choice of modes of transport;
- as to likely changes in travel patterns over the catchment area of the development;
- any significant environment impacts – which may arise where an out of town scheme having a floor area of some 20,000 sq. metres gross or more is proposed, as at this size the development may be sufficiently significant to trigger the need for *environmental impact assessment* (and see further the subsequent chapter).

An assessment of economic and transport consequences may also be needed for smaller developments for example a development likely to produce a major impact on a small market town. These should be drawn up consensually where possible with the developer and the planning authority agreeing relevant data to as great an extent as possible – *e.g.* as to population levels, expectations of turnover, *etc.*[53]

The Secretary of State has also indicated in the guidance that he will continue to be prepared to 'call in' for his decision applications raising issues of more than local significance, particularly, bearing in mind the cumulative effect of proposals. Thus under the Town and Country Planning (Development Plans and Consultation) Direction 1992 authorities are required to notify the Secretary of State of applications which depart from the terms of development plans where they consist of more than 10,000 sq. metres gross retail floor space, or where by reason of their scale, nature, or location they would prejudice to a significant degree the implementation of development plan policies and proposals. Similarly under the Town and Country Planning (Shopping Development) (England & Wales) (No 2) Direction 1993,[54] local planning authorities are required to consult the Secretary of State on any application for a retail development with more than 20,000 sq. metres gross floor space, and may not grant planning permission until at least twenty one days after that consultation. However, such consultations need not take place where an authority determine to refuse the application.[55] The Guidance in PPG 6 is reinforced by that in PPG 1 'General Policy and Principles' issued in a revised form in February

1997, see particularly paras 26-27. Maintaining the vitality and viability of existing centres is to be a general policy and principle of land use planning.

All in all, the 1996 version of PPG 6 represents a major revision of central policy on retail developments with a clear general presumption against the development of new off-centre retail outlets of the out of town variety, a presumption in favour of town centre development and a case by case approach to edge of centre developments. Furthermore all of this is set in the context of the wider sustainable development strategy which *inter alia* seeks to reduce reliance on travel by private car, thus reducing levels of pollution and the consumption of resources.

Background to the change of policy: a tale of unnecessary panic?

Why was there such a change of policy in what was such a comparatively short period of time from 1988 to 1996?

'Straws in the wind' might have been observed as early as 1989. It will be remembered that a major plank of urban strategy under the Thatcher Governments were Urban Development Corporations (UDCs), created under the Local Government, Planning and Land Act 1980, to regenerate run down inner urban areas. Retail development within these areas formed an early part of the regeneration initiatives adopted. Some of these reused older buildings while some were new shopping complexes. Among the proposed developments were retail warehouses, for example the 1987 Merseyside UDC proposal for 245,000 sq.ft of retailing space in disused docklands to house 'DIY' home improvement, carpets and floor coverings, white goods, cars, caravan and boat outlets, but not food. The UDC for Teeside, however, planned a 350,000 sq.ft leisure complex and 450,000 sq.ft of retailing space, including a 72,000 sq.ft food superstore, nine other retail units, of between 25,000 and 40,000 sq.ft, six shops of 10,000 sq.ft and 8,000 car parking spaces – though major public transport facilities were also to be included.

Hostility from local authorities

However, while new 'speciality' shopping schemes were welcomed as attracting new customers to some areas, and while in others new shopping facilities were generally welcomed where existing facilities were poor, the enthusiasm for whole new swathes of retail development was not generally shared. Cardiff City Council expressed early concern about major retail developments proposed for the Cardiff Bay area, pointing out in 1989 that 10 per cent of the existing retail floorspace in Cardiff centre already stood empty. Liverpool City Council became concerned by the Merseyside UDC proposal outlined above because they had already designated land for three other retail warehouse parks in suburban areas which had already attracted some support, which had the potential to expand, and which were designed to concentrate retail activity in areas of the city which were generally accessible. They were also concerned about the effect of the UDC's proposal on the existing city centre.

Even greater local authority concern arose over proposals for certain new out of town shopping complexes. Cleveland County Council was concerned that the Teesside proposals outlined above could result in a 10-15 per cent reduction in trade in Stockton which could jeopardise two further major retail development proposals in that town's centre, while Middlesbrough, it was feared, would also suffer a loss of investment and business confidence.

One major problem experienced by all the aforementioned authorities was, however, the lack of any developed impact assessment technique for determining the effect of new retail proposals on existing centres.[56]

The effect of recession

The recession of the late '80s, however, affected even food retailing and by 1991 there were arguments that even the three largest developers of massive off-centre foodstores, Sainsbury, Tesco and Safeway, were coming to the end of their greatest development phase, and that the dream – to some a nightmare – of a network of giant foodstores on out of town sites might not be achievable because the arterial roads serving those stores could be clogged with traffic. It was thought there could be fewer new stores and more competition between existing ones.[57] However, it was perhaps then too early to predict the end of new store development, while the evidence continued to mount of the deleterious effect of off-centre development on existing towns.

The Merryhill effect

Probably few places have been so badly affected by off-centre development as Dudley in the West Midlands. Dudley is an old settlement whose central market trading area had grown gradually over a period of hundreds of years, so that by the '50s it had buildings dating from the 16th century to the '30s all being used for brisk retail trade. The local authority had planned a redevelopment scheme in the '30s but this was disrupted by the Second World War. A limited redevelopment scheme of rather unfortunate architectural appearance was carried out in the early '60s which destroyed much of historic interest. Subsequent industrial decline in Dudley and the surrounding 'Black Country' led to very considerable areas of land being available for redevelopment. One such area was a former steel works site at Brierley Hill, south of Dudley. (Brierley Hill was an existing urban centre which had been incorporated in Dudley some years previously.) This site became the Merryhill development which opened in phases between June 1986 and November 1989 finally comprising 1.39mn sq.ft of gross retail floorspace, together with non-retail uses such as a 10 screen cinema – effectively a whole new town centre in retail and leisure terms. Some 450,000 people live within a fifteen minute drive of Merryhill, and 1.3mn within 15-30 minutes drive, while within the 45 minute drive band there are 3mn people. By 1993 some 50,000 people daily were visiting Merryhill with 72,000 on Saturdays – the great majority (between 84 and 93 per cent) travelling by car. The development has had a severe impact on Dudley, though Stourbridge, Halesowen, Kidderminster, West Bromwich, Brierley Hill and Cradley Heath have also suffered qualitative declines in retailing. But Dudley, which, it must be added, was a town in decline even before Merryhill was commenced, lost major multiple retailers, so that by 1993 its market share was less than one third of the 1989 level. Merryhill had also had an effect on employment. Though 3,370 people were employed there by 1993, 69 per cent were part/time casual workers.[58]

1993, of course, also saw the issue of the first revision of PPG 6 which was intended to restrict the development of out of town shopping centres. But that alone could not, of course, prevent the development of sites for which existing planning permissions existed, often for food stores. At the end of 1993 the National Sensitive Sites Alliance claimed that Tesco, Safeway and Sainsbury were each building one new store every two weeks – some 80 stores a year.[59] Obviously a major retail food store development does not have the same impact as a whole retail park or regional centre , but there was concern that major retailers were moving out of town centres (following the lead of the food retailers) to edge of centre or edge of town locations leaving behind their former premises empty and derelict.

By the beginning of 1994 there were 4 major out of town shopping centres already built and in operation – The MetroCentre in Gateshead,

Meadowhall in Sheffield, Merryhill in Dudley and Thurrock Lakeside in Essex. Also consented were Dumplington (Trafford Centre) in Manchester, Cribbs Causeway in Bristol and Bluewater Park, Dartford. Rejected or abandoned proposals were Digby Hospital, Exeter and Centre 21, Leicester, though here a smaller development, Fosse Park (since much extended by incremental growth) had been consented.

A further major development in policy on such centres came in early 1994 when the Secretary of State refused planning permission for major retail developments at Ludlow and Duxford near Cambridge. The latter refusal was in respect of a 'sub-regional shopping centre' with space for 4,500 cars, two departmental stores, a food supermarket, shops, restaurants, food court and petrol station. The proposal, which, of course, predated the 1993 revision of PPG 6 and reflected the more favourable terms of the 1988 version, along with two others in the Cambridge area, went to a four month public inquiry beginning in 1991. Permission was refused by the Secretary of State *inter alia* on the basis of the damaging effect the proposal would have on the vitality of Cambridge as a retail centre.[60]

However, by then many radical – some argued catastrophic – changes in retailing had taken place with consequential effects for town centres and employment prospects. The statistics are: that in 1945 there were 500,000 shops in Britain, by late 1993 there were 230,000; in 1945 there were 32,000 butchers and 10,000 fishmongers, with 13,000 and 2,000 respectively in 1993; the first 25,000 sq.ft grocery store opened in 1964, by 1993 there were 760 with 1,000 predicted by 1996 and actually in existence by the end of 1997. The first 'shopping centre' opened also in 1964, but by 1993 there were 950 such centres (though the term is only vaguely defined) with 15 per cent of UK retail selling space. The first out of town retail park opened in 1982, by 1993 there were 237 out of town developments. By 1992 one third of money spent on shopping was spent in such centres.[61] And the saga continues, for by the end of 1997 there were only 10,000 independent retailers left of the 40,000 that existed a generation earlier, with grocers closing at a rate of 800 per annum, butchers at 1,000 per annum, and a halving of the number of market traders between 1993 and 1997. Similarly the number of master bakers has declined over forty years from 12,000 to under 4,000. Meanwhile travelling to shop has gone up by 300 miles per person per annum over the years 1977 to 1997, with the percentage of car-borne shopping increasing from 32 to 50 per cent. Likewise the 90 per cent of milk delivered to the doorstep in 1972 had declined to 37 per cent in 1997. (This, incidentally, has considerably affected the use of re-usable glass bottles, as supermarket milk is largely sold in cardboard cartons or plastics containers.) As something of a counter argument to the foregoing statistics, however, it must be remembered that the disappearance of at least some of the small retailers was traceable to the slum clearance programmes in housing in the '50s and '60s, whereby many communities were swept away, and with them the network of shops they supported. A similar tale of decline could be told by the licensed victuallers – but no-one would accept that the nation has in consequence become more abstemious.

Furthermore, the stand against off-centre developments by central government was argued by some to be no more than a pause in the move to out of town shopping. The reasons for this lie, arguably, in deep and irreversible changes in the fabric of society. First of all the population has moved away from many established urban areas, while that population has become car-borne, with a very large number of working women wanting once a week 'one stop shopping' of the sort out of town developments can offer. Furthermore the format of out of town developments, with their large warehouse style buildings, enables retailers to sell much greater quantities and ranges of profitable lines of goods than is possible from High Street stores – what is more at a lower price to the retailer. By 1994 rents on out of town sites were at least 50 per cent lower than High Street rents, some £8-£10 per sq.ft as against £25 to £35 per sq.ft. The out of town development, some argued, enabled retailers to sell to consumers at lower prices and still make an adequate profit. There was, moreover, evidence to suggest that while central policy had turned against the development of large sub-regional shopping centres, it was not nearly so averse to smaller retail park developments.[62] In addition a new departure were proposals for up to 16 'Factory Shops' developments in England and Wales, and 2 in Scotland. These American style schemes were effectively retail developments where leading goods manufacturers lease space to sell their branded goods at bargain prices. And while in theory the good sold are 'end of line', in the USA it is clear that manufacturers have begun to make goods specifically for such developments. One such proposal was for a 200,000 sq.ft, 25 acre site near Junction 28 of the M1 at Mansfield in Nottingham.[63]

Since the late '80s factory 'village' or 'designer village' outlet centres for the sale of discounted surplus goods, ends of ranges, cancelled orders and, in some cases, 'seconds' have been created in a number of places. They sell branded name goods and 'designer labels' in fashions, shoes, jewellery, china, soft furnishings, sportswear and leather goods. Such developments exist *inter alia* at Bicester (Oxon), Clarkes of Street (Somerset), Cheshire Oaks (Ellesmere Port), Great Western, Swindon (Wilts), Festival Park, Ebbw Vale (Gwent). The Great Western development is on old industrial land – the former Great Western Railway Works. Clarkes' village attracted 850,000 visitors in its first fifteen weeks of trading – more than had been predicted for a whole year, with 46 per cent of customers travelling over 50 miles or more to reach it. The development has ties with local tourist attractions at Wells, Glastonbury and Wookey Hole. Cheshire Oaks opened in 1996 and has since attracted 7mn visitors. Festival Park opened in 1998 combining shopping units with restaurants and a country park. Only the Great Western development could be said to be 'town centre', and is the only one completely under cover. All the others are specifically designed for car borne shoppers. The most recent addition to this band appears to be the designer outlet MacArthur Glen in Derbyshire, one mile from Junction 28 on the M1.

The situation in 1994 reviewed

Both Government and Parliament considered retailing in published reports in 1994. The Urban and Economic Development Group (URBED) published a report undertaken as part of the DoE's Planning Research Programme, *Vital and Viable Town Centres: Meeting the Challenge*.[64] This examined the perception of decline experienced by a number of town centres, both those in expanding market towns, and those in contracting industrial areas. It also argued that while the most easily perceived threat to existing centres came from off-centre developments and the 'new' forms of retailing, as already argued, the main cause of decline is more deep seated. As the population of older urban areas declines and disperses, and the economic base of society changes from production to service industries, people became more mobile while town centres are not necessarily 'car friendly'. However, the study also accepted that as retailing moves away from town centres other economic functions may follow, and thus existing centres could follow the pattern found in some areas of North America where town centres have become contracted 'downmarket' places. It was further concluded that in general terms the dispersal of trade from existing retail centres was not being sufficiently checked by public policies, and that policy was also failing to direct investment into existing centres. However, the study concluded merely negative policies are insufficient to preserve the viability of existing centres: a much more positive approach is required. This must be based on proper understanding of the 'vitality' of existing town centres, *i.e.* their degree of 'business', and their viability, in other words their capacity to attract ongoing investment.

Parliament considered the issue *via* the report *Shopping Centres and their Future*.[65] This began by welcoming the new more cautious approach to retail development ushered in by the 1993 revision of PPG 6, and while it accepted that planning law and policy are not in place to inhibit competition and innovation in trading, it called for a more subtle and refined approach to retail development and more informed and consistent planning decisions within the development plan framework. The report went on to make a number of recommendations, some of which are now reflected in the 1996 revision of PPG 6. Briefly the recommendations were as follows.

- Clear and consistent planning guidance is needed for all concerned, and this should be based on a 'sequential test', *i.e.* retail development should not be allowed off-centre if there is a suitable central site.
- There is a need for consistency, in central guidance, for example over the issue of car parking space in town centres and PPG 6 and PPG 13 as they stood in 1993/94 were inconsistent in this regard. The report recommended their revision.
- Where a development could result in harmful damage to a centre a retail impact study should be required.
- There should be enhanced regional guidance on retail development to act as a framework on which development plans should be based.
- There should be a 'handbook' of detailed guidance on retail development for planning inspectors and local authorities to prevent ad hoc decision making and to promote consistency of decision taking.
- Automatic call in should apply to any large retail development which is a departure from development plans and which the local planning authority has determined to consent.
- There should be further criteria for determining whether to call in an application for retail development, such as where the development will house uses clearly competitive with existing centres in their non-food and specialist rôles, or where the development could have a regional effect, or where shopping patterns could be polarised to the disadvantage of a considerable number of consumers.
- There is a need to develop new measures for determining the vitality and viability of existing centres.
- Existing centres also need to be more promotionally managed, and to become safer, cleaner and more attractive shopping venues. Those appointed to managed town centres need to have sufficient seniority and authority to give them the 'leverage' to influence town centre management strategies.
- More work needs to be done on how to fund town centre management

initiatives, particularly by encouraging partnerships in this respect between the public and private sectors.

- Various fiscal regimes could assist in funding positive management of town centre such as giving tax relief to private sector investment in town centre improvement schemes.
- Local authorities should be given enhanced powers to facilitate approved town centre development schemes.

The preceding recommendations on the whole may be characterised as stressing the need for positive management of existing centres. The report next turned its attention to placing restrictions on off-centre development.

- An urgent study should be undertaken on the effect of off-centre development on town centres, and in the meantime no proposal for a superstore or other large retail development in or around a market town should be considered without being accompanied by a comprehensive study of its effects on retailing over the proposal's catchment area.
- There should be more detailed guidance given on how to assess shopping impact studies.
- Authorities should be encouraged to restrict development of retail warehouse parks where these sell comparison goods (*e.g.* clothes) in competition with town centres.
- There is a need for a national strategy on retail warehouse parks.
- Where restrictions are placed on the ranges of use permitted in a retail park these should not normally be lifted over time.
- Warehouse clubs should be dealt with in the same way as other retail development proposals, similarly factory outlets (see above) should be made subject to restrictions (*e.g.* by way of planning conditions) to prevent them from becoming mainstream shopping centres, or from retailing normal-range merchandise.
- Development plans must be up to date and must create a proactive framework within which retail development is appropriately located.
- Where a development is consented it should respect its local context by use of local themes, styles and materials.
- There should be a presumption in policy guidance that food superstores are best located in central or edge of centre situations.

The report also dealt with the vexed question of planning gain consequent on the development of major retail units – an issue to be returned to later at greater length.

- Where planning gain occurs on a cross boundary, *i.e.* inter-authority, basis, authorities should co-operate in apportioning it, and perhaps should create trust bodies to receive and apportion financial benefits arising as planning gain.

- However, no amount of planning gain can make acceptable what is fundamentally unacceptable in planning terms.
- The then current guidance on planning gain (DoE Circular 16/91) was in need of clarification and revision, and further guidance needed to be given to authorities on the development of policies on planning gain in the local context. (See the following chapter.)

The report also included a number of general recommendations on amassing appropriate data bases against which impact studies etc made in connection with particular proposals could be measured. It welcomed the creation of a retail statistics working party to review the need for further data on retailing and the potential for use of existing data, and also the release by the DoE of data on town centres and floor space. More particularly it recommended:

- that there should be a nationally consistent system of retail data collection, published regularly and including data on town centres and off-centre developments to enable a more informed, effective and efficient system of adjudication on development proposals;
- more independent research into the impact of retail developments, particularly where these have a cumulative effect on existing centres to feed into development plan making and decision taking;
- that there should be an enhanced flow of information from central government on the numbers of retail development applications that have been departure applications from development plans, and also the amount of land taken by retail developments – particularly in the green belts;
- that there should be greater research into consumer and residents' attitudes to retail developments and their preferences for particular types of development.

Finally the report addressed a number of issues which *inter alia* set the issue of retail development in the context of the wider environmental debate on sustainable development – a policy to which the Government has been committed since signing up to it at the 1992 Rio Conference on the Environment and Development.

- Decisions on sustainability issues are currently made without anyone knowing how sustainability is to be quantified. This is a matter requiring urgent attention.
- Future public transport systems must offer better choices to shoppers if the latter are to be weaned away from their cars – and that will require major new investment.

It is clear that both the URBED report and the Environment Committee

Report favoured a re-emphasis on reviewing and supporting existing urban centres, seeing positive town centre management as a major contributory factor in this, with town centres finding new rôles and functions in order to enable them to survive as vital and viable areas. The Environment Committee, however, took a rather more fundamentally restrictive line on out of centre developments and saw that almost as the necessary concomitant of positive centre management and promotion.

A contrary voice?

Many of these issues were also developed by Geoffrey Smith in his paper 'Vitality and Viability of Town Centres'.[66] Smith sought to rebalance the arguments over off-centre development by questioning the increasingly hostile 'received wisdom' on out of town developments which followed from the revision of PPG 6 in 1993. Smith pointed out that by 1994 the Secretary of State was already putting a gloss on PPG 6 as it then stood by stressing needs to reduce travel and to protect the vitality and viability of existing centres, and that this 'gloss' was informing decision taking. He argued that by 1994 there was a change of policy on retailing expressed not just in PPG 6 but also in PPG 13 on transport, the combined effect of which was to doubt the need for out of town development in order to provide for competitive retailing. Though the Secretary of State himself somewhat resiled from this policy stance, Smith concluded that PPG 6 could not be taken at its face value and that instead one had to look to a whole series of speeches and appeal decisions to discover policy on retail development (as opposed to documents issued after due public discussion). Smith further concluded, however, that the real impetus for the change of policy on retailing came not so much from the desire to give positive support to active town centre management but rather from a desire to reduce travel. Smith found this disturbing because of the lack of clear commitment to positive town centre management which had been identified as needed by the URBED research, but also because PPG 13 on transport issues can be attacked as failing to give a good factual basis for transportation policies.

Smith, however, then somewhat shifted the focus of attention to argue that for a number of years the perception of the danger caused by off-centre *foodstore* development had been mistaken, and indeed he argued it was very hard to think of towns where edge or out of centre foodstore provision had had long term damaging effects, and produced evidence to support his argument from a number of places. He argued that even developments involving the retailing of bulky durable goods at off-centre locations have not, overall, harmed the vitality and viability of existing centres. As some evidence for this he cites the City of Leicester where the development of retail warehouses at Fosse Park has, in his view, not deleteriously affected the city centre where the major retail development of the Shires Shopping Centre has taken place and is trading satisfactorily. It may be added that Leicester's other existing central shopping centre, the Haymarket, was also in 1996 refurbished, and a major new retail development on the site of the former Lewis's store has also been erected. However, the current evidence in the case of Leicester may not entirely support Smith's thesis. Further retail development at Fosse Park has replaced commercial warehousing initially erected along with the first wave of retail outlets, while there remains clearly visible evidence of void properties in the city centre – some of them in former prime shopping areas. To a certain extent the void problem has been alleviated by a considerable conversion of commercial retail units into catering establishments, bars, public houses and a comedy club night spot, which can be seen as a positive move to give the city centre a new functional identity. In addition some of Leicester's 'unwanted' central locations have been brought back into use as the more prosperous late '90s have succeeded the depressed years before them – evidence, perhaps, that central allocations are now particularly vulnerable to changes in the national economy and may be less able to withstand downturns than off-centre locations catering for people less affected by economic change. Nevertheless there must be a continuing concern in Leicester, as in other similarly affected towns and cities, that a gradual diminution in central retailing may lead to other functions moving out of the centre to peripheral locations.

Smith's argument becomes even more open to question, however, when he deals with the impact of regional and sub-regional shopping centres on established towns and cities. Though he was right to argue that positive town centre management can prevent over-much adverse impact from a major new centre (such as has been the case in Ilford with the Thurrock Lakeside Centre and Newcastle with the MetroCentre), it is arguable that he does not deal convincingly with the impact of Meadowhall on Sheffield and Merryhill on Dudley. True, in both cases there were central area problems before the new centres opened, and, certainly in the case of Dudley, a more positive rôle for the existing centre could have been planned. Nevertheless Smith was wrong to deny that Dudley is an historic centre, and to claim that 'its core continues to have a robust retail rôle',[67] and he clearly has not given due weight to the findings of the 1993 Merryhill Impact Study. Furthermore it is not enough to dismiss the impact of Meadowhall and Merryhill simply on the grounds that there was long term decline previously present in Sheffield and Dudley. The new centres have accelerated and contributed to that decline, massively so in the case of Dudley, and that is sufficient reason to cite their existence as instances of the real threat that major new regional and sub-regional centres can pose to existing town and city centres.

Moreover, there is an even more compelling reason to express concern over developments such as Meadowhall and Merryhill. Both represent a 'short termist' response to industrial decline, being built on former 'heavy' industrial land. As the nation has shed old industrial capacities so the gap that was left has been filled, in at least these two cases, by a form of economic activity which, though undoubtedly able to create wealth, does not immediately add greatly to the overseas earning capacity of the nation. There are not many foreign shoppers likely to visit either Meadowhall or Merryhill – though there is evidence of a flow of Scandinavian shoppers into Newcastle. In addition the jobs created by major retail developments may well be part time and do not adequately replace those lost by the decline of older industries. The core problem posed by these two shopping centres is that they represent a failure to replace old industries with new ones.

Having disagreed with Geoffrey Smith on a number of detailed issues, it is gratifying to be able to agree, at least in principle, with the overall thrust of his argument which is that town centres can *in general* resist the pressures of off-centre retail development but only if they are positively managed with a framework of co-operation between central and local government and the private sector. However, before examining this conclusion in greater depth it is important to complete the narrative of events down to the revision of PPG 6 in 1996 and its immediate aftermath.

Further debate and development

A major attack specifically made against the major supermarket chains was contained in the report *Off Our Trolleys*.[68] While many of the findings of this report are more germane to the question of monopolistic domination of the food shopping market discussed elsewhere in this book, its authors claimed the supermarket chains have been active supporters of the road building lobby as more roads and greater use of cars indirectly subsidise the operation of supermarkets and disguise the real cost of out of town shopping facilities. Thus between 1975-76 and 1989-91 numbers of shopping trips grew by 28 per cent and the total for distances travelled in shopping rose by 60 per cent. The report argued that food superstores increase travel, and hence the consumption of resources, and lead to more demands for road building and the emission of pollution in vehicle exhausts; while at the same time encouraging the growth of other environmental disbenefits such as disposable packaging.

In February 1995, however, the Government reaffirmed support for vital and viable town centres in its response to the Commons Environment Select Committee considered above. *Shopping Centres and Their Futures*[69] indicated that there would be a sustained shift of emphasis in retail development planning, with the Secretary of State reaffirming his commitment to use his planning powers to support local efforts to maintain town centres, and particularly their retail viability. In particular the Government agreed with most of the recommendations made with regard to the 1993 version of PPG 6. This has led, of course, to the current version already considered above with its greater emphasis on the 'sequential test' whereby developers should, in general, look to town centres first for development sites and then edge of centre before looking out of centre. The Government was less keen, however, to accept automatic call in for central decision of all large retail developments which are departures from development plans, arguing that call-in decisions should be taken on a case by case basis, as it is for local authorities primarily to make decisions on retail development applications, and the Secretary of State should intervene only where there are compelling reasons for this. Nevertheless the Select Committee's recommendations were broadly reflected in the proposals to: revise PPG 6 to clarify policy on the location of retail developments; clarify the 'sequential test'; make guidance on car parking issues clearer; emphasise a plan-led approach to development issues; promote mixed use development; amplify support for positive town centre management. The Government further undertook to commission 'good practice' guides on town centre management, town centre car parking and on quality design for centres and their car parks. Furthermore a review of possible ways of funding town centre improvements and management was promised, though the promise here was not particularly specific. The Government did, however, indicate its resolve to address problems concerning land assembly in relation to providing adequately sized sites for town centre developments. Further undertakings were given to commission yet more research on the impact of superstores on market towns, the impact of new types of retailing, such as retail clubs, and consumer attitudes and preferences for different types of retail development. Many of the Environment Committee's recommendations were thus translated into policy, but a number were made subject only to 'further research' undertakings, and other forms of action less than that for which the committee had pressed.

The draft revision of PPG 6 appeared in July 1995, and once again the Secretary of State reaffirmed Government determination to revitalise town centres by encouraging private sector investment, not just in shopping developments but also in offices, other businesses, entertainment, leisure uses and higher education. What was not included in the draft was a proposal to encourage people to live once again in town and city centres – a notable omission! Reaction to the draft was mixed. Those opposed to out of town developments generally welcomed the proposals, but pointed out that the draft guidance did not impose a total ban on off-centre development, nor was anything said about the many existing proposals for such development already granted planning consent. Even so there was general agreement that the draft was a great advance on the 1993 PPG 6, being more categorised and detailed. Some environmental campaigners were, however, dismayed by the proposals on car parking. As part of the town centre management programme the draft guidance advised authorities to provide attractive and reasonably priced car parking in town centres with appropriate parking tariffs to encourage those who drive into town to shop. This was condemned by those who believed that public transport should be improved to provide the main access to town centres.[70]

'An idea whose time has come'

On 22nd June 1995 the Secretary of State was reported as saying: 'Town Centre Management is an idea whose time has come'.[71] This no more than embryonic 'science' is, of course, concerned with a wider range of issues than land use planning only. The basic concept is to ensure town centres are attractive to all sections of the community by *inter alia* improving cleanliness and security as well as ensuring the existence of a wide range of shopping and service functions, and by encouraging a feeling of civic pride in town and city centres. However, there are formidable obstacles in the path of positive town centre management. Town centre businesses are subject to a tax on their premises in the form of Uniform Business Rate, but this is not then spent locally. Many generally attractive specialisms in town centres such as traditional public houses have been converted to follow 'theme' formats which are attractive only to the young. There is a strong public perception that town centres have decreased in cleanliness and have increased their rates of crime and vandalism, while the high cost of parking in town centres deters many motorised shoppers. Clearly changes in planning laws alone cannot by themselves reverse such perceptions. Equally it appears that it is not possible for the public sector by itself to bring about such a reversal – there must be a partnership between public and private sectors. 'Flagship' High Street traders such as Boots and Marks & Spencer are essential partners if town centre management schemes are to thrive. But they are only likely to be willing to participate and invest if there is strong commitment and investment from local government. Some private sector investment looks, however, set to continue. Since the launch of the Tesco Metro stores in 1989 (the first being in Covent Garden) Tesco has developed 35 such food stores in town centres designed to catch the 'top up on the way home' city centre worker by opening late. The average size of such stores is about 12,000 sq.ft. Marks & Spencer in 1997 announced plans to increase its central food outlets by a further 25, bringing the total to 60 in a £2.1bn expansion programme designed to create 4,500 - 5,000 jobs, and a 33 per cent increase in retail space which will be spread over town centre stores, smaller central food stores and off-centre superstores.[72]

By mid-1995 a group of major retailers and developers – Boots, Sainsbury, Marks & Spencer, Somerfield, The Halifax, Thorn Security, the Prudential, the Nat West Group (Group Property) and Land Securities – were associated with the Association of Town Centre Management whose objective is to share good practice, ideas and experience on the future prosperity of towns with particular reference to issues such as retailing, property, regeneration, and training. The Association had by then identified no less than 200 schemes of town centre management in the UK. At the same time a number of major retailers had appointed their own heads of town centre planning. Other 'big names' supporting town centre regeneration include W H Smith, Sears, Kingfisher, Debenhams and House of Fraser. From the 'public side' of the management equation, however, there must come a willingness to employ persons with experience of trading who are able to advise others on how to compete with off-centre developments. Other functions a town centre manager may discharge include: advising small town centre businesses on reducing their business rates; promoting an appropriately sited town as a one day shopping trip to visitors from the continental mainland; ensuring that pigeons are scared away from central areas so that mess is reduced; improving communications between small businesses and local authorities; bringing together public and private sector funding for town centre development initiatives; devising 'shop mobility' schemes to enable elderly and disabled shoppers to shop in town centres, and co-operating with the police in pressing the case for bye laws prohibiting anti social drinking in centres.

But though there is clearly a range of opportunities available to town centre managers, again it has to be stated that such management alone is not a panacea for all ills. Management and planning controls have to develop here a hand in hand approach to problems. Planning controls must be so operated as to accept that not all retailers can be successfully accommodated in existing centres, but where an edge of centre development does occur it should be complementary to the traditional centre. This is most likely to be achieved where new development is channelled alongside existing shops. At the same time, without a long term strategic commitment by major retailers to working with local authorities on town centre schemes such management initiatives are unlikely to achieve much. Furthermore those owning town centre properties must do more to manage their holdings in a more positive way. However, positive management of property is difficult where sites are in fragmented ownership or are subject to inflexible leasehold arrangements. There is also a continuing problem of attracting investment into town centres. The great advantages of off-centre developments are that they are efficiently laid out, have controlled environments with plentiful free parking and are provided with a dedicated management structure. To combat these advantages a much more dynamic style of town centre management than that currently existing must be developed. Thus of the 130 or so town centre managers in post in 1995 none appeared to have any real executive power or high executive status. There was also a reluctance on the part of local authorities to fund town centre management posts to a sufficient level to attract the most dynamic and business oriented managers – instead authorities prefer to invest in schemes that may be more short term socially attractive – such as child care or social housing schemes. At the same time businesses, apart from the handful of committed major players, can be resistant to putting in funding to management schemes and managers' salaries. Many businesses argue they pay high business rates yet receive poor services, such as street cleaning, by way of return. They also argue that their capital investment in the infrastructure of their shopping units is a sufficient investment – why should they contribute more?

It appears that while town centre management is an idea whose time has come, it is one that will not develop unless it is supported by sufficient funding. To do that developments within the tax system appear to be needed such as ring fencing part of business rates to channel part of that money into town centre initiatives or giving capital tax allowances to those prepared to invest in town centres. Economic instruments must also take their place alongside planning and enhanced town centre management if established centres are to thrive. These arguments have been reinforced by the latest official investigation, *Town Centre Partnerships*.[73] This concluded that though town centre management is essential for the continued vitality and viability of centre areas, and must depend on a partnership of the public and private sectors, currently it lacks a structure. Though there are more than 200 management initiatives, fewer than half have a distinct budget and many are merely liaison bodies. The lead in creating effective town centre management must, it was concluded, come from the local authority who have to show their commitment to their central areas if private sector interest is to be stirred. Both senior officers and leading members of authorities must be prepared to champion the town centre and to give it concerted attention directed to its improvement: this demands a shared vision and a clear strategy, together with an initial budget to ensure some 'early wins' in the improvement programme. Thereafter trust with the private sector needs to be built up. It is essential that people should be able to see how the improvement strategy will progress from conception to infancy, growth and maturity, with attention being given to tackling the most obvious problems first, and every effort being made to deliver results with resources being concentrated according to a common agenda. To achieve success a formal partnership between the public and the private sectors is commended, with an agreed programme of shared responsibilities. This is not easy to achieve but where it is, it is characterised by the '5 Ms' – membership, mission, money, management and measurable results. It is possible to add to this a corporate 'Town Trust' which relates to a specific area and has its own business plan, full time staff, progress monitoring system, and a broadly based board of management able to secure accountability. Any partnership scheme, however, should seek the best possible information about its area – current vacancy rates and property values, levels of service provision and expenditure on services, car park usage, sales, investment, *etc.* must be monitored – as must the output of town centre promotion, improvement and economic development.

However, the key to achieving a successful partnership is probably the question of finance: where should the funding come from? The evidence to hand suggests that the most successful partnership improvement schemes have drawn up a 'cocktail' of funding from a variety of sources. These include:

- Contributions from major property owners *if they feel they can benefit directly from the investment* – s 106 planning obligations may be helpful in this regard, though clearly not if the private sector investment is no more than a 'bribe' to allow developments otherwise unacceptable.
- Government grants payable under the City Challenge and Single

Regeneration Budget Schemes.

- Private finance under the Private Finance Initiative whereby the private sector takes on the provision of what were previously public services. Currently this type of funding is largely confined to transport schemes and it is not known whether builder/developers will wish to remain as service managers.
- Local authority funds may be forthcoming as government is more willing to allow the sale of assets whose proceeds can then be reinvested. Some authorities, however, are wary of relinquishing income bearing assets.
- EC funding. A number of towns have benefited from EC grants, but these can only go to eligible areas. Their effect can be to distort trade as eligible recipient towns are improved so much more than other, perhaps neighbouring, ineligible ones.
- Regional agencies may within their areas be able to provide funding.
- Miscellaneous sources of funding include English Heritage which may fund a Conservation Area Partnership, while the National Heritage Lottery Fund may play a larger rôle in the future. Housing Associations through their funding bodies – *e.g.* the Housing Corporation – may be able to participate in schemes including new housing. Businesses can also give general support by giving help in kind, such as the printing of newsletters, or maintaining bus shelters, benches and toilets, *etc.* in return for advertising space.

However, the current system for putting together funding packages is wasteful with too much time taken up in abortive bids, and too many bids based on inadequate research and consultation. Money received may also be too thinly spread across too many activities. Much funding also comes in on an ad hoc basis. The private sector makes a major contribution, but most of this is for specific projects, while there are major variations in the current practice and level of resourcing between partnerships. For the future a clear distinction has to be made between capital and revenue expenditure. Considerable amounts of money have been spent on capital projects such as street improvements and pedestrianisation schemes, and more of this is planned, but it appears harder to find funding for ongoing revenue expenditure such as extra staff and other costs associated with maintaining the promotion of central areas – for example it is little use installing closed circuit security TV if there is then no money to maintain it. Ongoing revenue expenditure cannot be easily funded by *ad hoc* contributions. Are existing financing mechanisms adequate to deal with the scale of expenditure required?

There are a number of funding options.

- The Business Improvement District (BID) is a North American concept whose core notion is that a supplementary levy is charged on taxes already paid by property owners (say 5 per cent) which is then spent on town centre improvement by a body run by the private sector. BID funding can be used to supplement local authority services, often to create 'clean, safe and friendly streets', but it may also support cultural and promotional events. A BID association may also run a retail and business development programme, especially tackling voids, and may take on parking and traffic management, physical improvements and maintenance. A BID may exist within a wider partnership organisation applying to a larger urban area than that covered by the BID.
- The Investment Priority Area (IPA) is a concept whereby public expenditure is concentrated in a particular area to create a critical mass of finance that then exerts leverage on the private sector, particularly where this is reinforced with tax incentives which appeal to the profit motive. This notion has been developed in Ireland where in Dublin the scheme was formalised by the creation of an area based regeneration agency with power to take over and redevelop property.
- The Town Improvement Zone (TIZ) is a British concept which develops the Town Trust idea by giving it a statutory mechanism. A Corporate body is created which encourages investor confidence with a board of directors representing local businesses and property owners, and a minority representation for the local authority. This body may receive funding from town centre parking charges, and on-street trading that it itself runs. There will be a business plan, and this will encourage private sector contributions to the budget. A TIZ could in addition to meeting revenue expenditure raise capital finance by way of bonds. However, a TIZ (which could be initially established for 5 years) can only work where there is a clearly designated area within which there is a common interest in securing improvement. That demands prior private sector commitment before the TIZ is created, and therefore might need a favourable ballot by affected landowners. The TIZ may also receive funding in the form of a town centre service charge collected by the local authority, much as with a BID, while contributions from the private sector could be set against tax. However, there can be no room for 'free riders' in a TIZ. All those in the TIZ need to contribute, and to see their contributions not as a tax but as a form of service charge contributing to the future viability of the area.
- Reforming Business Rates.

Ever since 1973 capital expenditure by local authorities has fallen as a proportion of domestic expenditure. Immense changes in the structure of local authority finance under the Conservative governments in the '80s saw rate capping, then the introduction of replacements for rates which have eroded the ability of local government to spend in a discretionary fashion on capital improvement, with such money as there is largely being concentrated on housing and education services. Furthermore the local tax on businesses – the Uniform Business Rate – is only collected by local authorities who pass it to central government which then redistributes it. However, business rate payers actually still fund 25 per cent of local authority expenditure via this mechanism. They are unwilling to make further local contributions unless there is some form of 'top slicing' or hypothecating business rates so that a prescribed proportion is spent locally. While business rate payers resent paying rates in return for what many see as poor local services, the reality is that authorities are merely channels for finance and have no incentive to direct funding to town centre improvements. At the same time the current system of funding which allocates capital to town centre initiatives *via* the single regeneration capital budget not only is competitive, so that some authorities fail to gain funds, but is also time limited in that there is no element of ongoing revenue funding. A regeneration scheme may lose its skilled managers once the funding ceases. In addition the burden of business rates falls particularly heavily on small businesses in contrast to larger concerns able to relocate in off-centre sites where they can generate more income to meet their obligations because of ease of parking, *etc.* At the same time larger towns and cities with historic centres to maintain, and other heavy public costs such as pedestrianisation schemes, do not appear to receive commensurate funding under the current redistribution system for uniform business rates. Finally business rates are a burden on the occupiers of property who are not necessarily its owners and the latter frequently have little interest on an ongoing basis in the general state of a town centre around their property until it falls vacant, at which point they must pay the rate and find another tenant.

While the Uniform Business Rate is an attractive tax for central government, raising £13bn in 1996-97, it remains unrelated to local priorities, and gives hardly any discretion to its collectors to vary its incidence – for example by lowering it in areas with large numbers of void properties. The local tax system could – and arguably should – be utilised to fund local projects, and to shift the incidence of burdens so that rates are lower in central locations than in peripheral areas, thus making the former more attractive to business and commerce. Rateable values could be raised in line with changes in trading conditions and property values, while local authorities would be given a discretion to vary rate values by +/-10 per cent within their areas. At the same time an element in business rates should be identified as being a 'local service element' which should relate to the amount spent by an authority in its central area, while funding from rates could be used to 'match' contributions from businesses to TIZ schemes. Central government could also review the way in which it redistributes Uniform Business Rate funds to reflect the needs and costs of town centres. There could also be a move away from property taxes generally towards local pay roll taxes or higher VAT.

The foregoing, however, are unlikely to occur without a radical commitment by central government to review local taxation and the acceptance of the principle of hypothecation of taxation.

The City of Coventry in October 1998 took the step of setting up City Centre Company (Coventry) Ltd as a non-profit making organisation with an annual £5.5mn budget from the City. This company must, however, meet specific targets if it is to retain that funding, such as a 5 per cent reduction in shop lifting, reversing the decline in the numbers of people visiting the centre and increasing it by 3 per cent, reducing overall crime in the centre by 5 per cent and enhancing cleanliness. The City invited shopkeepers to join in the company's membership scheme. In return for a £500 contribution they will receive enhanced security and pursuit of thieves *via* criminal and civil courts, and business promotion events. CCTV cameras will also be installed to enhance security. Uniformed staff are also to act as business ambassadors to welcome shoppers.[74]

Coventry's lead appeared, however, to be lacking in legislative support despite interest from other cities. Lord Jenkin of Roding introduced in 1997 a private member's Bill into the House of Lords – the Business Improvements District Bill – to give effect to some of the proposals outlined above. This, however, failed to reach the statute book. Furthermore the money released by the Government in the early and middle '90s under the City Challenge and Urban Pride initiatives to tackle central area decline, and under which collaboration with the private sector by local authorities attracts extra funding from the Single Regeneration Budget fund and/or from English Partnerships, does not appear to have been directed principally towards shopping centres. Certainly in Leicester the money was used to clean up old railway land for housing, student accommodation, University buildings, offices and leisure facilities.

But even if such a panoply of measures were to be put in place on a nation-wide basis it can be argued that they would be too little too late. The 1995 report *Survival of the High Street* found that the most affluent shoppers prefer off-centre retailing. 64 per cent of the survey group were attracted by the 'under one roof' nature of off-centre developments, 58 per cent were attracted by easy parking and 53 per cent by free parking. Conversely 42 per cent of those surveyed said that free parking would entice them back to town centres, while 35 per cent said that a greater range of 'big shopping names' in centres would attract them.[75] The problem, confirmed by the report, is that UK shoppers are car borne and have become accustomed to using their cars for shopping, while they also like the ability to conduct a major shopping expedition on a Sunday. While the research concluded there could be a different future for town centres in providing 'top up' shopping facilities coupled with more service outlets such as legal services, estate agents, restaurants, speciality shops and doctors, it also argued that for general retailing to thrive a much more restrictive planning régime is required – even than that proposed by the government in 1996 for the revision of PPG 6, namely a freeze on extensions to existing off-centre retail outlets and new developments. To support that the report pointed to the creation in 1995 of 17mn sq.ft of new retail space, of which 11mn sq.ft was in out of town retail parks.

Where do we now stand?

1996 opened with a number of confusing messages – some pessimistic others more optimistic. However, for every optimistic sign there were countervailing indications to indicate that policy thinking had not advanced sufficiently to contemplate taking the truly radical steps necessary to curtail off-centre developments and to concentrate new development in existing centres. Thus on 22nd April 1996 the UK hosted the First World Congress of Town Centre and Downtown Management at Coventry Cathedral organised by the Association of Town Centre Management with assistance from the International Urban Development Association and the International Downtown Association of the USA and Canada. Addressing this gathering the Secretary of State for the Environment argued town centres were fighting back and that UK government policy is to support this. Quite correctly he stated it is not state initiatives alone that lead to town centre regeneration and vitality – partnerships between sectors and between government agencies and individuals are essential. He pointed to the change in UK government planning policy whereby the balance has been tipped in favour of town centre development, while also arguing that local partnership initiatives can produce a sufficiently unified force to counteract the single management body advantage enjoyed by off-centre retail parks. He pointed in particular to Coventry where retailers, local businesses, leisure and training organisations have joined with the local authority to set up one company responsible for city centre management of litter removal, eradication of *graffiti*, landscaping and paving, car parking, lighting, closed circuit security television and entertainment. He also expressed interest in the North American model of the Business Improvement District whereby levies can be raised directly related and dedicated to town centre management and improvement. He also stated, and this was one of the most significant items in his speech, that town centres should be places where people want to shop, to be entertained, to meet friends and 'perhaps most important of all – to live'. That was an early statement of a policy to which the Secretary of State has subsequently returned, namely that future residential development should largely take place in existing towns and cities rather than in villages and on greenfield sites – a planning policy driven by overall sustainable development principles and one designed to reduce resource consumptive travel. Indeed in the future it might well be that the real key to revitalising town centres will be seen to be getting people to live back in and near them, though some very radical policy and legal changes will be needed to achieve that.

What, however, the Secretary of State did not say was that he was prepared to impose a freeze on off-centre developments, or to consider the enhanced use of economic instruments to promote town centres by ring fencing part of business rates to pay for a much more dynamic and effective style of town centre management. It was therefore all the more interesting to note the then Labour opposition proposals that there should be a revival of inner urban living by means of a campaign to use the estimated 80,000 to 100,000 currently empty flats over existing shops once more for housing. To further this campaign it was argued the 50 per cent reduction in council tax payments landlords currently enjoy on such empty properties should be removed. Housing Associations would also receive enhanced grants to renovate such properties and bring them back into use. The Labour Party further proposed that planning powers should be used to ensure the incorporation of residential accommodation in new shopping developments.[76]

Nevertheless on the launch of the revised PPG 6 in June 1996 the Secretary of State, while declaring the object of the guidance is to encourage a wide variety of development in town centres, returned to the issue of setting town centre development and regeneration within an overall framework of the wider sustainable development policy. He further stressed the need for new residential development to take place within existing urban centres: 'Towns are where most of our population live, work and shop. It is where many of the 4.4mn households projected for 1991 to 2016 will need to go'.[77] However, in shrinking from announcing a total freeze, or even a lesser degree of restriction, on off-centre development, the Secretary of State declared that the new guidance would encourage a more positive rôle for planning as part of a system of revitalising existing centres. The object is for authorities to plan positively, to identify sites for new developments, to adopt a partnership approach to working with developers, to lay down a clear and certain framework within which all can work and take investments decisions. Even so it was also accepted by the Secretary of State that:

> some uses, such as shops selling bulky goods or certain large scale leisure developments, may be able to establish that there is a need for their development which cannot be accommodated in the town centre.[78]

While it is clear that the implication of those words is that there is a burden of proof – a considerable burden – on those arguing for off-centre town development, and while it is also clear from subsequent words that the Secretary of State expects those who wish to develop off-centre to do so by combining with other out of town facilities and by providing improved public transport to their developments, nevertheless the door is still left ajar for off-centre development to take place. And where planning policy's door is left ajar economic pressures may cause it to open.

Hard on the heels, however, of the launch of the revised PPG 6 came the inception on 18th July 1996 of the largest – and *maybe* the last – out of town centre. This is the Bluewater development near Dartford in Kent which was consented before the tightening up of policy on out of town retail development. By 1999 the Bluewater development would have a cinema, cafes, restaurants and 275 shops including Marks and Spencer, House of Fraser, John Lewis, Boots, C & A and W H Smith. It would have 13,000 car parking spaces, coach parks, a bus station and rail terminal. It would cover 1.6mn sq.ft, and, as in the case of the Meadowhall development in Sheffield and Merryhill in Dudley would occupy former industrial land, in this case an ex-chalk quarry. It was expected to create 7,000 jobs during its construction phase, 6,800 permanent on-site jobs and might attract 30mn visitors each year. Interestingly the foundation stone of Bluewater was laid by the Deputy Prime Minister, Michael Heseltine, while the Secretary of State for the Environment was absent, though a Junior Environment Minister present, Mr David Curry, said it was *possible* that the development was the last of its size to open. In Scotland one further such centre at Braehead near

Glasgow is under construction.

The Trafford Centre in Manchester also appeared in September 1998. This *quasi*-Roman, almost Disneyworld, cost £600mn, has three miles of shops and is expected to attract 30mn shoppers per annum, spending £13bn, and travelling to it by road, especially the M60. Units in the development have been taken by Debenhams, Boots, C & A, Bhs and Selfridges (their only store outside London). There is a 60 bed hotel in the complex, with permission granted for a further 150 bed hotel, while just at hand is land for a 150 acre regional sports complex. The centre was designed not just to appeal to the 5.3mn people in the 45 minute drive band, but also to be a tourist attraction for the Midlands and North of England. The centre was built only after a protracted public inquiry and litigation going to the House of Lords – the entire planning process taking 14 years. However, shopping impact studies have predicted that trade will be deflected into the centre from nearby towns, at rates as high as 27 per cent for Altrincham and Stockport, and over 20 per cent for Warrington and Wigan. To counter this small traders in 27 towns in the area have formed a consortium with a £1.5mn budget to promote their claim to trade. Even so that response has something of a 'poor little 'un' against a 'good big 'un' feel about it. Though few in number, major regional shopping centres cater for the affluent in our society, and there are many of them – in fact most of us. People are prepared to travel to them, and thus alter the pattern of trade nationally. And if such a centre can be the 'star' of a successful television documentary series, as that at Thurrock was in 1998, then it is highly arguable that despite planning policy 'we are all Lakesiders now'.[79]

The spectre of the slow erosion of town centre vitality by off-centre development certainly did not, however, go away with the launch of the 1996 version of PPG 6. In November 1996 the press indicated that new threats were being posed to the vitality of many historic 'classic' market towns (Cirencester, Great Malvern, Hexham, Clitheroe, Tavistock, Okehampton and Leominster) by out of town and edge of town retail developments. The local authorities in question argued that, even as revised, PPG 6 gives no guarantee that out of town development will be halted. As the ring of off-centre developments around our larger towns and cities is completed, so major retail developers are now looking to develop and compete with one another around smaller market towns. This had led the Government to commission research into the deleterious effects of off-centre development on small market towns – towns which may suffer particularly as many of their town centre retailers are food outlets which find it impossible to compete with major supermarket chains. In the case of some of the towns concerned past permissions for off-centre food stores have already been implemented with noticeable results on the vitality of central trade. Yet other past permissions wait to be implemented.

What discernible effect, if any, did the defeat of the Conservative government and the return to power of the Labour Party in 1997 have on retail development policy? The indications are somewhat confusing. On 3rd July 1997 a major expansion of Merryhill, comprising 30 new shops and 2 large stores, was refused planning permission by the Secretary of State following strong local opposition to the proposal. There were, however, certain other consequences of this decision for it was reported on television shortly thereafter that cash 'sweeteners' from the disappointed developers which would have gone under agreements made with the local planning authority to fund improvements in Dudley, Stourbridge, Brierley Hill and Halesowen town centres, had been lost. These packages would have been worth some £6mn, and would have been used to release matching funding from central government.[80] Then on 20th July 1997 there were press reports that, despite local opposition, ministers had approved plans to build a major new Sainsbury store between Richmond and East Sheen. This was interpreted by some as a reversal of the policy of the previous government – a view strengthened by a Prime Ministerial remark that the preference of shoppers for out of town shopping was recognised. This interpretation continued into the Autumn of 1997. The Prime Minister's apparent preference for consumer choice as an element in development control policy was coupled in some minds with the approval of the Richmond superstore as a resiling from the previous strict line on such developments. This was further coupled with the allegations in November 1997 that David Sainsbury, then head of the supermarket chain, and ennobled by the Blair government in August 1997, had donated an undisclosed sum of money to the Labour Party (certainly over £5,000), while in October 1996 representatives from Sainsbury, Tesco and Safeway had met with Mr Blair, then Leader of the Opposition, in his office in the House of Commons to argue for a softening of central policy on off-centre development. These allegations, however, were considered at the time to be no more than a political embarrassment for the government, and certainly not evidence of impropriety by any donor, the payments having been made in solely a personal capacity.[81] The restrictive attitude of the Major government towards off-centre developments was also estimated to have built up a backlog of 150 applications for retail developments all seeking approval, with estimates that a further 600 applications could be made down to 2002.[82] So what of the official policy?

New Labour: new policy?

Reference has already been made to the House of Commons Environment Committee's investigation of retail development in 1994. That Committee reconsidered the issue during the Parliamentary Session 1996-97, and in response to its arguments the incoming Blair government issued *Shopping Centres*,[83] which laid down central policy on the issue. This may be summarised as follows:

- The government remains committed to applying the 'sequential approach' contained in PPG 6, and this will not be altered as both developers and planning authorities need time to gain experience in applying this approach. However, as a matter of principle the onus of showing that more central sites have been thoroughly assessed before an off-centre site is put forward for development lies clearly with the developer, who must convince the decision taker that the task has been done. Where there are rival proposals for retail development of more central sites it is again incumbent on developers to show that these sites are both available and suitable.
- The same sequential approach will be equally applied to large scale leisure developments – which may, it should be noted, often be associated with major retail developments. It is for authorities, after consultation with the leisure industry to lay down local policy on the siting of leisure development – where appropriate grouping it in 'leisure quarters' within or at the edge of town centres. The impact of a large leisure development should also be assessed by reference to relevant development plans; by reference to impact on the vitality and viability of existing town centres; by reference to its accessibility by a variety of means of transport, and in terms of its impact on overall travel patterns. A large off-centre development should always be assessed according to the principles of PPG 6.
- Currently certain impact study information has to be provided in respect of proposed retail developments over 2,500 sq. metre gross floor space, and further research is being undertaken as to whether there is a need for this requirement to be extended. This may be necessary where a retail development less than 2,500 sq. metre gross floor space could have a significant impact on, for example, an historic market town. Further research may also be undertaken to consider whether the reliability of impact studies can be improved, though as a matter of practice it is accepted that neither applicants nor authorities have either the inclination or the resources to review an impact study's accuracy at the stage of the

application. Thus the need is to provide in future improved methodologies for undertaking impact assessments so that they are more transparent and their findings less open to debate at a planning inquiry.

- It is not policy to conduct, as a matter of priority, research into the cumulative effect of a series of consented developments on an existing centre.

  [Many would argue that it is impossible to consider the effect of a proposed development without setting it in the context of past developments of a like nature, and that the notion of 'cumulative impact' should be an important determinant in the planning decision process where appropriate. To support such arguments quite extensive new research is needed, but clearly the need for that is not accepted by central policy makers who simply assert that a proper application of the sequential test should ensure that individual applications are appropriately assessed:

  > Proposals for out-of-centre developments, which might previously have proceeded because of lack of evidence of cumulative effects, still need to follow a sequential approach in the choice of sites, which means that the assessment of cumulative impacts is not a first order issue.[84]

  There is something not quite convincing about that assertion. The sequential test is surely primarily concerned with site selection and suitability not with setting the proposed development in the context of historic economic changes affecting an existing centre. A town centre development which would clearly satisfy all the criteria of the sequential test would also have a cumulative impact effect on other existing central sites. Nevertheless policy makers appear to have turned their faces against early research into the cumulative effect issue.]

- Where planning permission for a retail or leisure development has been granted on a temporary basis, when permission 'runs out' and a renewal application is made it should be determined in accordance with the up-to-date development plan, and, if this has been overtaken by events, with due regard to relevant central guidance, which means the application of the sequential test.

- Central policy will concentrate on town centre regeneration as a development priority coupled with enhanced provision of public transport to and from such centres in conjunction with the Government's intention to pursue an integrated transport policy which emphasises public transport at the expense of private car use.

  [It must, however, be asked whether providing better public transport to regenerated town centres can do much to dissuade car borne shoppers from using their vehicles to visit existing off-centre retail developments. Both the cars and the developments exist, and while better public transport and improved town centres may go some way to ensuring lower growth in both car use and off-centre development, they do not ensure that now established patterns of shopping will be reversed. The government furthermore accepts that further consideration is needed of arguments that off-centre car parking spaces should be taxed in order to make their use less attractive, conceding that car parking costs are ranked below issues of easy access, proximity to destination, and security by shoppers when asked to indicate why they choose to drive to particular locations.]

- Further consideration will be given to promoting positive town centre management, including expanding entitlement to tax relief on private sector contributions to approved town centre improvement schemes.
- Further consideration will be given to reforming the planning system so that development plans may be more speedily prepared and revised to take account of changing circumstances, probably by ensuring the use of shorter and more easily understood plans, prescribing time limits for the various stages of the plan making process and promotion of consultation between planning authorities and objectors to plans so that objections may be resolved in advance of a formal inquiry into a plan.

An assessment

'New Labour' appeared to be holding very much to the 'Old Conservative' line adopted in PPG 6 – in particular the use of the 'sequential test'. It could, however, be suggested that the likely line of policy under the Blair government will be to resist major off-centre developments – particularly out of town developments and major regional centres. A major test, however, of the Government's resolve, arose in 1998 when Brent London Borough Council resolved to grant permission for an extension of Brent Cross by 28,335 sq. metres, providing 1800 further parking places, improved junctions with the M1, A406 North Circular Road and the A41. A diversion of the River Brent would also occur. Though planning obligations would also impose requirements for improved bus services, on 30th September 1998, acting under s 77 of the Town and Country Planning Act 1990, the Secretary of State called in the proposal for his decision following its referral to him under the Town and Country Planning (Shopping Development) (England and Wales) (No 2) Direction of 1993 as a proposal to provide additional gross shopping floorspace over 20,000 sq. metres. The basis for call-in was that the proposal could conflict with policies in PPGs 6 and 13, and policies for sustainable transport in the White Paper 'A New Deal for Transport: Better for Everyone'.[85]

The Blair Government's apparent policy would not, however, prevent the development of new stores within the 'urban envelope' of existing towns nor, necessarily, at edge of centre locations. In particular central policy makers are unlikely to intervene, so as to limit site availability, in any struggle between the major food supermarket chains – Sainsbury, Tesco, Safeway and Asda – to develop new stores in existing urban areas, even where these are of the very large 'hypermarket' variety (familiar in France) comprising not just a foodstore but other outlets such as 'own brand' clothing, cleaning services, banking, florists, travel agents and other types of trading such as electrical goods. Both Asda, which has experienced a resurgence in trade by operating 'hypermarket' stores some 50 per cent larger than those of its rivals, and Sainsbury through their Savacentres, have followed such a path of development. Tesco entered the arena in June 1997 with a 103,000 sq.ft store at Pitsea in Essex (this should be compared to 70,000 - 80,000 sq.ft for its 'ordinary' stores), and has been said to have plans for a further 50 'Extra' hypermarkets, with alternative proposals for extensions to existing stores to raise these to hypermarket size as it may be easier to gain planning permission for these as opposed to new developments.[86] Certainly Tesco was in 1997 granted planning permission for two major new stores, one at Weston Favell in Northampton – an expanding commuter suburb – and one on an old brickworks site at Peterborough. That latter grant may also point to the continuance of a policy well developed under the Conservatives, namely that where there is a derelict industrial site retail redevelopment will be allowed, particularly if no other use can be found for the land. Indeed though local planning policies, and residents' groups, may be opposed to such developments it could be that the chief constraint on the development of the hypermarket in the UK may be the problem of finding large enough tracts of land to develop them – though in that context inner urban derelict land may become attractive. It should also not be forgotten that the growth of such stores is driven not only by changes in shopping habits on the part of car borne customers but also by the increasing need of the major traders to compete with each other and to find evermore new ways to boost their sales.

Policy affirmed – questioned – and re-affirmed

Research published in September 1998 supported the government's restrictive attitude to out of centre development, yet at the same time demonstrated weakness in current guidance.[87] The research looked at smaller urban areas, particularly market towns, where increasing development pressure has been felt from the major foodstore operators seeking to increase market share and increasingly being restricted in this desire in larger urban areas by the consequences of PPG 6. Concentrating on the impact of both edge of centre and out of centre foodstores on established centres, the research discovered a range of impacts of between 13 to 50 per cent on principal established food retailers on the opening of a new off-centre foodstore, leading to closures and vacancies in premises. The impact was not confined to food retailing, for off-centre stores frequently also offer services such as pharmacies, dry cleaning, a post office and cashpoints, thus affecting also comparison and service shopping. The research also accepted that the cumulative impact of a series of off-centre developments can weaken a town centre over a number of years. Central food retailers will close stores where these fall below particular levels of turnover and profitability, as Safeway did in 1994 when it closed 17 town centre stores nation-wide. Even the potential threat of an off-centre development can dent town centre retail confidence, leading to decisions not to invest, or even to close.

The research also showed that off-centre food superstores, on average, have a negative effect on retail employment in an area, attract more car borne trade than central stores, do not encourage linked shopping trips by customers whereby food shopping is joined with other purchasing, and do not, despite operators' arguments, generally claw back trade to a town which it has lost to other centres.

The report, however, highlighted the current paucity of methods for assessing the impact of a proposed off-centre development, and called for a new survey based system with a consistent framework which combines both retail and transportation impacts in a new Combined, Retail, Economic and Transport Evolution (CREATE). It also recommended that on the next revision of PPG 6 the issue of whether there is need for a new foodstore in market towns and district centres should be more clearly defined, and questioned whether the current distance limit of 200-300 metres for definition of a development as edge of centre is too great for small market towns.

Further proposals in the report were:

- that all foodstore proposals over 1,000 sq. metres net sales at edge of or off-centre sites in market towns and district centres should be accompanied by a CREATE survey;

- that PPG 6 should be further revised to include as indicators of vitality and viability in a centre issues such as retailer representation (*i.e.* the range of retailers present) retailer performance, vacancy levels and the state of a town's central environment;
- in the case of market towns and district centres impact assessments should take account of the cumulative effect of developments – a most important proposal – and where a town already has a well established provision of off-centre foodstores, a cautious approach to further non-central development is warranted;
- proactive planning and positive town centre management are, however, essential for the continued vitality and viability of smaller centres.

The direction of EC policy on urban areas is to stress the integration of functions in the planning and design of urban areas so that they are attractive and sustainable places to live, being mixed, diverse, lively meeting places for all activities at all times.[88] This is echoed in UK policy in 'Planning for the Communities of the Future'[89] which stressed higher density residential developments in town centres as a part of a new concept of Sustainable Residential Equality, which is *inter alia* concerned with harmonising urban management measures with planning policies so that social innovations such as car pooling schemes go hand in hand with land development proposals to reuse existing urban sites. This illustrates a new stress in policy on concern over extensification of cities, growth of land take, separation of activities leading to increased travel and traffic growth, and growth of peripheral developments. With particular regard to peripheral shopping development ministerial policy was reaffirmed on 5th November at the British Council of Shopping Centres Annual Conference. Pointing out that in 1980 5 per cent of retail turnover was in out of town centres, while by 2000 the figure could be 33 per cent and rising, the Planning Minister, Richard Caborn, reaffirmed that policy is not concerned with striking a balance between central and off-centre shopping; town centres, are to be given priority and that applications for out of town development will continue to be called in, where necessary, for central decision. He stressed that the corner stones of policy are regeneration of existing centres, equality of access and sustainability, with goods being brought to the people, not the people to the goods.

We may not see another Merryhill: we shall continue to see major new supermarkets and hypermarkets. Many of these, together with other retail outlets, may, however, now be built in existing centres. By late 1997 there were 17 town centre shopping schemes schedules to be completed by the end of that year, while there were only four off-centre shopping complexes so scheduled. There was an emerging concern among developers that PPG 6 in its 1996 guise had continued the slow down of off-centre development which was, some argued, apparent through the '90s. The great complexes such as Meadowhall and Merryhill were the product of the '80s, no such developments have been proposed in the '90s; while by 1997 proposals for town centre shopping space stood at their highest level since 1991. 1997 schemes ranged from 50,000 to 750,000 sq.ft of shopping space, though the proposed redevelopment of Birmingham's Bull Ring would provide 1.2mn sq.ft. This move back to central redevelopment is paralleled by European Community and Local Authority initiatives to boost town centre retailing, for example £600,000 from the EC to enable North London traders to improve their competitiveness in the face of competition from the Brent Cross and Lakeside shopping centres, while both Barnet and Haringey London Boroughs have also undertaken similar initiatives.[90]

Can this apparent turn round be ascribed solely to changes in planning policy, however? It is argued the answer must be 'no'. It is the overall state of the economy that is the real cause of change. In the '80s there was an apparent belief on the part of central government under Mrs Thatcher that financial sector business (including retailing) were more important to the nation's economic health than manufacturing businesses – and planning policy was subordinated to this belief to allow off-centre development. The rather more balanced attitude of the Major and Blair governments, coupled with the ending of the late '80s recession, have paralleled a return to economic prosperity – and it is that which is primarily fuelling the resurgence of town centres – not hindered, of course, by current planning policies. Certainly the affluent over-35 market appears to consider well located town centre department stores with a range of comparison goods and good services to be desirable places to shop.[91] Even so, there is a lesson to be learned here.

Retailing reflects the state of the national economy. Where the economy is weak, or out of balance, or in a state of flux it is folly for planning policy to be relaxed to allow over much off-centre retail development for that will then be reflected by dereliction and decay in areas most vulnerable to the wider economic changes around them. Such areas may take years thereafter to recover. This is the bitter lesson of Merryhill and Meadowhall, *et al*, but it is also apparent, though to a lesser degree, in other places where off-centre retail development has taken place. Though planning policy should not retreat into a wholly negative attitude towards non-central retail development (which is mere 'defensivism' unlikely in itself to revive central areas), it must reflect the realisation that retailing alone cannot lead the way out of a recession, nor provide a new economic and industrial base for the nation. Believing that was the mistake of the '80s.

Conclusion

At this point it is instructive to return to the arguments of Geoffrey Smith already considered above[92] as we consider where planning policy and law now stand, what they could accomplish and what are the limits to which they are subject. Smith, it will be remembered, was somewhat sceptical about the trend of retail planning policy development following the 1993 revision of PPG 6. He considered that there were certain myths prevalent in urban retail development planning. These myths were that: town centres cannot compete with out of town shopping developments; town centres decline because of out of town developments rather than as a result of wider social and demographic changes; positive and comprehensive town centre management is not needed, and even if it were to be there is no need for public research to be committed to it; the behaviour of shoppers can be changed by planning policy; a negative approach to off-centre development is an alternative to the positive promotion of vital and viable town centres, and, finally, shoppers will visit town centres even when they cannot park there. Since Smith wrote in 1994 events have moved on somewhat. Policy on retail development is now clearly placed within a wider policy commitment to sustainable development, one part of which is a need to reduce resource consumption by travel, while another is a desire to re-use existing urban land for new residential developments in order to save rural greenfield sites. Policy on retail planning has thus come, at least in part, to be driven by wider environmental forces. Whether Smith would applaud that must remain an open question; he would almost certainly applaud the more positive approach to town centre management increasingly visible since 1994, but would probably decry the continued lack of a national policy commitment to devote resources from the public purse – at either central or local level – to positive town centre management. Smith would probably also applaud the rather more pro-active approach to retail planning evident in the 1996 revision of PPG 6, but might still be dubious whether alone it can change the shopping habits of the nation which are shaped by powerful social, economic and demographic forces – and by the availability of cheap, personal motorised transport.

Currently, however, planning policy on off-centre development – and that drives the legal machinery of planning decision taking – is clearly generally opposed to major off-centre retail developments of the size of Meadowhall, Merryhill and Bluewater. Even so it cannot be assumed that there will *never* be another one of these major developments. Though there are not many of these regional centres, their impact is out of all proportion to their number because of their size, accessibility and the areas over which they attract customers. Bluewater might well attract day shoppers from France and Belgium when the UK section of the high-speed Channel Tunnel rail link is completed, which would feature a new international station near to the development with a possible rapid transit link into it. Planning policy is less averse to edge of centre development but that is a notoriously vague term because everything depends then on what is defined as 'the centre'. Consider the following case.

In Leicester the redevelopment, completed in Summer 1997, of the former cattle market site as a major leisure and retail development with a public house, restaurant, multi-screen cinema, bingo club and major food supermarket has taken place at some distance from the historic medieval city 'core' – certainly arguably beyond walking distance for a person wishing to shop in both places, and particularly so in view of the numerous busy major roads a pedestrian would have to negotiate. The prime emphasis was on leisure development, and while the food supermarket is of a size lacking in Leicester's historic centre, its principal customers could be residents of the terraced inner city housing nearby, together with a large adjacent council estate, in addition to city centre workers shopping on their way home – by car, of course. On the other hand in the same county the redevelopment of the former cattle market in Market Harborough with a major supermarket, market hall and a range of other shops and catering facilities was contiguous with, and formed a natural extension to the historic core which appears to be generally revitalised. That latter phenomenon could be equally – may be more so – explained by the growth of Market Harborough as a residential settlement. However, in both cases the vague definition 'off-centre' can be applied as a generic classification.

In any case we should be wary of concentrating thinking too much on what are generally classified as 'off-centre' developments with the associated sub-classifications of 'edge of centre' and 'out of town'. The truth is that any large retail development anywhere has the potential to alter trading patterns. While public concern with retail developments often focuses on off-centre developments it must not be forgotten that planning law and policy must apply equally to all types of such development no matter where they are proposed.

Planning law and policy intertwined

Though the statutory rules of planning law can be stated as reasonably terse propositions, they only provide a framework within which planning policy operates and where planning decisions are taken. It is policy that is important and policy remains, even after the 1996 revision of PPG 6, somewhat soft on retail development.

In a free market society it is unacceptable for planning policy and law to discriminate positively in favour of certain named retailers either in legislation or in statutory plans, though the outcome of the decision taking process will inevitably be to advance the interests of some retailers and consequentially diminish the interests of others. Even so, the past practice of planning concerning retail developments, particularly over the last thirty years or so can be characterised as regulatory, reactive and restrictive – in sum defensive.

It has been regulatory in that it has been concerned with trying to take land use decisions on individual plots of land, on something of a 'command and control basis' rather than trying to establish an overall vision of the needs of communities. This needs some explanation. Historically, the possession of land carried with it *inter alia* the right to develop it. Such a right was hardly articulated as such, probably because it did not need to be. Those who possessed land were subject only in individual circumstances to restrictions arising out of the existence of rights of way, or the terms of their leases where appropriate, or, from the mid-19th Century, the imposition of restrictive covenants. Under the Town and Country Planning Act 1947 the right to develop was taken away and replaced by a right to seek its recovery by way of a grant of planning permission, coupled with a policy presumption that such a grant would be made unless to grant permission would cause unacceptable harm to an interest of acknowledged importance. This placed a discretionary regulatory power to adjust land use patterns in the hands of local planning authorities. In the vast majority of cases planning permission is almost routinely granted, yet there are times when it is refused on grounds of wider public interests, or is granted only subject to conditions to protect a wider interest. While it is true that planning practice attempts, wherever possible, to proceed on a consensual basis with developers and authorities, and, to a lesser extent, the public, agreeing together on the best way to utilise land, wherever permission is refused clearly consensus has departed, and another interest has been considered superior to restoring the historic right to develop. Planning authorities have seen themselves not just as arbiters in the land development process, but also as representatives for other public interests they have perceived as being threatened by proposals for retail development, particularly on an off-centre basis. Hence we have a readiness to refuse permission – a 'command and control' stance in terms of regulatory management.

This, however, is largely the consequence of the other features of planning, which has been reactive in that, to a considerable extent, development decisions have been taken as a consequence of decisions taken elsewhere and general policy trends – and this is nowhere better illustrated than by the shedding of industrial manufacturing capacity and the re-use of its sites not for new industries but for shopping. It has been restrictive in the sense that, at the local level, planning authorities have found themselves caught in a series of policy and economic developments at national level which have conflicted with their perceptions of the needs and aspirations of their areas. They have tried using local policies to resist forces in many ways outside their control.

Planning policy is currently moving towards a more proactive stance on retail development. However, major questions remain as to whether policy can shake off its defensive past, especially when it must continue to express itself through the basically regulatory form of current planning legislation. Proactive planning policy should include financial instruments to enable a properly funded, truly executive system of town centre management to emerge. There would be ring fencing of at least part of the business rate to provide moneys to be spent locally on priorities determined by local authorities and the traders in their area. There would be nationally determined financial incentives in the form of tax breaks and allowances for developers prepared to develop in town centre locations. There would be more pump priming finance from central government for local authorities to carry out land assembly packages *via* the mechanism of compulsory purchase to enable the provision of suitable central development sites freed from the restrictions of leases, and capable of being subject to a unified management system once developed – particularly where there is the prospect of the return, over time, of that initial finance to the public sector from a private sector development partner. In the absence, however, of such positive financial instruments, given the force of law by special legislation, it is hard to see how the present system of planning can be truly proactive with regard to town centre development.

Even assuming such financial instruments were to be put in place, however, it still remains questionable whether the factors that have, so far, driven the off-centre retail development revolution can be curbed and reversed. There are powerful social, economic, demographic and mechanical forces at work. Ours is a society where women no longer stay at home while their menfolk go out to work: the ability for most women to do a 'daily shop' has been lost. Shopping, particularly food shopping, is now done on a weekly or even monthly basis. Secondly, our society is generally more affluent than ever before. Those with money demand a wider choice of goods than previous generations could have thought of. Thirdly, ours is a society in which cheaply available motoring is open to an increasing number of people from their mid-teens well into their seventies and even beyond. Finally, we have moved out of large towns, and continue to move residentially in the direction of small towns, outer suburbs and villages. Residential development is largely concerned with the creation of opportunities to assume particular lifestyles – and the desirable lifestyle for the many of us able to afford it for the best part of the last twenty years has been rural – albeit the *pastiche* rurality of nostalgic yearning for a falsely imagined past. For those less able to afford rurality there has still been the lure of the outer suburbs. These features of society combined together produce a highly mobile, affluent, convenience orientated – yet perhaps time constrained – body of shoppers. They look for one stop shopping with ample parking – they do not always find it in town centres. This does not mean that town centres are doomed, but it does give reason to doubt how successful even a properly financed system of town centre management and planning could be in preventing new off-centre development. Indeed it may be that we shall only stop the outward march of retail development when we are prepared positively to reverse the outward march of residential development. But to do that we need a vision of towns and cities as positively desirable places to live, and the will to devote resources to making a reality of the vision.

In the meantime we do well to heed evidence[93] that some inner urban areas – and also some villages – are becoming 'fresh food deserts' for those without cars who are forced to rely on a few corner shops selling high priced packaged 'convenience' goods as other independent retailers have given up the struggle against supermarkets. This poses particular problems for the elderly , the housebound and the poor. Department of Health officials 'mapped out' these food deserts, and the matter was examined by a special 'social exclusion unit' in the Cabinet Office. This inquiry was headed by Sir Donald Acheson, a former chief medical officer for the Government who discovered inter linked problems of poverty, health and poor nutrition which were exacerbated by the growth of out of town shopping and the decline of local shops. In areas across the UK, some of them inner urban areas in major cities, including London and Liverpool, there are 'food deserts' where cheap varied food cannot be purchased. The major supermarkets control 80 per cent of the retail food market, yet 10 per cent of the population have no easy access to them, and though the major chains claim to retain a number of 'High Street' stores, these may be no nearer to some areas than the off-centre developments which have largely replaced small local retailers. The major chains, moreover, appear to be unwilling to move into areas where crime and vandalism are perceived to flourish and expect a lead first from government before they invest. As much was admitted by a representative of Safeway stating that 175 stores had been opened from 1988 to 1998, only one third of which were 'High Street' shops, while 56 stores had been closed, mainly small stores. He added:

> That is what the customers wanted: one stop shopping. You cannot get the same access or car park facilities in town stores...we have abandoned these [deprived] areas, frankly because of the problems of crime and vandalism.[94]

A range of policy options may be considered such as relaxing planning rules so that retailers can be encouraged to set up in deprived urban areas, outlying housing estates and remote rural areas, encouraging village shops and local produce centres to run on a co-operative basis and examining partnership schemes between major retailers and local authorities whereby food can be delivered to elderly, infirm and housebound people with free bus services provided for others to reach existing supermarkets. Retailing is an issue not just in planning but in health and social justice.

Whether the warnings outlined above will be heeded and the vision previously called for will emerge must depend to a considerable degree on political will, and a readiness on the part of politicians to seize on other social and economic opportunities as they arise and to use them to aid in the task of town revitalisation. It is, for example, government policy that in the next five years, for example, 4.4mn new homes need to be built. The Major government considered 60 per cent of these should be on 'brownfield' sites. Under the Blair government after May 1997 it appeared that rather more new building might take place on 'greenfield' sites, and there was considerable opposition from counties such as Cheshire, Devon, Dorset, Gloucestershire, Hampshire, Hertfordshire, Oxfordshire, Somerset, Surrey, West Sussex and Wiltshire – most of them in the South and South East – to the targets centrally laid down for new 'greenfield' housing sites. However, by late 1997 it emerged that the Secretary of State for the Environment,

Transport and the Regions and Deputy Prime Minister, John Prescott, had declared a policy that more than half of the new homes should be built in existing urban areas. This would be essential if UK government undertakings to reduce emissions of greenhouse gases given at Kyoto in December 1997 were to be met as much of the reduction would have to come from cutting the use of private cars for transport. It was, however, further accepted that dwellings alone would not be enough and that a range of community facilities such as small schools, local hospitals and shops would have to be provided in the newly conceived 'urban villages'. It was realised that the best way to provide those shops would be by persuading the major supermarket chains to open small outlets selling a range of goods of a quality and price equivalent to those in superstores. Ministers thus realised their vision could only be realised by gaining the active co-operation of the retail sector.[95]

The future

Whether planning policy will be able to resist development of new off-centre retailing by major supermarket chains may depend to a considerable extent on internal changes within the supermarket sector. This is dominated by Tesco, Sainsbury, Asda and Safeway. Each of these is determined to create a particular identity for itself, but each is dependent on reading the 'mind' of the client. In the future will the trend be away from queuing at supermarket checkouts towards more automated shopping with home delivery services available *via* 'phone, fax or the internet? This was a market already tapped by Tesco's 'Direct' service which by the beginning of 1998 had some 15,000 customers. Such a development could lead to mass redundancies in retailing and to pressures to create a service network of massive warehouses to hold and distribute goods. Alternatively the future may be in the re-creation of the High Street under one roof following the example of the US mall, and that also would require even larger units – a development apparently expected by consumers who favour convenience and one-stop shopping. Tesco and Asda, for example, have built and wish to build such stores with floorspace of up to 60,000 sq.ft. At the same time each of 'the big 4' is re-inventing and renewing itself by diversifying its trading operation and also targeting what it identifies as its core clientele. For example, Safeway aims for families with children aged 0 to 5. Safeway also has in-store pharmacies and dry-cleaners, as does Asda; Sainsbury has gone into banking, opening 12,000 accounts a week by the end of 1997; Tesco sells designer label clothing, while Asda has its own 'George' clothing line. In time superstores may well include estate agencies, dentists, opticians and travel agencies; by early 1998 there were experiments in that direction. More superstores may also open for 24 hours a day.[96] Such changes would have repercussions. Initially they would almost certainly confirm the continuing decline of the independent trader already noted above. Secondly they would impact upon the 'second rank' superstores such as Waitrose, Morrisons, and Iceland who would find it hard to compete. Indeed that realisation almost certainly partly prompted the merger of two such 'second rank' stores, Kwik Save and Somerfield, confirmed on 19th February 1998. This £1bn merger created the fifth largest supermarket group with 1,400 stores, though it was thought that number could reduce as the new group rationalised its outlets, and 120 stores could close. That could affect poorer households disproportionately as Kwik Save has largely operated from High Street locations and has sold goods at discount prices some 5-6 per cent cheaper than those of Sainsbury and Somerfield, a mid-price chain which is likely to be the dominant partner in the new group.[97] Thirdly they would lead to yet further changes in the food production and supply sector for national retailing chains prefer to deal only with national suppliers who can guarantee continuity and quality of supply, to the detriment of local suppliers. Food is also likely to have to travel longer distances between its point of creation and point of sale with associated environmental travel disbenefits and the need for more food preservatives. Fourthly, of course, there would be yet more demand for new off-centre retail sites.

It is arguable, therefore, that no matter how retailing develops, the combination of food selling with a range of other products and services, and its concentration in a smaller number of hands, must lead to pressures on planning to allow the creation of larger units within which the activity can take place – whether in central or off-centre locations.

These pressures were intensified by the proposed acquisition of Asda by the US Wal-Mart chain in June 1999. Wal-Mart's 'Supercenters' number 715 with an *average* square footage of 160,000. These are based on the hypermarket pattern – a concept best described as a store that is off-centre, very large and retailing almost as many non-food as food items. Such stores devote space to high profit margin goods such as clothing and run on comparatively few staff. On the Continental mainland Carrefour opened a '*hypermarché*' south of Paris in 1963, and such stores are now familiar throughout France and other Western European nations. Sainsbury introduced the concept into the United Kingdom, by joining with British Home Stores (Bhs) to create 'Savacentres', the first opening in County

Durham in 1977. Sainsbury now has 13 such stores, but has tended recently to concentrate more on food retailing in them – up to 80 per cent of the retail space being devoted to food, as opposed to the more usual hypermarket limit of 60 per cent. Tesco in its 'Tesco Extra' stores has gone some way along the hypermarket route, with 5 such stores with an average square footage of 80,600, but including the 102,000 sq.ft hypermarket at Pitsea in Essex. However, it is Asda which has promoted the hypermarket concept most in this country, with 20 stores having an average square footage of 60,000. Even so the hypermarket is rare in the United Kingdom compared to France, Germany and North America. Nevertheless fears have been expressed that, following its acquisition of Asda, Wal-Mart could seek to persuade the government to relax planning policy to allow the erection of stores built along the lines of its target 220,000 sq.ft outlets.[98]

It must be remembered, however, that it is not just giant stores that have the capacity to alter radically local trading and economic conditions. In the late '90s Tesco applied for planning permission to build a food superstore just outside Saxmundham in Suffolk, a town with 81 foodshops retailing goods from 300 local producers who together employed 548 people, 317 of them part time. Those opposed to the proposal conducted research, subsequently confirmed by the local planning authority's own findings, showing that this local economy would be destroyed by the building of the superstore, balanced only by the creation of a small number of jobs in the new store. That application failed, but a number of similar ones were at the same time current at Kirkby Lonsdale (Cumbria), Romsey (Kent) and Sherringham (Norfolk) and the National Retail Planning Forum claimed that the creation of one food superstore can lead to the loss of 250 local jobs in retailing and food production; 93 such stores opened between 1991 and 1995 having led to a net loss of 14,500 jobs.[99]

Government policy, however, appeared to remain clear that, despite speculation that a new wave of hypermarkets might be built, there would be no change in retail planning policy which would be directed towards promoting the viability of town and city centres.

Speaking on 17th June 1999 the Planning Minister, Richard Caborn, stated:

> We expect new retail development, as the first choice, to be in town centres. This is consistent with our policy to regenerate our town centres and to make sure that everybody has access to a range of local shops whatever their choice of transport as part of our key objective of social inclusion.[100]

It will be noted, however, that the minister did not say retail development should be restricted to existing centres, and while there is money to be made out of off-centre retailing, coupled with an affluent population much swayed by the advertising notion of 'shop until you drop', and in thrall to the private car, we may expect existing centres to remain under pressure from new non-central forms of retail development.

Notes

1. 'Sundry Minor Operations' are given automatic permission under the General Permitted Development Order, 1995, SI 1995 No 418 and, more importantly, certain changes of use of existing premises, as opposed to new building, are permitted under The Use Classes Order SI No 764 Class A1: Shops. See further H. Norris, 'The New Use Classes Order' [1987] JPL 89.
2. Cmd 6153 (1940).
3. Cmd 6386 (1942).
4. Cmd 6378 (1942).
5. The Report of a Committee of Inquiry appointed by the Nuffield Foundation, London, chapters 8 and 9.
6. As witness the Marsh Mills saga to be examined later in the context of planning obligations.
7. London, Routledge, 1994 at pp. 77-79 and 90-91.
8. Guy C, *op. cit.* p. 91.
9. Guy C, *op. cit.* ch. 6.
10. Guy C, *op. cit.* p. 183 *et seq.*
11. *The Best Butter in the World*, Williams B, Ebury Press, London (1994) p. 169 *et seq.*
12. Guy C, *op. cit.* p. 158 *et seq.*
13. Guy C, *op. cit.* p. 129 *et seq.*
14. Guy C, *op. cit.* p. 121.
15. Tesco did, however, gain planning permission for a major foodstore at Hamilton, a new settlement to the north east of Leicester which opened in July 1999, At the same time Tesco closed their small store in Oadby, which was originally built in 1966 in the face of competition from the Co-op and Kwik Save. Competition from the large Sainsbury and Asda stores was not mentioned as a reason for closure: *Oadby and Wigston Mail*, 27th May 1999.
16. Guy C, *op. cit.* pp. 129-143.
17. Guy C, *op. cit.* p. 146.
18. Guy C, *op. cit.* p. 169.
19. Guy C, *op. cit.* p. 178.
20. Guy C, *op. cit.* pp. 186-187.
21. *The Times*, 23rd April 1997.

22. Guy C, *op. cit.* p. 178.
23. See MOHLG Circular 64/69, MOHLG Circular 6/53, DoE Circular 9/76, DoE Circular 22/80, DoE Circular 14/85, Planning Policy Guidance Notes (January 1988) No 11, para. 15.
24. Mr William Waldegrave speaking during *Question Time* in the House of Commons on 20th April 1998, see *The Times*, 21st April 1988.
25. DoE Circular 71/72. Development Policy Control Note No 13.
26. DoE Circular 96/77, Development Policy Control Note No 13.
27. Development Policy Control Note No 14.
28. DoE Circular 21/86.
29. Made under Articles 10 and 15(4) of the Town and Country Planning General Development Order, 1977 (as amended).
30. PPG 6 (1988 version) para. 4.
31. *Op. cit.* para. 6.
32. *Op. cit.* para. 7.
33. *Op. cit.* para. 10.
34. *Op. cit.* para. 8.
35. *Op. cit.* para. 17.
36. *Op. cit.* para. 18.
37. PPG 6 (1988 version) was here reinforced by PPG 2 'Green Belts'. PPG 2 para. 3 in its 1988 version pointed out that 'green belt' designation applied to 4,500,000 acres, or 14 per cent of England, and that one of the purposes of green belt policy was to preserve 'the special character of historic towns'. The guidance was clear that: 'Inside a green belt, approval should not be given, except in very special circumstances, for the construction of new buildings...'
38. PPG 6 (1988 version) para. 7.
39. PPG 6 (1993 version) para. 47.
40. Guy C, *op. cit.* p. 78.
41. PPG 6 (1993 version) paras 36-38.
42. See also Town and Country Planning Development Plans (England) Direction 1992, London HMSO.
43. PPG 6 (1996 version) para. 1.1.
44. PPG 6 (1996 version) para. 1.3.
45. PPG 6 (1996 version) para. 1.9.
46. PPG 6 (1996 version) paras 3.4 - 3.5.
47. PPG 6 (1996 version) paras 3.6 - 3.9.
48. PPG 6 (1996 version) paras 3.12 - 3.17.
49. PPG 6 (1996 version) para. 3.14.
50. PPG 6 (1996 version) paras 3.18 - 3.19.
51. PPG 6 (1996 version) paras 3.23 - 3.25.
52. PPG 6 (1996 version) para. 4.10.
53. PPG 6 (1996 version) paras 4.12 - 4.14.
54. DoE Circular 15/93, London HMSO 1993.
55. PPG 6 (1996 version) paras 4.15 - 4.18.

56. Jones P, 'Retail Development within the UDCs' 1989, vol. 44, no. 1, *Housing & Planning Review* 10-11.
57. Pincombe R, 'Megastores at the Crossroads' *The Independent*, 26th November 1991.
58. Tym R. & Partners 'Merryhill Impact Study' DoE/HMSO, London 1993.
59. *The Independent*, 7th September 1993.
60. *The Times*, 8th February 1994.
61. *The Independent*, 8th November 1993.
62. *The Times*, 29th March 1994.
63. *The Times*, 4th May 1994.
64. London, HMSO, 1994.
65. House of Commons Environment Committee Session 1993-94, 4th Report, HC 359-1, London HMSO.
66. Journal of Planning & Environmental Law, 'Planning Icons: Myth and Practice', Sweet & Maxwell, London 1994, pp. 91-106.
67. Smith *op. cit.* p. 100.
68. Lang, Tim and Raven, Hugh, London, Public Policy Research, 1995.
69. Cm 2767, London HMSO 1995.
70. *The Independent*, 20th July 1995.
71. *The Times*, 22nd June 1995.
72. *The Times*, 5th November 1997.
73. A report for the Association of Town Centre Management, London, Department of the Environment, HMSO, 1997.
74. *The Times*, 13th October 1998.
75. London, Mintel, 1995.
76. *The Times*, 27th December 1996.
77. DoE London Environment News Release 267, 20th June 1996.
78. *Loc. cit.*
79. *The Times*, 5th September 1998.
80. *Midlands Today*, 10th July 1997.
81. *The Independent on Sunday*, 16th November 1997, *The Sunday Times*, 16th November 1997.
82. *Financial Mail on Sunday*, 20th July 1997.
83. Cm 3729, London, HMSO, 1997.
84. Cm 3729, para. 20.
85. Cm 3950, London, HMSO 1998.
86. *The Times*, 11th September 1997.
87. 'The Impact of Large Foodstores on Market Towns and District Centres', CB Hillier Parker & Savell Bird Axon, London HMSO, 1998.
88. Commission of the EC: 'Towards an Urban Agenda' COM (97) 197 final, Brussels, CEC.
89. Cm 3885, London HMSO 1998.
90. *The Independent on Sunday*, 16th November 1997.
91. *The Independent*, 11th August 1997 and *The Independent on Sunday*, 8th November 1997.

92. Smith *op. cit.*
93. *The Times*, 5th November 1997 and *The Independent*, 16th October 1998, 17th October 1998 and 21st October 1998.
94. Quoted in *The Independent*, 21st October 1998.
95. *Independent on Sunday*, 14th December 1997.
96. *The Independent*, 29th December 1997, 30th December 1997, 31st December 1997, 1st January 1998.
97. *The Independent*, 20th February 1998.
98. *The Times*, 19th June 1999.
99. *The Times*, 17th June 1999.
100. DETR News Release 580, 17th June 1999.

6 Policy into practice: the law in operation

Though national policy as outlined in the previous chapter has been a major determinant in setting the overall course of planning law's approach to retail development, individual planning applications are, initially at least, decided at local level by local planning authorities

The relationship between planning policy and planning law is complex. Arguably law should be the servant of policy; yet policy cannot be translated into practice without law, and while in most instances law merely provides the formal framework within which decisions are taken, there are occasions when law influences policy to a considerable extent. The historic general philosophy of regulation amongst planners in the United Kingdom in the 20th century has been to ensure the prevention of urban sprawl, the eradication of nuisances and the preservation of amenity. This has been accepted by government as the basis of planning policy. In addition, however, policy has added the all important 'gloss' referred to in the previous chapter of the presumption in favour of development, *i.e.* that development should be allowed provided it will not cause unacceptable harm to interests of acknowledged importance. This, of course, is productive of conflict for there is ample room to disagree as to what is 'unacceptable harm' and what is an interest of 'acknowledged importance'.

It is *via* the door opened by the potential for conflict that the influence of law has penetrated planning policy and practice. Historically English land law gave a general right to landowners to do what they wished with their land provided they did not harm others in the process. That right was taken away by the Town and Country Planning Act 1947, and was replaced by a regulatory system which declares landowners cannot develop their land unless they have a grant of planning permission – an essentially restrictive system, which has to be modified in practice by the grant of extensive permitted development rights and, of course, the presumption in favour of development. Nevertheless gaining planning permission is generally an essential prerequisite to exercising the ability to develop land, and where there is disagreement over whether a development will cause unacceptable harm to an interest of acknowledged importance there is the potential for conflict which may only be resolvable in court. This is why the courts and the law which otherwise are peripheral to the day to day operation of planning practice are important. Through those conflicts which have ended up in court the judges have brought to bear on planning law – and hence also planning policy and practice – a set of traditional legal values whose application has resulted in constraints on what planners and planning can achieve. Despite the apparently wide wording of the legislation what can be done under it is trammelled by the meaning given to the words of the statutes in court.

This would not be too much of a problem if it were not for the fact that the principles applied by the judges are themselves couched in general terms, while their application can often depend on the attitudes taken by individual judges – especially as many cases never go beyond the level of a single judge in the High Court. Thus while any first year law student should be able to recite the general principles of administrative law with ease, namely: that administrative agencies should only do what their powers allow them to do; that they should obey the procedural requirements laid down in statute; that they should generally behave fairly towards those subject to their powers; that they should only act on the basis of relevant considerations and should eschew irrelevancies; and that they should behave reasonably (*i.e.* in a way which is not oppressive towards those subject to their powers), the actual application of those principles is far from easy. There is, for example, an element of circularity in them. If an authority must consider only what is 'relevant' and must not consider what is 'irrelevant' then the argument centres on determining what is 'relevant' and what is not. Even more notoriously if an authority is to behave 'reasonably' it must do what a 'reasonable authority' would do!

On the whole judges seek to avoid at all costs becoming embroiled in the merits of a planning dispute. Questions of whether a particular development should or should not be consented are not justiciable and should be left to planning authorities. The rôle of the judiciary, it is often claimed, is to ensure that in making such a determination planning authorities stay within the legal limits of their powers. Yet even when the courts seek to distance themselves in this way from questions of merits, by making the foregoing claims, they cannot entirely escape from such issues. If, for example, a planning decision is struck down on the basis that an 'immaterial' (irrelevant) consideration was taken into account, it *may* be possible for the same decision to be reached without the offending issue featuring in the determination process. However, if that issue was fundamental to the initial decision, then the subsequent exclusion will probably lead to a different conclusion being reached. In this way issues of legality can affect factual outcomes. In addition because of the English doctrine of precedent a rule laid down in one case becomes normative for all similar factual situations thus adding a constantly growing mass of case law to what is already a considerably complex statutory framework. In addition ministerial appeal decisions in cases where planning permission has been refused, though not 'precedents' in the strict legal sense, add yet another layer to the 'geology' of decision making, and much time can be spent in searching for and arguing over the applicability of past decisions whether taken in court or by ministers.

Furthermore the application of general legal principles often depends on whether the judge has a basically positive or negative view of how authorities should go about their business; *i.e.* does the judge believe that when Parliament entrusts powers to authorities it intends them to get on with the job subject to as little supervision as possible, or, that no matter what statute says, there are clear limits to legality within which authorities must stay. The result is a confusing plethora of case law decisions, largely created by the fact that a lot of money turns upon gaining a permit to develop. Those decisions constrain what planners can do, from deciding what constitutes development, through the decision making process, to the imposition of conditions and obligations on developers, and thence to the stage where challenges may be mounted to decisions taken. In addition though the courts regularly reiterate that questions of fact and the application of planning judgement are matters for authorities as 'decision takers', yet what constitutes a matter of fact and the limits within which planning judgement can be exercised are matters of law.

Thus the *interpretation* of a particular policy document is a matter of law, while its application to a set of facts is a matter of fact for the decision taker, though even here there is room for disagreement. There is authority for saying that it is only for the courts to determine what the words in a document are capable of meaning, with the decision taker being able to determine the actual meaning within the acceptable range of meaning.[1] However, once planning permission is granted the meaning of that permission is a question of law for the courts, and authorities have no discretion to alter that meaning.[2] Similarly though the weight to be given to any planning policy or other relevant consideration is a question for the decision taker, a failure to give reasons for a particular finding, or to fail to make a particular finding, which is fundamental to the subsequent decision is a matter of law, and a legal challenge can be mounted to the failure.[3]

In most of England and Wales decisions on planning applications will be reached formally by the district council (in England), though in London the matter will be one for the London borough council, in the former metropolitan county areas such as the West Midlands, Merseyside, Greater Manchester, South and West Yorkshire and Tyne and Wear, the metropolitan district council and, where such an authority exists and appropriate provision has been made under ss 14 and 17 of the Local Government Act 1992, the unitary authority. (These latter have increasingly been taking up their new powers since April 1997. They are principally large towns which lost their county borough status in 1972, for example, Leicester, Derby and Nottingham.) These authorities take the formal decision to grant or refuse planning permission. That decision will, however, normally reflect (a) a very considerable amount of informal discussion and negotiation with the applicant before a formal application is made and, no doubt, a deal of planning bargaining, of which more later, and (b) local policies on retail development. In Wales, it should be noted, under the Local Government (Wales) Act 1994 there are 22 'Principal Councils' that are the planning authorities – 11 counties and 11 county boroughs all of which are unitary authorities, see ss 1 and 18 of the 1994 Act.

The rôle of the development plan

In coming to a decision on an application an authority will be much guided by its 'development plan', which in some cases will consist of more than one statutory plan.

Ever since the commencement of the Town and Country Planning Act 1947 statutorily required plans have been a major feature of the planning system. However, plans have not since 1947 been regarded as 'blueprints' for development. They are flexible documents, both as to their provisions and as to the ways in which they may be changed. They do not directly control development; rather for most of the period since 1947 they have been background guides in relation to granting or refusing planning permission. At first there was only one 'development plan' for a planning authority's area, but since 1968 various types of plan have made up 'the development plan'. Furthermore the identity of these plans varies from one part of the country to another. In some areas there will only be one Unitary Development Plan (UDP) – this will be the case in London boroughs, metropolitan districts, some English unitary authorities where the Secretary of State has so determined under ss 14 and 17 of the Local Government Act

1992, and in the case of the Welsh authorities under s 10A of the Town and Country Planning Act 1990 and Schedule 1A. In most of England, however, the 'development plan' will be, under s 54 of the Town and Country Planning Act 1990, the 'Structure Plan' made by the relevant county council and the 'Local Plan' made by the district. (It is not appropriate here to go into any level of detail concerning the process of making these various plans. The interested reader is further referred to Hughes, *Environmental Law* 3rd Edition, London, Butterworths 1996 pp. 154-167 and Moore *A Practical Approach to Planning Law* 6th Edition, London, Blackstone 1997 chapter 4.) However, there are certain national requirements which all plans should reflect. Under Planning Policy Guidance Note 12 (PPG 12) plans should provide guidance to developers, indicate preferences and aversions for particular types of development, while making realistic provision for the development needs of their areas; which means adequate opportunities for needful development must be provided. All plans must, and this is a statutory requirement, include policies on nature conservation, natural beauty, preservation of amenity, improvement of the physical environment and traffic management. Structure plans should additionally indicate the overall balance struck between development and conservation, and how development will be served by transport infrastructures. The structure plan should contain general policies on *inter alia* the rural and urban economy, which will in the present context include policy on retail development. Indicative guidance should be given on the level and general location of development opportunities for particular types of activity, though detailed guidance is the preserve, where appropriate, of local plans. In areas where UDPs exist the distinction drawn between structure and local plans will be mirrored in the division between Parts I and II of the UDP. Plans should also *inter alia* generally strike a balance between 'greenfield' and 'brownfield' development, should seek to promote urban regeneration and should consider the impact of development on particular sections of society, together with the need to preserve and enhance employment opportunities. All of these policies are clearly relevant to retail development. PPG 12 further stresses the need for all plans to reflect the overall commitment of the nation to a sustainable development policy, and in the particular present context, this means maintaining the vitality of existing urban centres, limiting car use by siting new developments so that use of cars is reduced or rendered unnecessary – which clearly militates against grants of permission for out of town developments – and relating development to public transport networks.

Thus in general terms the 'development plan' will either be a collection of documents or a single document, but in either case it will contain 'broad brush' and detailed 'brush stroke' elements. On the one hand there will be a strategic policy framework underpinning local planning and development control, and an attempt to ensure an overall realistic provision of development opportunities that is internally coherent and also consistent with national and regional policies, while on the other there will be specific allocations of land for particular purposes; though there will not, of course, be a rigid zoning 'blueprint' for future development. The development plan may also be supplemented, as is recognised by PPG 12, with a whole range of non-statutory supplementary planning guidance (SPG) drawn up by local authorities. SPG cannot have the same significance as the development plan though it can be a material consideration in relation to any given planning decision. Where it exists, central guidance insists it must be clearly separate from the development plan; it should not introduce policies which have not been subject to public scrutiny, and should be consistent with the statutory plans. Furthermore where it is relied on its status must always be made clear. Such SPG can range from design guides through to quite detailed 'planning briefs' for particular sites. Its nomenclature is not standardised, and developers frequently claim it is confusing and inconsistent.

Development plan policies and retailing

Traditionally plan making presented an opportunity for an interventionist rôle for local planning authorities as there were attempts to influence both the overall growth of retailing and its location. From the first issue of PPG 6 in 1988 central government indicated its dislike of the former style of intervention but the latter is still commonly encountered.[4] Thus most structure plans will contain policies on retail development because of its economic significance and potential for creating and retaining employment opportunities. Similarly local plans will contain retail development policies both for the economic reasons already mentioned and because such local plans have a considerable locational significance. Indeed the plan making process is likely to give rise to public inquiries into the likely need for and suitable location of particular sorts of development, including major new retail developments. In practice plan policies have been dominated by a hierarchical notion whereby planners have attempted to specify a 'system of retail concentrations within urban areas which appear to satisfy consumers' requirements for access to shopping'.[5] They have tried to ensure relationships between the size of any given shopping centre and the extent of its catchment area – though this is hardly possible where a major regional shopping centre is under consideration as its customers may be drawn from a very wide area indeed. Planners have tended to disfavour such types of development as running counter to their hierarchical notions. Planners thus tend to favour existing town centres as against new off-centre developments, and the reuse of existing developed sites in an attempt to prevent the outward march of urban areas. Plan policies have included, and may still include:

- restriction of total retail floor space, *i.e.* a limit on planned floorspace provision derived from forecasts of 'shopping need' for an area at a future date;
- allocation of 'shares' of the total floorspace to particular areas or types of shopping centre;
- policies for the specific creation of new retailing outlets to meet forecast needs, possibly with a particular location in mind;
- provision on conditions to be attached to grants of planning permission for retail development;
- safeguarding of existing shopping centres, either by general restrictions on new retail developments, or, more positively, by making provision for the upgrading of existing centres with the local planning authority having *inter alia* a co-ordinating rôle for various private sector initiatives.

Such policies are quite commonly encountered in local plans as district councils seek to protect their existing centres.[6] Indeed, since the tide of central government thinking turned against off-centre retail development with the 1993 revision of PPG 6, it is now possible to encounter highly detailed policies in local plans on retail development. These may take a positive form with subsequent restrictions. For example a policy may exist that permission for retail development will 'normally' be given, though subject to the restriction that this will not be allowed where the development in itself, or cumulatively with others, would seriously affect the vitality or viability of a nearby town centre. Alternatively retail development of particular sorts may be positively targeted to go to particular locations, but again subject to restrictions relating to single or cumulative impact, the types and extent of advertising designed to attract the public to the area, and the range and type of goods to be sold. In some cases the restrictions may be imposed on the grant of planning permission. Where this cannot be done the restriction will be sought by way of an obligation under s 106 of the Town and Country Planning Act 1990, see further below.[7]

Any policy on retailing can exist in a more or less restrictive form. In the '70s the general attitude towards off-centre development was highly restrictive, but that changed (particularly under the influence of central policy, see the previous chapter, and the need to adapt to rapidly altering economic circumstances) to a less restrictive attitude in the '80s. In some cases authorities actually encouraged off-centre development as a way of improving shopping provision in their areas generally, or as a means of relieving existing inner urban congestion. The degree of control which was exercised by central government over structure plans – a degree of control not relaxed until amendments to the 1990 Act by the Planning and Compensation Act 1991 took away the need for their central approval – meant, however, that in some cases over-restrictive policies on retail development were modified, or even deleted, by the Department of the Environment (DoE) during the plan approval process. This made it hard for county planning authorities to restrict new shopping developments or to confine their growth to existing centres. Even under the current law the Secretary of State has power under s 35A of the Town and Country Planning Act 1990 to 'call in' a plan for his approval, and potential modification. PPG 12 further makes it clear that this power will be used where a plan is considered unsatisfactory, particularly with regard to applying national or regional policies, or where a plan is controversial and raises issues extending beyond the boundaries of the plan making authority.

The reasons for the historically restrictive attitude of local planning policy towards off-centre development are well known and stem from perceived needs to maintain existing shopping centres, particularly in central areas. This is reinforced by arguments that off-centre development encourages the use of private cars and is not accessible to non-car owners, being both consumptive of resources and unfair in operation, and that it will 'stand alone' and be unrelated to other commercial and cultural centres. It is further argued that land may be devoted to shopping use that should be, and may be under plan policies is, devoted to industrial use. Finally there is a perception that off-centre development frequently takes place in 'greenfield' sites. Thus local policies in general range from: strong presumptions against development (the closest to a categoric 'no' that can exist); through a general policy of non-allowance, or non-allowance on land scheduled for industry or warehousing, or only on an individual merit basis, to rather more cautious policies that may allow development in or near to an existing retail centre (in some cases, however, only where specified criteria are met) or on designated sites only or on fringe sites; then to rather more liberal policies that allow specified types of development away from existing centres, and finally to policies allowing development away from such centres provided certain criteria are satisfied. The most restrictive policies were commonly encountered in plans drawn up in the late '70s and early '80s, with more liberal policies being encountered as a result of overall policy change throughout the later '80s, see the previous chapter. Furthermore, there is a hierarchy of reasoning justifying particular policies on off-centre retail development given by planning officers. The effect on other outlets is the most potent justification usually given, followed, in descending order, by questions of 'need', accessibility, effect on the supply of industrial land, the necessity of supporting existing shopping hierarchies, amenity issues, public transport availability, innovation, the generation of traffic, maintaining existing town centres (particularly against competition from new centres) and questions of employment. Clearly planning officers time and time again are concerned with issues that can be described as 'shopping impact', *i.e.* the effect of new developments on existing ones and in particular their effect on existing retail centres.

It should not be supposed, however, that there is an uniform trend of opposition to new retail development, even where local planning policy as formally expressed is averse. In any given case a development may be allowed for a variety of reasons. Thus before 1980 under the planning legislation as it then stood certain applications for permission for larger new stores had to be determined by county councils as 'county matters'. These tended to fare badly as structure plan policies were generally averse to such developments. With such applications being entrusted to district councils since 1980 a number of applications have been successful which might not otherwise have been. While district councils are statutorily required to make their decisions conform generally with structure plan policies, and must inform county councils of major retail applications so that county views may be expressed and considered, nevertheless 'exceptionally' some applications have been granted. Individual districts have sought either to enhance their 'retail profile' or to prevent a development going to some other district in the county. Districts have also taken into account issues such as the availability of general environmental improvements consequent on the retail development of an 'old' site , and the possibility that jobs may be created, even though many of these will only be part time, and may be 'purchased' at the cost of other jobs lost in other parts of a district or in other districts. It must therefore always be remembered that while national policy may have swung against off-centre development, and while a particular authority may be opposed to such development in its own area, between themselves local authorities are in competition for trade, particularly upmarket middle class trade. It can be hard for an authority to resist the blandishments of off-centre developments if it is known refusal may lead to the same development being proposed, and possibly consented, in a neighbouring district.

One phenomenon that at a particular time in the '80s appeared to indicate distinct possibilities of differences of policy between authorities has since receded. This was the apparent trend for planning permission for large new stores to be more easily obtained in the north than in the south, and, more particularly, for permissions to be concentrated in less affluent areas. The figures from the early '90s indicate a levelling of permissions across the nation – again reflecting the liberalisation of local policy in the light of what was then central policy.[8]

The special case of the Urban Development Corporations, Enterprise Zones and Simplified Planning Zones

Urban Development Corporations (UDCs) were a favourite tool of the Thatcher government for regenerating large areas of inner urban land, being designated by the Secretary of State under Part XVI of the Local Government Planning and Land Act 1980, particularly s 136. They existed outside the normal framework of local government and were set up *inter alia* in London's Docklands, on Merseyside, Trafford Park and Central Manchester, on Teeside, in Tyne and Wear, in the Black Country, Leeds, Sheffield and Bristol. Their period of designation has now drawn to its close, but in their time they were powerful agents for redevelopment of their areas. They were able to take over planning functions for their areas if so designated by ministers, though, as will later become clear, in this capacity they were required to act objectively and were not to allow their regenerative function to override their objective planning function. One of their principal tasks was nevertheless to attract private sector finance into their areas, and they tended in doing this to favour new retail development, particularly on an off-centre basis (see further the previous chapter) often in the face of opposition from 'dispossessed' local authorities. Enterprise Zones were also introduced under the Local Government and Planning Act 1980 and utilised a combination of tax advantages with specific development rights granted by the scheme of ministerial designation as a means of urban regeneration prompted by local initiative, as opposed to central imposition as was the case with the UDCs. They have since been superseded by simplified Planning Zones (SPZs) originally introduced by the Housing and Planning Act 1986, see now ss 82 to 87 of the Town and Country Planning Act 1990.[9] SPZs are designed to promote urban regeneration in older, depressed areas, and grant permitted development rights by virtue of their scheme of designation, subject only to limited conditions to protect health and safety, preventing polluting emissions, regulating vehicular access, specifying height and density requirements and laying down parking and landscaping conditions. These zones, according to Guy[10] have had an 'important impact upon retail development'. While in most cases normal planning controls have been retained over such developments, 'in a few zones permission has been allowed either for any type of retail development or for any development below a certain size limit'.[11] The important point to remember is that wherever such development was promoted by a UDC or allowed under a zone designation it takes place outside the jurisdiction of the local planning authority, and could even be opposed by planning authorities as contrary to local planning policy.

Local policies and the historic impact of central guidance

Structure, unitary and local plans may be relevant to the location of new retail developments. For some years in the '80s making of local plans progressed but slowly, though many are now being made: in terms of large store development it can still be the structure plan that is more relevant. However, a plan, of whatever sort, is only one factor to be taken into account when deciding a planning application, albeit an important one. Furthermore, its relevance to any given application can vary with its age. While s 54A of the Town and Country Planning Act provides that 'where in making any determination under the planning Acts regard shall be had to the development plan, the determination shall be made in accordance with the plans unless material considerations indicate otherwise', a provision clearly designed to give an enhanced status to plans, they by no means act as blueprints for development. Moreover the cardinal determining principle remains that in s 70(2) of the 1990 Act: 'the authority shall have regard to the provisions of the development plan, so far as material to the application, and to any other material consideration.' The case law indicates that the effect of s 54A is as follows:

- where a proposed development accords with the plan the presumption will be to grant permission;
- where the development is clearly in major conflict with the plan the presumption is to refuse permission, save where the progress of time and events has overtaken the plan or there are other convincing reasons for allowing development;
- where there are no other material considerations and the plan covers an issue it will be determined according to the plan;
- where there is no clear conflict, or where any conflict is only minor, or an

issue arises on which the plan is silent, the decision must be made on the basis of all relevant considerations.[12]

In sum, a decision taker must take into account all relevant or 'material' considerations, including the general presumption in favour of development not causing demonstrable harm to interests of acknowledged importance, and should decide the issue in accordance with the plan save where 'material' issues otherwise indicate. As there will always be such other issues, as PPG 1 points out, the plan is only a starting point and the other factors have then to be considered before a decision is made.[13] Furthermore the plan may not carry much weight where its provisions are out of date, having been overtaken by subsequent central guidance or other factual events.

Plan making thus has only certain restricted functions in relation to the siting of retail developments. It was clear from the initial version of PPG 6 that plans should take account of forecasts for plan periods of retail expenditure, on a county and district basis, and the implications of those forecasts. In *exceptional* circumstances where the viability of an existing town centre would be jeopardised by competitive development elsewhere within an area, the cumulative effects of recent and proposed developments could be reflected in a plan. Plans should reflect the need that existing centres have to maintain diversity and activity, but should *not* be drawn up in consideration of the possible effects of major developments on existing individual retailers. They should not prescribe rigid floor space limits for new retail developments, either overall or for particular areas.[14] This was a considerable change of policy: the *Memorandum on Structure and Local Plans* DoE Circular 22/84 had stated at para. 4.22:

> Policies and proposals for shopping should include a broad guide to floor space provision... Authorities will wish to avoid substantial over provision of shopping facilities and take account of the likely impact of new development on the continuing viability of established town centres.

That circular had stressed that while the task of planning is not to regulate competition, nor to prevent new forms of retailing from evolving, there was a need for access to adequate shopping facilities for everyone to be convenient. In the Lee Donaldson *Superstore Appeals Review 1988*, significant comment on the policy change was made:

> The suppression of floorspace estimates and controls eliminates a major aspect of the argument concerning shopping needs, and is consistent with the shift in onus or burden of proof to the local planning authority to demonstrate harm to interests of material importance.[15]

The policy guidance as then drafted, however, reflected judicial pronouncements. In *Great Portland Estates PLC v Westminster City Council*,[16] the House of Lords restricted the range of planning considerations to be taken into account in plan making, pointing out that plans should not be made on the basis of protecting individual traders, though it was (and is) lawful to have constraint policies designed to preserve an overall balance of land uses within an area. This may have the indirect effect of protecting an individual's trading position.

It was also a contentious question whether plans could place 'burdens of proof' on developers to make out cases for grants of permission. In *Urban Planning Law* Grant argued that:

> An out-of-town superstore, for example, may draw trade away from existing town centres, causing shop closures, general economic deterioration and a loss of service to town centre dwellers who lack the necessary mobility to take advantage of the new competition... The issue of competition and the existing state of supply of a commodity or service often arises in the context of restraint policies which require the developer to make out a case for the grant of permission, in terms of demand. It is thus not a regulation of competition, but the policy may have that indirect effect at least in the restraint area.[17]

But there was no consensus on this issue. Some commentators have been of the opinion that developers should not be made to establish need in public interest terms for retail developments.[18] It is indeed debatable how far it is legal to impose a burden of proof. In *Federated Estates Limited v Secretary of State*[19] a major extension to an existing shopping centre was proposed. The relevant structure plan policy was that such proposals should be refused permission unless justifiable as exceptions to policy by reference to various specified criteria, including adverse impact on existing shopping patterns. Permission was refused. At the subsequent appeal the Inspector concluded the new area would be a risk to existing shopping facilities and that, in line with structure plan policy, permission should be refused. The question was raised as to whether it was lawful to impose a burden of proof on a developer by means of a plan. The court disposed of the issue by finding that nothing in the plan placed such a burden on the developer. However, in view of statements in *Pye (J A) (Oxford) Estates Limited v Secretary of State*[20] that the concept of 'burden of proof' is appropriate to civil litigation but *not* within a planning appeal, there has been doubt as to how plans can place burdens on developers. This was reinforced by central guidance which has regularly reiterated the view that there is a presumption in favour of development unless it would cause demonstrable harm to an interest of acknowledged importance, which in the present context does not include the trading position of an individual. Constraint policies, though allowable, were (and are) not automatically overriding factors. Indeed it is clear, from the treatment received during approval procedures by plans regarded as being excessively restrictive by the DoE in the '80s, that inclusion of 'hard line' policies severely restricting development of new retail outlets was hardly possible.[21] However, as central policy in the '90s turned its face more and more against off-centre developments – save in accordance with declared principles, see the previous chapter – local plans could begin once again to be more constraint based. It nevertheless remains clear law that policies may not operate to discriminate in favour of given individuals as such, nor is the concept of a 'burden of proof' appropriate within the context of planning.

The issue of prematurity

Plans are not fixed 'once-for-all' documents, being subject to regular revision and replacement, new proposals often being referred to as 'emergency plans', which clearly have a relevance to decision taking. The question can arise whether a proposed development should be refused because it is 'premature' in that it could prejudice such an emerging plan. The question arose in *Boulevard Land Ltd v Secretary of State for the Environment*[22] in the context of an application for retail development which might have pre-empted a decision on shopping policy for an area which should have been considered in the light of a review of the relevant local plan. In particular there were fears that the decision would pre-empt the incorporation of shopping policies reflecting the current state of PPG 6. PPG 1, however, is clear that the pre-maturity argument should only be utilised where a development plan is actually being prepared, or is under review and consultation proposals have been issued. This was not so in the instant case. The decision was therefore contrary to PPG 1 in its approach to prematurity, and the guidance was a material factor which should have been taken into account. Because of the apparent failure to consider that material consideration the decision was quashed, though, as the learned commentator on the case in the 'Journal of Planning and Environment Law' points out, had the matter been taken into account there would have been no bar to the decision-taker reaching a conclusion that nevertheless pre-empting fundamental decisions on shopping policies was a sufficient reason to refuse permission.[23]

Development Control: the process

In deciding applications for planning permission (and indeed in determining appeals against refusals) it is clear the process involved is *qualitative* in nature, involving coming to a judgement on *all* relevant factors, and not determined solely, for example, by *quantitative* arguments based on the impact a development will have on existing trading centres.[24] Many factors will be relevant to this stage of the process. What are these other 'material' or relevant considerations? They may vary according to the development proposed which will range, in the retail context, from constructing new shops or extending existing ones, through altering the existing use of premises to retail use, or from one retail use to another, carrying out ancillary works such as the construction of car parks, to altering the existing retail outlet. Over 80 'considerations' have been identified in relation to such matters, of which over 50 may be employed in any given situation.[25] The considerations can be considered as 6 groups – (1) Amenity, (2) Arrangement, (3) Efficiency, (4) Co-ordination, (5) Quantity and Distribution and (6) 'Other'. These are further divided into sub-groups – (1) site characteristics, design, physical impact, operation, relationship to surroundings; (2) on-site layout, off-site relationships; (3) on-site use of resources; (4) phasing of development, on- and off-site, and operation and time issues; (5) quantitative issues, distributional and location issues, and (6) 'other'. Under the subgroups are ranged the specific factors which may be considered relevant in any given case: (1) topography, landscape, presence of historic buildings, archaeology, architectural style, scale and mass, external space arrangement, daylight, sunlight, any hazardous uses, the hours of operation, litter generation, obstruction of traffic, impact on other buildings or protected land, the fact that a use may be non-conforming; (2) layout and capacity of site roads, the layout and capacity of parking, pedestrian movement, and new routes for pedestrians, disabled access, refuse collection, whether 'backland' development is involved, security issues, any use incompatible with another off-site, proximity and capacity of local highways, proximity and capacity of utility services; (3) conditions under the surface of the site, the conditional conversion potential of existing buildings, the presence of vacant land; (4) links with other uses on site, and proposals to link with off-site developments, any temporary uses proposed; (5) the loss of an existing use, increases in use, expansion of premises, employment generation, impact on off-site uses (taking into account not just an authority's whole area but also sub-areas); (6) planning gain, the need of the applicant, need for site assembly, precedent. It will be noted that the fears and other views of local residents and traders are not specifically mentioned in the foregoing list though undoubtedly they play a part politically in determining the minds of elected members of authorities as they come to make a decision, and can be material considerations in the decision making process.[26]

In deciding a development proposal a planning authority must exercise discretion in a genuinely independent and fair way, free of predetermination, and not primarily motivated by hope of gain for themselves. This is so even where the authority is an interested party in the development.[27] This obligation does not, however, extend to rival retailers opposed to a proposed development. This is clear in a report that objectors to a Sainsbury development in Islington ('The Stop the Store Alliance') received contributions to their costs at a pubic inquiry into the proposal held in April 1996 from other store operators. It should, however, be noted that the rival operators all had stores in a previous development which would have been threatened by the new store, while the alliance also included holders of shopping units in that previous development which they thought was protected against off-centre development by local guidelines.[28] Nevertheless the basic question for the planning authority is clear: the principal evaluative question to be asked is 'are there sound and clear cut reasons for refusing planning permission?'. It is clear following *Centre 21 Limited v Secretary of State*[29] that a plan policy *may* constitute such a 'clear cut' reason *if supported by other evidence in the matter*: it may not be assumed a plan policy of itself is determinative of the issue, especially given the case law on the effect of s 54A of the 1990 Act, see above. Certainly a mere general fear that to consent a development may create a precedent for future proposals is not enough by itself to justify a refusal. Though where creation of a precedent would prejudice the implementation of national or local policies the issue is different.[30]

The determination process must be generally fair, not only with regard to individual applications, but also, in cases where a number of developers have submitted proposals for retail developments, as between those 'rivals'. It may be necessary to co-ordinate consideration of conflicting proposals. This is particularly true in relation to proposals that go to appeal.[31]

This issue has been recently examined in *Asda Stores v Secretary of State for Scotland*[32] Here Sainsbury and Asda had competing applications for superstores in an area. Both were contrary to the relevant structure plan. Asda's application was refused, while the local planning authority indicated a mind to give permission to Sainsbury, but had to inform the Secretary of State as the application was contrary to the structure plan. There was at the time with the Secretary of State a proposed alteration to the structure plan which would have supported one further superstore in the area. Asda appealed against its refusal and the Secretary of State decided to determine the matter himself as the matter had implications for the consideration of the structure plan alterations. But he also decided not to call in Sainsbury's application, and Asda sought judicial review of that decision. The Court at first instance argued there was an obvious relationship between Asda's appeal and the proposal to alter the structure plan, and that it would be undesirable for Asda's appeal to be determined by the appeal process simultaneously with determinations on the revision of the structure plan. The Secretary of State was accordingly under an obligation to devise a process whereby Asda's interests were not prejudiced by the parallel proceedings, and that led to a conclusion that the Sainsbury application should also have been called in for all the issues to be determined together. On appeal, however, a very different view was taken. Asda's appeal had an implication for the outcome of the revision of the structure plan in that the implications of the appeal decision for the revision process would be a matter to take into account while deciding the appeal. However, there was no legal requirement for the Secretary of State to call in the Sainsbury application, nor was it, on the facts, irrational of him not to do so. That the facts disclosed a degree of preference on the part of the planning authority for Sainsbury over Asda was a matter the Secretary of State could leave to the authority, and he certainly was not bound to call-in both applications to assess their relative merits. In the instant case the Secretary of State was carrying out separate functions in relation to the various issues, and could not be required to conflate them, though it would have been otherwise had he as a matter of fact taken into account the merits of both applications and had then decided only to call in one.[33] The Courts are, furthermore, loath to interfere with the Secretary of State's decision either to call in an application under s 77 of the 1990 Act or to decline to do so.

This line of argument has been confirmed in *R v Secretary of State for the Environment, Transport and the Regions, ex parte Carter Commercial Developments Limited* a case involving three rival supermarket development applications. There is no overriding requirement of 'fairness' in that once one application out of a number has been called in, all the others must be dealt with in the same way. All the Secretary of State has to do is to have regard to the implications for the consideration of any other proposals as one of the considerations in his decision whether or not to call in an application. In the instant case the Secretary of State had acted properly in that one of the rival applications concerned a central site whose development would not have breached any national policy and so gave no reason for a call in, while the scheme of the applicant for judicial review was for an edge of centre development which breached the sequential test and so was justifiably called in. Even so it is interesting to note that the Secretary of State was holding a joint inquiry into the one application which he had called in, and one application which had been refused by the local planning authority and appealed, which indicates that co-ordinated consideration of the factual issues and merits is considered necessary.[34]

It is equally clear, however, following *R v Doncaster MDC ex parte British Railways Board*,[35] that the planning system is not operating neutrally when it grants one developer permission and refuses another. Dependent upon the number of new retail outlets an area can take, to grant one permission may inevitably determine refusing others. Each instance has to be determined on its merits, but those have to be evaluated against their context; that includes grants of permission for other developments that have effectively 'cornered' trade within the area. The courts seem to accept an issue on which policy guidance is not altogether clear: there is a point of 'saturation' beyond which it is simply not commercially possible to support the development of new retail outlets. As Schiemann J said in the *Doncaster* case:

> Problems could, and regularly did, arise in circumstances where several operators applied at more [or] less the same time for planning permission to erect a superstore in an area, each operator accepting that good planning required that no more than one such superstore should be erected in that area... If [the planning authority] granted one such application and refused the others, although the others had a right of appeal...that right was, in reality, worthless because their competitor had got a head start. In any event, by the time their appeals came to be heard there was a legitimate reason for refusal, namely that the area already had one superstore, which, it was the agreed planning judgement, was all that should be allowed.[36]

These issues were accepted also in the *Asda* case. Asda was 'prejudiced' by the readiness to grant permission to Sainsbury who thus secured a commercial advantage; but that was inevitable given the way the planning system operates, with there being no right of appeal against a decision to consent a rival application. The fact that all the issues were channelled through the Secretary of State did not mean that there was procedural unfairness in not giving Asda the chance to challenge Sainsbury's good fortune.

In *Fighting Planning Appeals*,[37] Lewis Keeble suggests *inter alia* the following as factors relevant to the process of determining retail development applications:

(a) Need 'to secure the establishment and continuance of business areas of appropriate size in appropriate locations...to ensure that everyone has every service as close to him as is economically possible in terms of minimum catchment populations needed if various facilities and services are to operate successfully';
(b) to limit numbers of such centres in order to preserve amenity for adjoining residences;
(c) to bear in mind highway factors, pedestrian and parking capacities;
(d) to make centres as compact as possible in order to minimise nuisance.

Keeble is also quite explicit that:

> Development control is about land and its use, not about the morality of people's behaviour or the encouragement of socially desirable uses and the discouragement of 'undesirable' uses. Nor is it about either the encouragement or discouragement of competition.[38]

Indeed, so far as past judicial dicta are concerned it is generally only where trading competition is likely to lead to the *decay* of an *existing centre* that it can be taken into account as a major determining factor. Schiemann J put it neatly in the *Doncaster* case:

> ...planning authorities were entitled to refuse planning permission for a large new outlet if its operation was likely to lead to...decay on a significant scale. When a refusal on such grounds was appealed to the Secretary of State an inquiry was held, at the conclusion of which the Secretary of State often attempted to quantify the degree of impact of the proposed new store upon the existing centres, and then made a decision as to whether that planning permission ought to be refused.[39]

Those words should not, however, be taken as a final pronouncement. Changes in planning policy as evidenced by PPGs and ministerial appeal decisions would inevitably affect any judicial opinion given today. In this context it is interesting to note that on 30th June 1988 the Secretary of State refused planning permission for the development of Centre 21 in Leicester – a proposal which would have rivalled either Merryhill or Meadowhall – (Application No 86/1337/1/OX). Highway, employment and wider environmental issues were considered, as well as the terms of the development plan. Insofar as that plan contained shopping policies the Secretary of State considered that it is important to protect the vitality and viability of existing centres where they have not so far decayed as to be incapable of new growth. Such vitality and viability, it was held, became threatened not only in circumstances where an off-centre development would result in absolute decline in a central area's turnover, but also where it would result in stagnation and a loss of investment in other central development initiatives.

A note on Environmental Impact Assessment

Environmental Impact Assessment (EIA) is the first major inroad into our planning law from the European Community under Directive 85/337/EEC, as amended by Directive 97/11/EC. The process was initially introduced into our law as 'Environmental Assessment' by SI 1988 No 1199. It has now been re-titled 'Environmental Impact Assessment' by SI 1999 No 293. This makes some changes to the previous law, particularly requiring a 'screening' process to take place to determine whether a proposed development is one requiring EIA, and also enabling guidance to be given as to the scope of any information to be given as part of the Environmental Statement (ES) which has to be submitted by the developer.

In brief, EIA is a technique whereunder wider environmental implications may be considered in relation to certain types of development. The skeleton of the procedure is that the would-be developer submits an Environmental Statement to the planning authority on the proposal. This will contain certain information about *inter alia* the site, design, scale and size of a development, its main effects on the environment and the measures proposed to deal with adverse effects. This ES will then be made subject to consultation with statutory consultees, for example the Countryside Commission, and also has to be made available to the public at reasonable cost. The consultation process generates 'Environmental Information' which then has to be taken into account by the decision taker when determining the planning application. EIA will only, however, be applicable to a very small number of off-centre retail developments, if at all. Such developments do not appear on the list of those for which EIA is in all cases mandatory. The process will then only take place where the project is determined (generally by the local planning authority) to be one with 'significant' effects on the environment and which *also* falls within Schedule 2 of SI 1999 No 293. This schedule refers to 'urban development projects', including the construction of shopping centres and car parks, sports stadiums, leisure centres and multiplex cinemas exceeding 0.5 hectares in size. Schedule 3 of the 1999 Regulations then proceeds to give an indication of the matters to be considered in 'screening' a Schedule 2 development to determine whether EIA is required. These include: the size of the development, the 'cumulation' with other developments; use of natural resources; production of waste; pollution and nuisances; risk of accidents; location bearing in mind matters such as the existing land use, the abundance, quality and regenerative capacity of natural resources in the area, the absorption capacity of the natural environment in the area, and the characteristics of the potential impact including its extent, magnitude and complexity, probability, duration, frequency and irreversibility.

Thus major off-centre retail development *may* be subject, in theory, to EIA, but in practice the issue does not seem to arise. Early in the history of EA as it was then known in UK planning law a proposal was put forward for development consisting of a retail park of 200,000 sq.ft, including restaurants, housing, leisure facilities, a hotel and car parking. This was a large scale development close to a city on a major motorway with high rise buildings which would have had major visual impact. It would also have required major changes to traffic flows and would have adversely affected certain geological features. The local planning authority considered this amounted to a development project which had a significant environmental impact and should therefore be subject to EA. The would-be developer disagreed and appealed – as is allowed by the regulations – against the determination. On appeal it was determined that the matter was indeed a development project falling within the regulations, but also that there would be no significant environmental effect such as to warrant EA.[40]

The literature reveals only a few instances of environmental impact assessment taking place with regard to proposed retail developments, and in those areas where it has occurred retail impact was not a prominent consideration. Thus in 1989 an application was made in respect of land at Slate Hall Farm, Lolworth, Cambridge for a sub-regional shopping centre of 50,000 sq. metres. The impacts considered were: recreation, socio-economic, highways, ecology and landscape. This application was refused in 1992.[41]

In 1993 an application was made to redevelop land in Hastings Town Centre for retail purposes. The impacts considered included: visual, noise and vibration, traffic, drainage, dust and air quality, archaeology, ecology and waste disposal. However, a further impact, that of 'planning' was also included as the object of the developers, in this case the local authority, was to redress retail imbalance between Hastings and other centres.[42] This development was consented. A proposal to develop a superstore with associated catering and other customer facilities was made in respect of land at Lambridge, near Bath. Retail impact was considered here, but it was considered that even on a cumulative basis the new development would not materially affect existing traders. Even so the application was refused in 1994.[43] The proposed mixed redevelopment of Salisbury Cattle Market to include a food superstore and retail warehousing was submitted for consent in 1993. Retail impact was not considered, but the proposal was approved in October 1994.[44]

It is therefore unlikely that EIA will play much part in the retail site development process. Other matters are likely to be of much more importance in the determination process.

The determination process

This essentially involves two stages. First comes establishing facts, including arguments about the shopping impact a retail development will have. The task of establishing facts lies with those who allege them. Where the argument about the impact of a development is employed it is extremely difficult to establish 'facts' because so much depends upon estimates; there is no agreed method for drawing up an 'impact equation'.[45] Only thereafter comes the evaluative decision: 'do the facts disclose sound reasons for a refusal of permission?' Over the years the answer to this has turned upon a wide range of facts. In the mid-'70s DoE Circular 71/76 examined reasons for refusals in a number of superstore applications. Out of 28 applications only nine were disposed of on the basis that adverse impact on existing facilities was unacceptable. Others were disposed of on a number of bases: need to protect green belt, and/or save agricultural land; to prevent congestion on inadequate roads, or to prevent inadequately scaled development, for example. In the '80s the same pattern of decision making seemed to continue. The 1986 Lee Donaldson *Superstore Appeals Review* surveyed 189 superstore appeals, some two-thirds of which were unsuccessful, and concluded there had been three main determining factors in these cases: land use (*i.e.* environmental factors such as need to protect green belts, and land supply issues), shopping (*i.e.* impact on existing shopping facilities and on policies on shopping), and traffic issues. Land use factors accounted for about half the refusals, four in 10 were disposed of on the basis of adverse shopping impact, while traffic issues and other matters accounted for refusals in one-eighth of cases.[46] In the one-third of successful appeals, however, it seems permission was granted because it was felt no sufficiently conclusive grounds to warrant a refusal had been adduced.[47]

The 1988 Lee Donaldson *Superstore Appeals Review*, however, revealed a success rate on appeal rising to 50 per cent. This was attributed to better site targeting; developers had learnt to avoid applying for sites where land use constraints applied and to seek sites within, or at the edge of urban areas, frequently choosing sites otherwise allocated for industrial development. Shopping considerations, however, had become the principal ground for refusal of permission. Lee Donaldson's *Superstore Appeals Review 1988*, additionally pointed out that during the '80s the stress within objections to retail developments based on shopping considerations moved away from their possible impact on existing outlets to the fear of prejudice to other preferred or approved alternative shopping proposals and developments. Indeed it was then Lee Donaldson's contention that:

> ...research controverts the general hypothesis that superstores entail widespread serious adverse impact upon the traditional shopping hierarchy. No study has found evidence of severe impact on surrounding shopping centres. The changes observed tended to be subtle rather than gross.[48]

Objections based on shopping policies may be, as stated earlier, supported by statements in the plans for an area, or by arguments that a new free-standing superstore would endanger nearby town centre development proposals, especially where these centre on an 'anchor' development of a large new foodstore. However, as Lee Donaldson's 1988 survey indicated, a countering tactic to such arguments has been for the developers to offer to take a tenancy of the town centre store in addition to their own free-standing store, concluding that different clienteles exist for each store.[49] Continuing practices lend some support to this argument. In Leicester, for example, Marks and Spencer, despite their major off-centre store at Fosse Park, in 1997 embarked on a 70 per cent extension to their town centre store, largely for food retailing. In part of the same redevelopment of the former Lewis's site Tesco, who have only been able to obtain planning permission for one major off-centre foodstore in Leicester, also created one of their 'Tesco

Metros', which caters *inter alia* for the needs of lunch hour food shoppers. Developers favour off-centre locations but clearly remain willing to invest in central locations where there is a market. In Leicester's case the growing number of students and other young people living and working within the central area may do much to explain this.

Certainly it has never been generally easy for a planning authority to show a direct causal link between the development of off-centre sites and a decline in central trading. Lee Donaldson's 1988 survey actually stated:

> ...although the local planning authority frequently argues that an appeal project is objectionable in terms of its likely impact, in no instance, despite the growth of superstores throughout the country, has the local planning authority been able to substantiate this objection on the basis of firm survey data and report demonstrating that a particular superstore has resulted in severe adverse impact.[50]

Authorities are, apparently, on firmer ground if they can show multiple objections to a development, for it can be argued that a superstore is now an established form of shopping, and the absence of such stores within an area is actually a *lack* which may need to be supplied. This argument can be appealing to both inspectors hearing appeals, and the Secretary of State who has gone further and has decided one case on the basis that:

> ...absence of need is not by itself a sufficiently strong planning objection to justify dismissing the appeal, unless the evidence shows that the store would seriously affect the viability of [the] town centre.[51]

That decision was explicit in arguing that restrictions on commercial competition could only be justified in exceptional circumstances.

Cumulative impact

The Lee Donaldson 1988 survey paid particular attention to the issue of cumulative impact indicating that planning authorities were concerned at the cumulative effect of proposals from developers to introduce further stores into an area, with specific regard to their impact on existing centres. No agreed criteria for an 'acceptable' level of cumulative impact exist, and the issue has become judged increasingly on the basis of measuring the cumulative impact of developments on a centre as a whole, measuring impact solely on food sales being less favoured.[52]

There can, however, be no doubt that the likely impact on local trade is a material consideration which can be taken into account by a planning authority. This was reinforced by a decision of the Northern Ireland Court of Appeal *In re F A Wellworth & Co. Ltd. In re Boots the Chemist Ltd.*[53] Here a developer had obtained permission to erect a food superstore in Coleraine and other buildings. A study of retail impact had been required by the planning authority – the Department of the Environment for Northern Ireland – based on the proposed superstore having a net floorspace of 28,000 sq.ft. No operator for this was identified and the developers adopted a notional turnover for the floorspace of £530 per annum per square foot at 1990 prices, and used this as the basis of the impact study. No public inquiry was thereafter required into the proposal and planning permission was granted. However, another developer then acquired most of the land in question and entered into an agreement with Sainsbury that they would operate the superstore. Further planning applications were also made in respect of the site, but no further impact study was required, and planning permission was given. F A Wellworth & Co. Ltd and Boots then sought judicial review of this decision arguing a material consideration had not been taken into account in that the increased retail impact of a store operated by Sainsbury should have been considered and a fresh impact study required. At first instance it was established that the turnover per square foot of a Sainsbury store might be materially higher than £530 per annum. This was accepted by the Northern Ireland Court of Appeal who argued that the business skills and experience of Sainsbury are such as to create a potentially much greater retail impact than would result from the operation of a foodstore by a small local operator. The identity of the proposed operator for a superstore also thus appears to be a material consideration, though it is clear that a planning authority should not penalise a large national company simply because it is more successful and more efficient than a small local concern.

The position following the revision of PPG 6

It is pertinent to ask how the revision of PPG 6 has affected the foregoing issues. Has the introduction of the 'sequential test' made it easier for authorities to resist proposals for off-centre developments? It is too early to give a definite answer in terms of survey evidence, and there is only some case law authority. However, the literature revealed one instance as a 'straw in the wind'.[54]

An application was made to erect a foodstore of 5,140 sq. metres gross/2,790 sq. metres net, its service yard and parking for 514 cars on 2.83 hectares of land in Trowbridge. The application was called in by the Secretary of State under s 77 of the Town and Country Planning Act, and while the inquiry inspector recommended (in 1995) a grant of permission, this was refused by the Secretary of State. The developers applied to the High Court under s 288 of the 1990 Act and following consideration of the arguments set out in their Notice of Motion, the Secretary of State agreed to have his decision quashed.

The issue turned on the existence of two alternative sites for the development put forward at the inquiry by the local Chamber of Commerce. The developers considered that neither of these was suitable, nor in practice were they available. Nevertheless the Secretary of State considered the disadvantages of these two sites were not insurmountable, and that it had not been shown that these other locations, which were either in or adjacent to the town centre, were unsuitable. He considered only a rudimentary sequential test had been applied, and neither the developers nor the local authority had carried out a survey of the area – though this was explicable partly because neither of the alternative sites was allocated for retail use in relevant plans. The Secretary of State concluded that despite the effort and expense involved, a survey was essential for the proper application of the sequential test, and that to allow the present development to go ahead without it would create a dangerous precedent undermining the future application of the sequential test.

The developers challenged this arguing that the Secretary of State had erected a barrier in requiring that developers should show that the problems associated with a town centre site were insurmountable before an off-centre site can be looked at, and by indicating that it cannot be said that an alternative site is unsuitable until it can be shown that its associated problems are insurmountable. This was accepted by the Secretary of State. It was further accepted that as central guidance stood at the relevant time there was no requirement that there should be a major exercise in overcoming the disadvantages of alternative sites; policy did not require – nor even support – that such suggested sites should be assessed in greater detail, or to the same level of detail, as the application site itself. The Secretary of State also accepted his argument (that to grant permission without a properly conducted survey of the area, and without a thorough investigation of alternative sites was unacceptable) was incorrect in that it conflicted with the draft of the revision of PPG 6 then current. That had stated that first preference should be given to town centre sites where these are 'suitable' and 'available'. (That is also the tenor of the final published version.) That did not require a developer to show that every piece of land in a central area had insurmountable problems or was otherwise incapable of being developed as proposed for there to be a proper application of the sequential test. Nor could it be argued from the draft guidance as it stood that a detached survey of alternative sites was required in respect of all applications for off-centre development. In the instant case the alternative sites would not have been capable of being used for the development proposed.

It therefore appeared arguable that what the sequential test demands is that before permission can be refused on the grounds that a centre or edge of centre site is available, that site has to be shown to be realistically available for development, and that it is suitable for the developer's purpose, even if not tailor-made for it. There appeared to be no requirement that the developer should conduct a minute search of an authority's central area in order to show that no other possible site might conceivably become available.

There was also a further case which turned on a rather different issue. In *Bannertown Development Limited v Secretary of State for the Environment and Cotswold District Council and Kimberly Securities Plc* two companies had applied to develop retail parks in Cirencester, and these were the subject of a 'called in' inquiry in 1996. Bannertown wished to develop 7,000 sq. metres of floorspace south east of the town with access to a bypass and a food superstore. Their proposal was for a large DIY unit, and for smaller electrical goods, furnishings and carpets etc, units, together with a car park. Kimberley wished to develop 8,000 sq. metres closer to the town centre. On the inspector's recommendation both developments were refused, but it was indicated that if one had been allowed it would have been Kimberley's. The decision took into account the draft PPG 6 and utilised a sequential test, and the principal reason for refusal was given as the possible 'likely impact' of the development on the town centre which could, potentially, have lost one third of its retail trade. The Secretary of State's decision was quashed on the basis that it had not been properly determined what the 'likely impact' would be – indeed the decision had said there was some doubt about the impact. Had the Secretary of State reached a conclusion on the issue of impact his decision might have been different, and thus it was fatally flawed in its reasoning and had to be quashed. The decision indicates that the sequential test needs to be based on firm conclusions properly determined if it is to be applied.[55] As the current version of PPG 6 refers to 'likely' impact it is thus important to determine whether impact would be small, great or something in between, and even the possibility of adverse impact may be enough to justify a refusal of permission. It may be a nice question of judgement to balance a doubtful or questionable 'likely' impact against the general presumption in favour of development.

The application of PPG 6: further judicial guidance

PPG 6 was considered in *Virgin Cinema Properties Ltd et al v Secretary of State for the Environment.*[56] Here applications were made for permission to erect a leisure development – to which PPG 6 also applies – consisting of a multiplex cinema, two restaurants, a family entertainment centre and car parking for 523 vehicles on one area of land in Eastleigh, and for a change of use of other adjacent land to car parking for 100 vehicles in association with the main development. The sites were in excess of 3 hectares and consisted of open land, though the larger site had permission for industrial and warehousing development. To the north-west of the land there was a warehouse and distribution building, a hypermarket and business park, and to the south-east there was a strip of land and then the M3 motorway. There was also extensive residential and office development in the area. On a called in application, the proposal being supported by the local planning authority, but opposed by the County Council, Southampton City Council and Fareham Borough Council, the Secretary of State decided, against the advice of his inspector who conducted the inquiry into the issue, that permission should not be granted. This decision was challenged on a number of grounds but that which is relevant in the present context was that the Secretary of State had misapplied PPG 6 by misunderstanding the operation of the sequential test.

PPG 6 requires that first preference should be given in relation to relevant developments to town centre locations where there is suitable land or buildings capable of conversion, then edge of centre, district and local centres, and only thereafter off-centre locations accessible by a choice of means of transport.

In the instant case there were initially three central sites identified for the relevant development and four edge of centre sites. Though it was not clear that these were the only alternatives, no other sites in or near the centre of Eastleigh were identified by the authorities who objected to the proposal. Of the central sites, one (an empty shopping unit) was considered by the local planning authority and the developer to be unsuitable on grounds of the cost of conversion, and likely adverse impact on existing uses around it; one (a redundant church) was rejected as being in too poor a structural condition to merit the cost of conversion; while the third (former railway land) was not easily accessed by foot and would in any case not provide easy car parking access. The inquiry inspector concluded that each of these sites had been properly considered on a sequential basis and none offered a reasonable prospect of being suitable or attractive for the development in question. Development constraints and disbenefits also ruled out the four edge of centre sites.

The Secretary of State, however, argued in his decision letter that commercial consideration should not over-ride national and development plan policies which favour the location of such development in town centres. His view of the sequential test was that it required examination of potential sites for development of the type in question 'of any size rather than concentrate on sites to accommodate development on the scale proposed'. In other words the sequential test required a search for sites that can accommodate a development of a more modest variety than that proposed by the developer, and this is to be given due weight in the decision making process '...the issue to be addressed is whether there are sites in Eastleigh capable of accommodating a cinema of any size'.

The Secretary of State's conclusion was attacked on three grounds:

- that he had ignored part of the wording of PPG 6 at para. 1.12 where decision takers are urged to be sensitive to business needs, and to identify sites along with developers that are viable for the uses they propose;
- that by stressing the need to examine sites of any size he had further ignored para. 1.12 where it says that sites should be suitable, viable for the proposed use 'and likely to become available within a reasonable period of time,' and that meant that there is no need to examine sites in the absence of evidence that they will meet the foregoing requirements;
- that he had misapplied the sequential test by requiring too high a standard of proof that the alternative sites examined were as a certainty the only other possible locations.

It was considered by the Court on the first ground that the Secretary of State had not misdirected himself. The proper reading of para. 1.12 is that commercial interests are not over-riding in themselves. They are not decisive; they must be considered. No more is required than that they be taken into account in the light of national and local policy. On the second ground the Court considered that the Secretary of State had merely argued that smaller as well as larger sites should be examined, he was not saying that there should be a time-consuming search for a site of any size that might be pressed into use, irrespective of its suitability, viability and availability. On the third ground the Court considered that, taken in context, the words used by the Secretary of State could not be taken as requiring a demonstration as a matter of certainty that no other site was available for the development in question.

So far the Court supported the Secretary of State's reasoning, the sequential test requires a search for town centre sites to accommodate a development of a more restricted nature than that proposed by the developer. It is not satisfied simply by looking for sites capable of housing only the development initially proposed. Where the Secretary of State's decision was, however, flawed, was that he ignored evidence in his Inspector's report that showed that none of the alternative sites was capable of accommodating *any* sort of development of the type proposed. The local planning authority had carried out a thorough, robust and realistic appraisal of sites and had failed to identify any site closer to the centre of Eastleigh which was suitable, viable and likely to become available in a realistic period for any sort of development of the type proposed. The Secretary of State had abstracted only certain information from his inspector's report and had taken it out of context and had then given it an interpretation it could not bear. On that basis the Secretary of State's decision was flawed and had to be struck down.

An interim summation

What does this important decision tell us about the application of PPG 6 and, in particular, the sequential test? It is clear that a developer cannot forestall the application of the test by proposing a development of a particular size and nature. There is a requirement that there should be a search for alternative, more central, sites capable of accommodating a more restricted development of the same sort as that proposed. However, where an applicant can show that all potential central site options have been examined, and none is suitable, viable and likely to become available within a reasonable period, the Secretary of State (nor indeed the local planning authority) cannot simply conclude that the applicant has not discharged the requirements of the sequential test without giving adequate reasons for reaching such a conclusion.

A second important case

William Cook Estates and Another v Secretary of State for the Environment and Others[57] concerned an application made by William Cook Estates (WCE) to Redcar and Cleveland Borough Council (RCBC) to develop a food superstore (to be occupied by Tesco), non-food retail units (including a DIY unit), a car showroom, a petrol filling station, a car park and access improvements at a site in Guisborough. This application was called in by the Secretary of State, and though unopposed by RCBC was opposed by Somerfield plc (S) who had 2 local food stores, off-centre in Guisborough and in-centre at Saltburn, and Safeway Stores plc (SS) who had a town centre store in Guisborough. A local inquiry was held which resulted in a recommendation, accepted by the Secretary of State that permission should be refused. WCE challenged this refusal alleging:

- PPG 6 had been misinterpreted and misapplied on two issues; first, the question of the meaning of 'easy walking distance' to and from a town centre with regard to what can be regarded as edge of centre, and secondly on the issue of 'need' for the development;
- that there had been mutually inconsistent findings in the inspector's report which vitiated the conclusions reached;
- that there had been undue consideration of the impact of the proposed development on Saltburn, as opposed to Guisborough where the development was to take place;
- there had been a failure to take into account the implications of the possible closure of S's off-centre Guisborough store, on which WCE had submitted evidence concerning the linkage of the proposed new Tesco store with the existing town centre (as compared to S's off-centre store) and also regarding the impact of the new store on all the stores of S and SS;
- the inspector had overlooked the 'package' nature of the proposed development which was to be situated as close as possible to Guisborough town centre and was in reality an edge of centre proposal (which was accepted by S but not by SS), with retail warehousing elements which would retain expenditure in the town which might otherwise go elsewhere, and would have linkages with shopping trips to other retail units in the town centre.

The last ground of challenge was rejected by the Court on the facts: there was ample evidence that the benefits of the packages of development had been duly noted and taken into account.

The Court then turned to the other grounds of challenge. So far as the first issue concerning PPG 6 was concerned, *i.e.* the question of 'easy walking distance', the Court pointed out that PPG 6 is only guidance, not a statute. The guideline distance of 200 to 300 metres from an existing centre is not to be applied as a statutory formula so that any distance within 200 to 300 metres is automatically to be regarded as 'easy'. Each case, the Court argued, must be considered on its merits, taking into account the terrain, the attractiveness of the route in question and of the town centre itself. On the facts of the present application, bearing in mind the justifiable conclusion that Guisborough town centre was only modestly attractive, the application site lay at the outer limit of what could be regarded as an edge of centre location, and thus it was unlikely there would be shopping linkages between the site and the town centre with a consequent impact on retail trade there. The inquiry, the Court held, could justifiably come to such a conclusion, even more in view of the relevant structure plan policies that there should be 'convenient' pedestrian routes between town centres and edge of centre shopping sites. In the present case the applicant's proposed pedestrian route could, on the facts, be categorised as not 'convenient'.

The next issue was that of 'need'. PPG 6 stresses that question of 'need' for particular types of development should be taken into account in the drawing up of development plans, but is silent on the same question with regard to an actual planning application. The inspector holding the inquiry into the application concluded that there was, however, a presupposition that 'need' for a quantitatively or qualitatively better store is a condition precedent to applying the sequential test when a planning application is made. WCE argued that this was an incorrect conclusion. Unfortunately the Court gave no guidance on this issue because it found that the inquiry report had not recommended rejection of the proposal on 'need' grounds. However, see further below on this issue.

The Court next dealt with the argument that there had been mutually inconsistent findings and conclusions in the inspector's report. The issue here turned on arguments as to whether permission should be refused because granting it would have an adverse effect on an existing town centre, or because granting it would promote unnecessary travelling to shop from other areas. The Court did not, however, consider these to be 'either/or' issues. A new store can have both an adverse effect on an existing centre, and then fall foul of the guidance in PPG 6, or it can promote an undue propensity to travel to shop, and thus offend PPG 13. The real issue is whether, given the overall trade potential in an area, a proposed off-centre development can trade to its likely potential without either affecting either the vitality and viability of an existing centre, or encouraging travelling to shop, or both. This is, as the Court accepted, a 'Morton's Fork' argument, but where there is limited trade potential it may be appropriately used, as there is no need to determine exactly how much trade will flow in from the existing town centre and how much from further afield.

The argument that undue weight had been placed on the impact of the proposed development on Saltburn was rejected on the facts by the Court. It was clear that the inspector had considered there would be some impact on Saltburn, but his principal conclusions related clearly to the impact on Guisborough where the development was to take place. He had reached justifiable conclusions that the development would have an undue effect on Guisborough town centre, affecting its vitality and viability, weakening the economic underpinning of the Conservation Area strategy that applied there, and putting at risk investor confidence in the town centre.

The argument that the inspector had failed to consider the possibility that S's store would close, and the effect this would have on trade, thus remained the outstanding issue, and it was here that WCE succeeded. S's existing store was off-centre, whereas SS's store was in the town centre. S's store was actually further out from the centre than the proposed new Tesco edge of centre store. S's store was likely to suffer adversely in competition with the new Tesco (whose customers would have the benefit of a larger and more modern store) and could well therefore close. This would actually free trade for both the edge of centre and town centre food stores. The inspector here failed to feed into the balancing exercise – that any decision in such circumstances has to be – any allowance for a capture of trade from S's store by the central area. This, the Court considered was an important issue that should have been developed and dealt with on a reasoned basis by both the inspector's report and the Secretary of State's subsequent decision.

Following *Save Britain's Heritage v No 1 Poultry*[58] and *Bolton Metropolitan District Council and Others v Secretary of State for the Environment*[59] there is a need to deal on a reasoned basis with the principal controversial issues in a decision. In the instant case the possible closure of S's store was not a subordinate issue but was a significant and substantial one, and should have been dealt with.

On the subsequent appeal, however, it was held that the High Court's decision had to be quashed on the basis that the arguments about the potential closure of S's store did not amount to a substantial point and were not a critical issue in the case simply because the evidence that had been placed before the inspector on appeal was too speculative in nature to require his attention.[60]

Commentators' conclusions on the Guisborough case

One issue seized on for comment by the editors of the Planning Law Case Reports is that the High Court's reason for upsetting the Secretary of State's decision was the failure to deal with a significant and substantial issue. In this the High Court appeared to have been swayed by the reasoning of the first instance decision in *MJT Securities Ltd v Secretary of State for the Environment*[61] which has since been overturned on appeal.[62] The current position is that in his decision letter after an inquiry the decision taker does not have to deal with every single material consideration. The obligation, rather, is to show in the decision that the principal, important and controversial issues have been dealt with. Obviously all material considerations have to be considered in coming to a decision but this does not require them all to be listed. The question might arise therefore in future whether a 'significant and substantial' issue is the same as a 'principal, important and controversial' one. The test may well be that one has to ask in any given case what are the main issues in dispute for it is those that must be dealt with in the decision letter. However, it is not easy always, particularly in the context of retail development, to separate main from subsidiary issues. Where, for example, a proposed development is capable of generating adverse impact on a number of existing centres, the impact on the centre most likely to be affected will clearly be a 'main' issue. However, does that mean that impact on other centres cannot be a 'main' issue? This surely cannot be the case and the inevitable answer is what is 'main' can only be determined on a case by case basis, with all the possibilities for dispute and litigation that that entails. This is reinforced by the comment made on the decision in the Court of Appeal. If a party at a planning inquiry wishes to make an issue a 'main' one, it must be fully argued and backed with detailed evidence.

A further issue thought worthy of comment was that left undecided by the Court, namely the question of 'need'. The editors of the Planning Law Case Reports point out that because of the presumption in favour of development, the longstanding assumption has been that where a development carries with it no planning disadvantages there is no burden on the applicant to show that it is needed. Conversely, they argue, where planning disadvantages are inherent in a proposal 'need' becomes a material consideration, for it may of itself outweigh any disadvantages. However, that will, of course be something the developer will wish to raise, there is no real question as to whether it is a matter developers should have to raise. In the present case it had been determined that the proposed development would bring some disadvantages with it and so there was no need for the Court to determine whether 'need' is now always a material consideration whose existence must be shown by the applicant. Certainly, however, in theory there is nothing to stop development plans from imposing a requirement that, for example, in relation to particular types of development an applicant must demonstrate need.

A third important case

The issue of 'need' was however, raised head on in *R v Hambleton District Council ex parte Somerfield plc*.[63] Here a local planning authority had granted planning permission for Safeway to develop a 3,250 sq. metre foodstore opposite an existing Somerfield store. Somerfield sought judicial review on the basis that the authority had not applied PPG 6 correctly. At an early stage in the proceedings Tesco became involved and became joined as a party, giving them the opportunity to argue the particular issue of whether there is a requirement for a developer to show a 'need' for a proposed store. Though Somerfield won on a technical issue, the decision is important for the comments made in the High Court on the 'need' point.

In considering this case it has to be remembered what changes the revisions made to PPG 6 in 1996 actually brought about. The document is, of course, not a statute and cannot be interpreted as such. Nevertheless there are pointers to its meaning in its structure and wording, and the present case fastened on those as not being as radical as might have been supposed, being largely concerned with clarification of issues not the introduction of major shifts of planning policy.

Thus the previous version of PPG 6 had stated planning permission for retail development should be withheld where there was clear evidence of adverse impact on the vitality and viability of a town centre as a whole. This rather crude test was replaced by a set of key criteria to be considered when an application for a new retail development is received, *i.e.* the impact on town centre strategy, investment implications, changes to the quality, attractiveness and character of the centre, the implications for the physical condition of the centre, impacts on the range of services offered and likely increases in vacancy levels. However, there is no clear and unambiguous statement in the revision of PPG 6 that a developer has to justify an unobjectionable proposal on the basis of need, and the Court in the present case seized on that point. It was accepted that under PPG 6 as it now stands an applicant who wishes to create an off-centre development faces many stiff hurdles, but having to show need as a precondition of a grant is not one of these; indeed need may not always be even a material consideration. Furthermore 'need' may simply be an incidental question, for where consideration of the likely impact of a development on a centre indicates a lack of impact it follows that there is spare local shopping capacity, while a considerable impact indicates there is likely to be no need for the development in question.

The Court furthermore considered that there is no requirement for the local planning authority to be satisfied that a new retail development will positively improve the health of an existing centre. PPG 6 accepts that a new development may cause a degree of harm to an existing centre – the issue for the planning authority is to decide how much, and whether the level of impact would be unacceptable. Though the overall objective of PPG 6 is to sustain and enhance the vitality of existing centres, it is implicit in the sequential test itself that there will be times when off-centre development has to be permitted, and that test is a facilitating measure in this respect. Again it is instructive to remember that PPG 6 itself does not clearly state the need for authorities to consider whether off-centre proposals will positively enhance existing centres. The Government, however, has now taken some further remedial action on this issue as will be detailed below.

The standing of PPG 6 after the cases

The foregoing cases were dealt with at length because they were the first reported decisions on the implementation of PPG 6. What was decided there laid down parameters within which planning decisions takers have to exercise their discretion. In particular it should be noted that:

- developers cannot forestall the applications of the sequential test by proposing developments of a highly specific size and nature;
- where a development is proposed there should be an initial, honest and robust search for a central site for it, even if such a site can only accommodate a more restricted version of the development that has been proposed;
- terms such as 'easy walking distance', 'town-centre', 'edge of centre' and 'off-centre' are not legal 'terms of art' and cannot be applied as if they were statutory formulae, each term has to be applied on a case by case basis, bearing in mind issues of locality, access, amenity, topography, *etc*;
- where a development carries with it no planning disadvantages there is no requirement for its proposer to indicate what the need for it is;

- development plans may impose a burden on developers to indicate need in particular contexts, such as, for example, by requiring a developer to demonstrate a need caused by population growth but that is not the case under the sequential test requirements of PPG 6. (See, however, further below.)

  Where that test applies an off-centre developer must only show that an honest but fruitless search for a more central location for a development generally of the type proposed has been made. There is no additional requirement to show that there is a qualitative or quantitative need for a development of the sort proposed;
- a proposed development may be considered undesirable either because it would pose a threat to the vitality and viability of an existing centre, contrary to the policy of PPG 6, or because it would generate unnecessary travelling to shop, contrary to PPG 13, or both (and where both there is no need for 'undesirability' to be mathematically apportioned between the two policy documents);
- where a proposed development would have an adverse impact on more than one centre, there is a clear obligation to take into account the impact on the centre principally affected, with impact on other centres being considered where this can be seen to raise important controversial issues;
- where an alternative site for a development exists and has to be considered under the sequential test, for that site to fail the requirement that it should be 'suitable' the developer does not have to show that there are insurmountable problems associated with its development;
- there is no requirement for a developer to conduct a minute search of a town's central area in order to show that no possible site may conceivably become available for the development proposed;
- permission for off-centre development can be refused where there is a central or edge of centre site that is realistically available for development, and generally suitable for the developer's purpose, if not tailor-made for the exact development proposed.

However, it is also clear that PPG 6, no matter what the intention of its framers might have been, did not radically shift the core notions of general planning policy to enable authorities to refuse off-centre applications where they consider that these will not positively enhance existing centres, or to impose on developers a positive obligation always to demonstrate need. 'Need' could come into play on the developer's side, raised as an issue in order to outweigh some other planning objection, or to justify a departure from a development plan. 'Need' could also be relevant in plan preparation in that authorities may have to include particular policies to meet specific needs. However, it remained a fundamental general principle that where a proposal is otherwise unobjectionable in itself there was no requirement otherwise to justify it in terms of need. Furthermore it was clear that 'need' would not always automatically be a material consideration in all cases.

If the framers of the 1996 revision of PPG 6 wished to bring about radical change they should have used clear, radical language.

Whether ministers have finally managed to use such sufficiently clear language remains to be seen. However, on 11th February 1999 in answer to a Parliamentary question the Planning Minister, Mr Richard Caborn, made a statement which must be taken, from its nature and the fact that the DETR chose to give it particular publicity, as a revision – albeit interim – of PPG 6. The statement was expressly said to add to and clarify PPG 6 in the light of recent litigation. The following points were made:

- Local planning authorities should adopt a plan led approach to handling applications for new retail and leisure developments.
- Where a need for such development exists it should be reflected in development plans which should be drawn up using the sequential test. Where there is no need for such development there is no need to identify additional sites.
- Proposals for new developments according with an up-to-date plan, or proposed for an existing centre, do not have to satisfy a 'need' test.
- Proposals which are 'edge of ' or 'out of ' centre and which do not accord with up-to-date plans, or which are in accordance with an out of date plan, *or a plan inconsistent with national guidance*, or one which otherwise fails to establish need for retail and leisure developments, should be requirement to fulfil *both* a 'need' test and the sequential test.
- 'Need' is to be demonstrated not just by showing physical capacity in an area or demand in terms of available expenditure in the area in question. These are merely factors to be taken into account by decision takers, who may consider other factors in determining whether need has been demonstrated. (What those factors could be was not stated by the minister but arguably impact on existing centres is a relevant matter – particularly that of a cumulative nature.)
- A refusal of permission is normally justified where there is a failure to demonstrate compliance with both the 'need' and sequential tests, save where there are weighty additional material considerations.
- In applying the sequential test the relevant places in which searches for sites are to be made will depend on the nature and scale of the proposed development and its catchment area. *The scale of any such proposals should also be appropriately related to the centre that is to be served –*

this is a clear statement that small settlements should not be dominated commercially by massive peripheral foodstores.

- The new guidance applies to both entirely new proposals and those for extending existing off-centre developments creating additional floor space. Once again a 'need' test will need to be fulfilled and a sequential approach taken.

It may be that this language is apt to show that the planning presumption is now *against* off-centre retail and leisure development, and that local planning authorities may normally expect the support of the Secretary of State should they refuse permission for off-centre development they believe is not needed. Certainly it is hard to see how the Blair government, which has proclaimed generally its commitment to the notions of urban renewal, reuse of 'brownfield' land, and encouraging new communities in older areas, could otherwise respond to the outward march of retailing and leisure facilities which PPG 6 in its various guises has so far failed to halt. Nothing, however, is certain in this area. PPG 6 even with 'ministerial pendants' remains only a policy document – a material consideration – and not a rule of law. While that remains the case we must expect developers to continue to argue their proposals satisfy its criteria and therefore should be consented. Equally it remains the case that local planning authorities may be tempted to take a generous line in the interpretation of the 'need' and sequential tests in order to attract to their areas development that might otherwise go elsewhere. The ability of third parties to attack such decisions remains, as will be detailed below, limited.

A further issue

It further appears that where an application is made to develop a site and this would have an adverse implication for sustaining an existing town centre, it is reasonable under the sequential test policies to PPG 6 to refuse permission where, though no alternative central locations for the development have been previously identified, there is a search being undertaken by the planning authority to check whether a suitable, viable and available site or sites could be found. The refusal in such circumstances enables the search to continue and thus the authority in such circumstances is not 'stampeded' into making a premature decision on the issue.[64]

The 'width' of a permission once granted

Unless a grant of planning permission is very carefully phrased (see also below on the rôle of planning conditions) an authority may discover it has given permission for a development which may grow beyond the authority's concept of it. Development control is in general a 'once only' matter, unless a development undergoes a material change of use, or is subjected to continued control by means of conditions. Thus in *R v Maldon District Council ex parte Pattani*[65] Tesco built a town centre store under a grant of planning permission; they then enabled a local pharmacy to relocate to a site within the store. Mr Pattani, another pharmacist, asked the local planning authority to use its enforcement powers to close down the in-store pharmacy as a breach of planning control by virtue of a material change of use. They declined to do so and Mr Pattani then sought judicial review of that decision (see also further below on protection of third party rights). Mr Pattani's argument was that Tesco had no permitted development rights to take on board the pharmacy under Part A of the schedule to the Town and Country Planning (Use Classes) Order SI 1987 No 764, as the permission there granted for a shop to be used for *inter alia* the retail sale of any goods (other than hot food) did not extend to the sale of pharmaceutical goods. In the High Court the application was unsuccessful. Collins J pointed out that many supermarkets now contain pharmacies, but that does not prevent them from being supermarkets. The permission to develop the site was a permission also to trade in any goods which are normally and properly regarded as obtainable in a supermarket which primarily sells food. Furthermore even though certain pharmaceutical goods require the prior provision of a prescription, the transaction in the case of a private prescription between the patient and pharmacist is still an ordinary sale. In the case of NHS prescriptions the supply of items corresponds to a retail sale. There was here no material change of use.

The issue of 'width' has come to court on other occasions. In one case planning permission was granted in outline terms for a residential development of 1,000 units, a primary school, a 'local centre' and other associated uses. The question subsequently arose of what the meaning was of a 'local centre'; and whether it could extend to cover a superstore which would obviously draw in trade from a much wider locality than the development otherwise permitted. In such circumstances the vague and imprecise term 'local centre' must be defined by reference to the context in which it is found. In the present case the words had to be interpreted in the light of the permission for residential development, and it was determined that the permission was simply for housing with associated ancillary residential services – a supermarket of 30,000 sq.ft of net retail floor space with car parking for 550 cars could not fit this description.[66]

Authorities may, however, find themselves in difficulties if an outline grant of permission is given without any limiting words. [A grant of outline permission, made in response to an outline application under Article 3 of the Town and Country Planning (General Permitted Development) Procedure Order, SI 1995 No 419, approves the principle of development and leaves detailed issues for later consideration.] In 1995 Leicester City Council gave outline permission for the redevelopment of a former power station as a small food store, large non-food store and leisure facility. This site was less than half a mile distant from a major foodstore development by Safeway on the former Leicester Cattle Market site. The grant of permission did not, however, in specific terms rule out the development of one of the large units as a food site, and an option to develop the land for an 83,000 sq.ft food superstore was obtained by Morrisons. In the absence of a specific prior condition in the outline planning permission Leicester City Council felt constrained in May 1998 to grant detailed permission to Morrisons, though their ability to proceed would be dependent on a decision to proceed by the site owner. Safeway also sought judicial review of Leicester's decision, but failed in the High Court. This was on the basis of their delay in seeking review, see further below on this issue. Safeway's further attempts to pursue the matter was again turned down on the same basis by the Court of Appeal on 18th January 1999.

The rôle of conditions

Planning authorities have an apparently extremely wide discretion to impose conditions on a grant of planning permission under s 70(1)(a) of the Town and Country Planning Act 1990 which enables them to grant permission subject to such conditions 'as they think fit'. Nowhere, however, has the interpretative power of the courts to place constraints on administrative power been more apparent than here. It is by now almost trite law that this power is subject to a number of limitations imposed by the courts, reinforced by ministerial inhibitions now contained in DoE Circular 11/95. Thus a condition must fairly and reasonably relate to the development permitted, and cannot be imposed to satisfy some ulterior object.[67] Conditions may only be imposed for a planning purpose, *i.e.* a purpose connected with the use and development of land.[68] They must not be such as no reasonable authority would impose; in other words they must not seek to impose what should be a public burden on the shoulders of the developer or seek to obtain unjustifiable advantages for the authority.[69] Conditions must also be certain, in other words their wording must have an ascertainable meaning,[70] and they also must not be unenforceable, *i.e.* they must relate to matters which it is within the powers of the planning authority to control.[71] Conditions must also be precise.[72]

Indeed so restrictive has been the judicial régime with regard to the imposition of conditions that planning authorities have been constrained to make much more use of negotiated planning obligations under s 106 of the 1990 Act, of which more will be said later. However, this is not to say that conditions have no rôle with regard to the control of retail developments. They will, of course, be imposed to cover a whole range of matters concerned with site layout and access, the prevention of nuisances caused by deliveries, the creation and illumination of advertising hoardings and other signs, *etc*. More particularly under s 75(2) of the 1990 Act where permission is granted for the erection of a building, the grant of permission may specify the purposes to which the building may be put. That power is particularly relevant to the development of retail parks. Ever since the 1993 revision of PPG 6 it has been recognised that a retail park can change its composition over time as traders leave, or go out of business and new ones come in their stead – which it may be entirely beyond the general power of the planning authority to control as the changes of use will normally fall within the scope of permitted development guaranteed by the Use Classes Order.[73] Where such changes could result in the creation of a development which would not have been consented in the first place because it would have an adverse impact on the vitality and viability of an existing centre, consideration may be given to imposing conditions in the original grant of permission to prevent any unacceptable change in the character of a development. These, however, may only relate to the main ranges of goods sold and may not control the details of particular products on sale. Local plans can elaborate the type of conditions which may be imposed on such developments so that it may be clear and patent before construction what the acceptable range of uses to which a development may be put are. That range may, moreover, be spelt out in detail with regard to the development of particular areas of land targeted for retail use. The 1996 revision of PPG 6 continues to counsel the use of such conditions, and indeed adds that 'conditions can be used to prevent the development from being sub divided into a large number of smaller shops and to limit the range or types of goods sold'.[74] Thus in *ICP Developments Ltd v Secretary of State for the Environment and Salisbury*

District Council[75] a condition was lawfully imposed (apparently by the Secretary of State on appeal against an initial refusal of permission) in relation to the construction of four retail warehouses. The condition was that the range and type of goods to be sold from the non-food retail units granted permission should be restricted to DIY, garden goods, furniture, carpets and floor coverings, camping, boating and caravanning goods, motor vehicle and cycle goods, and bulky electrical goods. These restrictions reflected the terms of the development plan, which consisted of the South Wiltshire Structure Plan 1993 and the Salisbury District Local Plan 1996, which *inter alia* sought to protect the vitality and viability of existing town centres against the individual or cumulative impact of near retailing developments.

Local authority involvement in retail development

Authorities, as has already been stated in the previous chapter, may be actively involved in retail developments from a promotional point of view, perhaps because their land assembly powers are needed to acquire a sufficient area for development, or because an authority has let it be known that they favour development of a particular sort. Authorities may wish to enter into partnership with developers. This raises the question of how far it is permissible generally for developers to enter into arrangements with authorities to overcome objections to development by including in the proposal some public benefit or planning gain – a practice viewed with extreme suspicion by those who see in it the disguised 'purchase' of planning permission.[76] This issue of planning gain has become increasingly contentious.

Grant in *Urban Planning Law* states:

> 'Planning gain' is an imprecise expression which has emerged in planning practice in recent years. In its most general sense it encompasses the process of balancing the likely beneficial and detrimental effects of a proposed development... But a more specific and more controversial approach to planning gain has flowed from this. Authorities have sought benefits from developers: for example the building of community facilities such as a swimming pool or public hall. Although characterised as a 'planning gain' the true effect is that the local authority is thereby relieved of the cost of providing the facilities itself... For the most part the bartering which lies behind such arrangements is done secretly and informally, and the requirements are expressed, not as conditions upon a permission..., but in contractual arrangement...[77]

In an article entitled 'Planning Gain Losing Ground', an article in the *Law Society Gazette*, Brand and Williams rather more bluntly stated:

> In practice the contentious planning gain issues tend to occur where the scheme proposed by the developer is quite substantial in size. In such cases the local planning authority may say, for example, 'We will grant planning permission for the retail and office complex you are proposing if you provide a swimming pool on site for use by the public'.[78]

It has already been stated that authorities may not seek to impose public burdens on private shoulders by means of conditions included in a grant of planning permission.[79] However, can the same end be achieved by means of what used to be known as planning agreements, and what are now called planning obligations? Authorities have secured valuable public benefits from developments, and the more orderly and efficient development of land: developers have, by conceding some planning gain, eased the passage of otherwise controversial major development proposals. There have been, however, others who, as has already been stated, have felt themselves prejudiced by the practice.

The development of an issue

The Property Advisory Group (PAG) of the DoE, commissioned to study this issue, produced their report 'Planning Gain' in October 1981. Bargaining for planning gain was generally condemned, and said to be acceptable in only two cases. First, where the purpose of the agreement under which gain accrues is to overcome otherwise legitimate grounds for refusing planning permission, for example lack of necessary infrastructure, and, secondly, in relation to certain 'mixed' applications for permission containing a variety of elements some of which, in isolation, would be objectionable, though others would promote positive planning objectives. In relation to such applications the PAG Report urged great caution stating:

> Where the proposed scheme contains an element which is so far contrary to established policy or would be so managing to amenity that it would, if taken in isolation, be refused outright, the authority should not allow itself to be tempted by the other collateral benefits to grant permission.[80]

These recommendations were effectively included in 'Town and Country Planning Act 1971 – Planning Gain', DoE Circular 22/83.

Central *policy* as then declared was that each application should be considered on its merits; permission should only be refused when this serves a clear planning purpose and the economic effects have been taken into account. Imposing obligations to ensure planning gain should only be considered where it would not be reasonable to grant permission on the terms on which it is sought: wholly unacceptable developments should not be permitted simply because of extraneous benefits offered by developers. It could thus be acceptable to seek an agreement in certain circumstances such as:

(a) works being needed to enable the development to go ahead, for example provision of adequate sewerage and sewage disposal facilities; or
(b) some financial payment being made towards costs of providing such facilities in the near future; or
(c) the work agreed on being so directly related to the proposed development that development should not be permitted without it, for example provision by developers of car parking space in or near developments; or
(d) the agreement is designed, in the case of a mixed development, to secure an adequate balance of uses – a somewhat vague term.

The *extent* of what is sought, it was stated, should also fairly and reasonably relate in case and kind to the proposed development. Furthermore what the developer was asked to provide, or help to finance, should represent in itself a reasonable charge on him.[81] This advice applied where either the authority or the developer initiated the bargaining process by seeking or offering, as the case may be, some planning gain.[82]

Bargaining generally for planning gain was thus officially regarded as unacceptable and discouraged. The *legality* of such bargaining was also judicially questioned in *Bradford City Council v Secretary of State*,[83] though only in an *obiter dictum.* Lloyd LJ doubted whether it would be possible to include in an agreement a provision that would be manifestly unreasonable as a planning condition. Against this had to be set the opinion of Nourse LJ in *Abbey Homesteads (Developments) Limited v Northamptonshire County Council*[84] that there were objections to an argument that an agreement conferring benefits that could not lawfully have been obtained by conditions was *ultra vires* the power of the authority. Arguably agreements, then made under s 52 of the Town and Country Planning Act 1971, were *primarily* designed to restrict or regulate the use of *the land*; though this is a wider concept than *the development on the land.*

Any other provision should only be of an incidental nature. It was seemingly legal for a developer to be asked, in the context of a retail development, to make a contribution towards the provision of parking facilities directly related to his development, and that was contemplated by PPG 6.[85]

The problem that arose was of a two fold nature: how far is it *legitimate* for an authority to seek gain in return for a grant of planning permission when this effectively circumvents the general presumption that a development should be consented unless there are substantial reasons why it should not be, and, secondly what was the *legal* extent of authorities' powers to seek agreements as part of an overall 'package' of permission? Though the issue was the subject of suspicion and debate, it rarely resulted in any legal challenge, largely because on the whole it 'suited the book' of developers to 'ease the passage' of what might otherwise have been controversial developments. Indeed the practice of including policies on seeking planning gain in relevant plans began to emerge.

The issue was further considered in *R v Gillingham Borough Council ex parte F Parham Limited*.[86] Roch J argued that an agreement had to be such that a reasonable planning authority could have imposed, and should only be imposed for a valid planning purpose, and not to further some ulterior or improper motive. Accordingly the answer to questions of the permissibility of developers entering into agreements or partnerships with planning authorities with a view to easing obtaining planning permission, seemed to be 'only in limited circumstances'. Similarly in *R v Wealden District Council ex parte Charles Church (South East) Limited*[87] it was also held the overall test for the validity of a planning agreement was that of simple reasonableness, not any requirement to show a fair and reasonable relationship to the development in question.

Section 52 of the Town and Country Planning Act 1971 became s 106 of the Town and Country Planning Act 1990, but this itself was soon replaced under the Planning and Compensation Act 1991 with a new s 106, s 106A and s 106B. Under these provisions some clarification of the law was made. The term 'planning agreement' was replaced by 'planning obligation' which could be either an agreement between the developer and the planning authority, or a unilateral undertaking given by the developer. Such an undertaking once given 'runs with the land' like a restrictive covenant in general land law, and may be enforced against the original covenantor, and anyone acquiring title from him. Furthermore, it was made clear that a planning obligation may include positive as well as negative obligations. The supplementary provisions allowed for the modification or discharge of planning obligations and for appeals against refusals to discharge or modify. Thus, by agreement or 'otherwise' a person interested in land may enter into an obligation with the relevant local planning authority whereunder the development or use of land is restricted, or whereby specified operations or activities may be required in relation to the land, or whereby a sum or sums of money may be paid to the authority at a specified time or times, or at stated periods. That money may be calculated by reference to a formula, and may be paid for either a limited time or indefinitely, though the payments need not specifically relate to the land or the development to be carried out on it. Obligations are enforceable by injunction, and may only be entered into by deed which states that the obligation is a planning obligation, identifies the land, and the person entering into the obligation and his interest in it, and the relevant planning authority. In a parallel attempt to deal with legitimacy issues the DoE issued Circular 16/91[88] to replace earlier guidance. This stated that a planning obligation should only be sought where this was necessary to the grant of planning permission, relevant to planning and to the development to be permitted. The guidance also stated that an otherwise unacceptable development should not be consented because of the offer of unilateral benefits by the developer.[89] In addition an obligation should satisfy a general test of reasonableness, and this was dependent upon what was required: *i.e.* was the obligation needed to enable the development to go ahead; or would it ensure the payment of money towards providing facilities needed if a development was to go ahead; or was it so directly related to the proposed development that the development ought not to be permitted without it; or was it designed, in the case of a mixed development, to secure an acceptable balance of uses or the implementation of local plan policies for a particular place or type of development; or was it intended to offset the loss or impact on any amenity or resource present on site prior to development.[90] Furthermore, a specific test of reasonableness also had to be satisfied, namely that what was required should fairly and reasonably relate in scale and kind to the proposed development, so that where infrastructure is needed that would not have been needed but for the development, a developer should only make a payment directly related in scale to the benefit which the development would derive from the facilities to be provided.[91] It was thus *inter alia* made clear that a planning obligation could relate to the provision of infrastructure relevant to a development, and that an obligation could relate to the implementation of local plan policies. What remained unclear was the extent to which 'community benefits' (as 'planning gain' had increasingly come to be called) could be required, or taken into account if offered by a developer.

A series of decisions of the courts was soon, however, to test this guidance to destruction.

The first case was *R v Plymouth City Council ex parte Plymouth and South Devon Co-operative Society*.[92] Here an area of largely derelict land initially allocated for industrial use became the site of rival planning applications by Sainsbury and Tesco, while at the same time the Co-op was seeking planning permission for a food store some distance away. In the outcome the planning authority granted permission to both Sainsbury and Tesco for one store each on the site, subject to s 106 obligations under which the companies undertook to provide, or to fund, various public benefits such as a tourist information centre, an art gallery display, bird watching hides, park and ride and crèche facilities, at a cost of over £3.6mn. The Co-op, which was initially unsuccessful in its application for planning permission sought judicial review of the decision to grant permission to Tesco and Sainsbury arguing that the planning authority had taken immaterial considerations into account in reaching its decision, namely the offer of community benefits. The Co-op further argued for a test of necessity in such cases, *i.e.* that a benefit needs to be necessary in order to overcome what would be a valid reason for refusing permission. However, the Co-op failed at both first instance and on appeal. The test of materiality applied in court was: does the benefit in question serve a planning purpose; does it fairly and reasonably relate to the development permitted, and is it reasonable in the sense could it be sought and/or accepted by a reasonable planning authority? It was considered the package of benefits in the instant case satisfied these tests. This approach was confirmed in *Good v Epping Forest District Council*[93] where the Court of Appeal held a planning obligation can go beyond that which is necessary in order to allow a development to proceed.

The next, and most recent case was *Tesco Stores Ltd v Secretary of State for the Environment*.[94] Here Tesco and Tarmac sought grants of permission for retail stores on the edge of Witney. The applications were considered together at a public inquiry and the inspector recommended that permission should be given to Tesco. In the event the Secretary of State only gave permission to Tarmac. At the inquiry it had been argued by the highways authority that a new link road would be needed if either of the sites was to be developed. Tesco was willing to pay for that road, but the Secretary of State considered that because of the distance between the new road and the Tesco site there was only an attenuated link between them. Furthermore, any increase in traffic on the new road flowing from the building and use of a store might not amount to 10 per cent of the overall traffic flows. The Secretary of State concluded that to accept full funding for the road from Tesco could fall foul of the terms of guidance requiring contributions to fairly and reasonably relate in scale to the development proposed. Indeed he considered that even to seek a partial contribution would not be reasonable. Tesco successfully challenged this decision in the High Court but lost in the Court of Appeal, largely on the basis that though it would have been wrong following the *Plymouth* decision to fail to consider Tesco's offer, the Secretary of State had in fact done so, but had decided not to accord it any weight. This decision was upheld by the House of Lords who considered that whether a proffered planning obligation is or is not a material consideration must be determined according to whether it has some real connection with the proposed development. If such a connection exists the obligation is material and has to be considered, but the weight to be given to it is at the discretion of the decision taker, provided the decision is not perverse or one that no reasonable decision taker could reach. In the final result it is clear that a planning obligation does not have to be 'necessary' in order for a development to proceed, though it is clear that the offer of benefits by a developer where these are wholly unconnected with the development is not a matter to be taken into account, and equally an authority should not seek benefits wholly unconnected with the development. Where, however, the various proposals are related it is quite proper for the planning authority to weigh the benefits against the disbenefits, and where there are two competing development proposals it is quite legitimate – and indeed lawful – for the planning authority to choose that one which offers the more attractive package of benefits (off-site or on-site) provided these can be seen to be linked to the proposed development.[95]

Subsequent policy developments

On 28th January 1997 the DoE issued Circular 1/97 replacing 16/91.[96] This made an initial distinction between legal tests for the validity and materiality of obligations, and central policy on the *use* of obligations. It accepted that planning authorities are entitled to seek to modify planning proposals by way of either planning conditions or obligations, but equally it is clear that planning permission should neither be bought nor sold. Accordingly it remains the core of *policy* that planning obligations should be: necessary; relevant to planning; directly related to the proposed development; fairly related in scale and kind to the proposed development, and reasonable in all other respects. The policy stress on 'necessary' should be noted, even though as a matter of law there is no such requirement. The implications of this will be returned to below, in the context of the enforcement of policy.

Fleshing out policy

Annex B develops policy on the use of obligations. A key question is to determine whether there is a direct relationship between the obligation and the proposed grant of permission: an obligation should not be sought where such a connection does not exist or is too remote. Equally an acceptable development should not be refused because the applicant is unwilling or unable to offer gains or benefits, the converse also being true, and so developers should not try to offer extra, *i.e.* unrelated, inducements as a means of overcoming what are good reasons for refusing permission. Where an obligation is put forward which goes beyond the limits countenanced by policy it may satisfy the strict terms of legality but should be given little weight in determining an application. If the bounds of what is 'necessary' are transgressed, the unnecessary elements in the offer should not affect decision taking.[97]

In addition planning obligations must satisfy a general test of reasonableness, and this requires an obligation to be tested against the following principles:

- Is it needed to enable a development to proceed, or, when it is an obligation to pay money will it contribute in the near future to the cost of providing facilities necessary for the development to proceed: or is it so directly related to the proposal that the development should not be permitted without it, *i.e.* will the development have such an effect on the environment or local amenity, or on national or local policies that planning conditions alone cannot ameliorate the impact and an obligation should be sought to overcome the difficulty?

  As an example of the foregoing the Circular cites providing or contributing to new access roads, junctions, car parking, new bus/rail stations, park and ride schemes, improved bus shelters. It also adds that contributions may be sought in the case of off-centre development where these make the development more accessible to the centre. However, in all such cases the facilities provided or contributions made must be directly related to the development proposed, must be necessary and must be related in scale and kind to what is to be developed.
- Is the obligation needed to ensure an acceptable balance of uses within a mixed use development?
- Is it needed to secure an element of affordable housing in a larger residential or mixed use development?

- Does it offset the loss of or impact on resources currently on the development site, or will it protect, or reduce harm to, sites or species of acknowledged importance? This may justify obligations where nature reserves are to be created, or trees planted, *etc*, or existing wooded land is to be replaced, again provided the other general requirements are satisfied, and it must be clear that there is a relationship between what is to be lost and what is to be provided. Thus a loss of open parkland will not normally be compensatable by provision of an indoor sports centre.[98]

There is then the need for any obligation to satisfy a particular test of reasonableness, *i.e.* it must be fairly and reasonably related in scale and kind to the proposed development. Thus developers may expect to contribute to the cost of infrastructure unnecessary but for the development, but their payments should be directly related in scale to the benefit their development will receive from facilities to be provided. They should not be expected to fund facilities needed to relieve existing deficiencies, such as generally inadequate local roads, though an exception arises where a development will exacerbate an already bad situation. Developers may also contribute jointly to the improvement of facilities, but only to the extent that their proposals create the need for those facilities, and each one's level of contribution should be fairly and reasonably related to the level of demand created by their own development. It is totally unacceptable to use planning obligations as a disguised form of levy on the profits of a development. Furthermore, authorities should not have 'shopping lists' of desirable benefits to put before developers, even where these may be considered as related to the proposed development.

Where a physical benefit is to be secured by an obligation its subsequent maintenance costs should be considered by the planning authority: who will have to pay for it in future? In this context the Circular points out that any payments from developers should be limited in time. Furthermore, there should be no attempt to impose a commuted maintenance sum requirement, save where additional highway works are an inescapable precondition of a grant of permission, or where public transport provision is to be made, or with regard to the maintenance of a small area of open space.[99]

Obligations and Plans

The Circular counsels that where an authority is likely to seek obligations either with regard to a particular sort of development, or with regard to a particular development site this should be the subject of a specific local plan policy. Such policies cannot, of course, guarantee that an obligation will always be successfully negotiated, nor may they lay down rigid formulaic requirements for obligations – any attempts to include such policies in plans are likely to be the subject of objections from central government. In particular there is likely to be central objection to any policies which fail to pay due heed to the terms of Circular 1/97, which seek benefits not directly related to particular proposals, or which are based on blanket formulations, or seek contributions to general funds which may be devoted to financing facilities not related to particular proposals, or which seek contributions in respect of the alleviation of existing problems (unless these problems will be exacerbated by proposals) or which seek to allocate precise costs in advance of proposals, or seek maintenance contributions as a general rule.[100]

Public involvement in planning obligations

It has already been stated that the use of planning agreements/obligations has often raised public disquiet over what is essentially a form of planning behind closed doors. Annex B of Circular 1/97 seeks to address such fears by arguing that the negotiation process should be as open, fair and reasonable as possible. Furthermore not only must all planning obligations be registered as local land charges, but the public should receive every assistance in searching for and examining planning obligations in which they are interested. In addition where an obligation is under consideration by a committee of an authority, the obligation and its related correspondence should be listed in the background papers for the committee, and only in very exceptional cases should authorities exclude the public from such committee meetings or determine that the public should be denied a view of connected correspondence. Should authorities fail to heed this advice the Circular warns that the Secretary of State could use powers under s 100 I of the Local Government Act 1972 to restrict their ability to confer exemption from access to information on relevant documentation.[101] This represents a major attempt to dispel the aura of secrecy surrounding obligations and the fears of those who believe that confidential dealings may work to their disadvantage. As a further development the Government has undertaken to introduce legislation when a suitable opportunity arises to make it a legal requirement that copies of planning obligations should be registered publicly along with the permission to which they relate. Until that is enshrined in statute, however, it is expected that such registration will take place as a matter of good practice, and similarly any existing agreements and obligations should also be placed appropriately on the register. This is designed to ensure that planning is perceived as a fair and open process in which all concerned may know the full basis for any given decision.[102]

Enforcement

It is one thing to lay down guidance in a Circular or Planning Policy Guidance Note, it is quite another to ensure that it is followed, and it is clear from case law that past circulars on the issue of gain, agreements and obligations have been treated on occasions with scant regard. How will the Secretary of State ensure that Circular 1/97 fares better than its predecessors? As a general principle it is declared that should a planning application come before the Secretary of State with which there is associated an obligation going beyond the terms of the guidance, little weight will be attached to it when a decision has to be made. Moreover if the matter has arisen by way of appeal and it is found that the planning authority has attempted to obtain unreasonable requirements from the developer the power to award costs against the authority may be used. In addition, however, to the other general requirement that the advice in the Circular must be borne in mind as a material consideration, authorities are further reminded of the Secretary of State's power to intervene in planning issues, either at the plan making or decision making stage – or by revoking or modifying grants of permission already given. 'The Secretary of State will give serious consideration to the exercise of his powers to intervene whenever he believes that the policies set out in this Circular are being ignored or misapplied'.[103] Assuming the Secretary of State can get to know of such instances – and presumably the enhanced publicity requirements considered above will help in this connection – this statement represents a very interventionist attitude on the part of central government. The issue of whether any given obligation stands or falls is not simply to be left to whether it satisfies the legalities as declared by the courts, but whether there is ignorance or misapplication of relevant central policy.

How this will work out in practice must remain to be seen, particularly the disjunction between policy and law over the need for a planning obligation to be 'necessary'. One leading commentator, however, has struck a note of caution. Considering the effects of the House of Lords' decision in *Tesco Stores Ltd v Secretary of State for the Environment*,[104] Moore argues that its practical effect is likely to lead to a polarisation between planning obligations which are *sought* by a local planning authority and planning obligations *offered* by a developer.[105] Although Moore acknowledges the attempt by Circular 1/97 to limit the misuse of obligations he states:

> ...the decision means that local planning authorities have the same freedom to consider, but then still decline to follow, any government policy statements on...obligations as...on any other matter.

and then goes on to conclude:

> No policy, however, can control the scope of an obligation a developer is prepared to offer in an attempt to seek planning permission, other than the public law tests of relevance to the development proposed and *Wednesbury* unreasonableness.[106]

He goes on to consider that the disguised 'purchase' of planning permission by developers is still a very real possibility, and draws attention to the expression in July 1997 of the unease of the Nolan Committee on Standards in Public Life over the wording of the current legislation, and whether it is apt to prevent the purchase and sale of permissions. That Committee also considered that there is a need for greater public discussion of obligations before planning permission is granted and that there should be free access to supporting documentation.[107] In response to the Nolan Committee the Government accepted the need for planning obligations to be placed on a publicly available register, though that would require new primary legislation. As to other issues arising out of the use of planning obligations, such as fears of 'disguised purchase' the Government response was rather more muted and the problem remains under scrutiny.[108] However, in advance of either Nolan or the Government the Association of District Councils in 1996 called for the long term phasing out of Planning Obligations and their replacement by a statutory scheme of betterment taxation of the profits earned consequent on grants of permission for major developments – somewhat along the lines of the Planning Impact Fee System found in the USA. This system relates 'charges' to the estimated costs of public facilities needed to accommodate a new development. The Impact Fee system exists within the context of publicly prepared, debated and examined plans. Such a change would, however, require primary legislation to be introduced into the UK.[109]

A continuing problem?

Despite guidance, the issue of gain and benefits for the public sector arising from grants of planning permission seems likely to be a continuing problem – one not just encountered with regard to retail developments, of course. There is evidence that it may be housing developers who are now particularly embroiled in the matter. Fierce competition for housing development sites in certain areas, coupled with an allegedly slow planning appeals system that discourages developers from appealing against refusals of permission where they have not been prepared to enter into an obligation places developers, in their own view, in a weak position *vis-à-vis* planning authorities. On the other hand authorities are hampered by public spending restrictions in general, and housing expenditure restrictions in particular. The result is that authorities continue to seek monetary contributions, and the granting of 'slices' of development sites to housing associations in order to build affordable homes for local residents. All this may be acceptable in the context of securing balanced housing developments, rather more controversial is seeking the provision of bus shelters, cycle tracks, green spaces, contributions to local transport schemes, such as 'dial-a-ride' schemes, and closed-circuit television surveillance. At the same time, however, retail developers may have turned away from the 'Plymouth' days of building bird-watching hides and tourist information centres, and such offerings may no longer be offered or sought.[110] This cannot be stated with certainty. In November 1997 it became public knowledge that two supermarket chains had both offered to build a new primary school in Settle utilising land given to the town and then owned by North Yorkshire County Council which had no resources available to build the much needed new school. Each chain wished to build a new supermarket in the town which is 16 miles from the nearest superstore. The matter divided the local community, opponents arguing the proposals would destroy the last greenfield site in Settle and would force existing local traders out of business. Both schemes were refused in November 1997.[111]

For the future some authorities argue that where their policies are made patent in their plans, and that it is clear that contributions will be sought in respect of certain types of development, then the cost of contributions will be reflected in purchase bids to acquire the land by developers who will not thereby be out of pocket. This may become general national planning policy – as may policies that 'greenfield' sites may only be developed where there is a balancing regenerative development of a 'brownfield' site, or a levy on greenfield development to fund urban regeneration, though this is less likely to be acceptable to central government as it smacks of hypothecated taxation.[112]

But the downside of planning obligations for local authorities cannot be dismissed either. In the mid-'80s Slough Estates built the Howard Centre in central Welwyn Garden City. At the same time a rival developer was building the Galleria development a short distance away, in which the local authority, Welwyn-Hatfield District Council, had an interest as both head lessor and planning authority. There was an agreement with Slough Estates, however, that the authority would, by use of its planning powers, maintain a particular tenant mix in the Galleria scheme. In 1991, on the completion of both schemes, Slough Estates obtained judicial review of the authority's decision to relax those planning restrictions, and then it transpired they had been informally relaxed in 1987, so that the Galleria scheme had been free to attract the type of tenants sought for the Howard Centre. Slough Estates claimed they would never have built their centre had they known this and sued the planning authority, obtaining judgement for £46mn in July 1996 on the basis that the authority had deliberately withheld information from the developer.[113] Clearly there could be very considerable repercussions resulting from a planning agreement/obligation that goes wrong. Authorities with comparatively modest annual budgets faced with considerable judgement debts such as Welwyn-Hatfield was, could be forced to dispose of capital assets, such as housing stock and land, and otherwise cut back massively on other capital projects.

A further problem for authorities who have granted permission for store development arises as a result of a recent, and as yet not fully reported decision. In *R v Secretary of State for the Environment ex parte Alnwick District Council*, a local planning authority had, some years ago, granted outline planning permission for a retail development to Safeway, though this had remained unimplemented. A little later, acting in line with changed policy on retail development, the Secretary of State had modified the grant, presumably under s 100 of the 1990 Act, which gives to him the same modification powers as the local planning authority have under s 97. Of course, such a modification has financial consequences under s 107 of the Act, and the supermarket company claimed a sum of £4mn, and that from an authority with an annual budget of £3.5mn. The authority sought judicial review of the Secretary of State's decision, arguing that he had failed to take into account the financial consequences for them of his decision to modify the grant. The High Court, however, held that the Secretary of State did not have to take that matter into account and so the authority are left to face the demands of the company.[114] This could, of course, have implications for authorities should the Secretary of State begin to make extensive use of the power.

The rights of third parties

Enough has been said to show that with regard to retail developments local planning authorities frequently negotiate a most tortuous course between the claims of competing interests. There may be competitive developers all seeking permission; there may be established trade interests seeking protection against incoming development; the planning authority itself may have an interest in the matter, either as partner in development or as the recipient of planning obligation, or because it is seeking to attract development to its area that might otherwise go to a neighbouring authority's area. This is the practical reality, the legal theory is otherwise. Planning law assumes generally that the local planning authority dispassionately and disinterestedly represents the general public interest in a planning decision, and does not seek to desegregate that 'interest' into the component parts of which in reality it is composed. To an extent the judges have recognised this, however, and do allow, in certain circumstances, third parties to challenge planning decisions.

There appears to be a well established judicial principle that planning authorities are required to operate the planning system fairly as respects the various interests of all those involved in a planning matter, though this begs the obvious questions 'what is fair' and 'what is an interest' in a planning matter? Such questions tend to be determined on a case by case basis. It is, however, reasonably clear that authorities must not mislead objectors as to their intentions in respect of a planning application; must not give special treatment to applicants while potential objectors are not even informed of a proposed development, and should inform any established objector to a proposal of any appeal against a refusal of permission so that he may continue to promote his case.[115] The obligation to behave fairly is even more important where the authority itself is implicated in the development as a land owner, land assembler, or, arguably, the recipient of other planning benefit as a result of planning obligations. However, before an objector can show a substantive ground of complaint, he must demonstrate that he has a 'sufficient interest' in the matter to be heard by the court. In other words he must have '*locus standi*' or 'standing'.

Thus in *J J Steeples v Derbyshire County Council*[116] a planning agreement between an authority and a commercial company to develop a massive leisure park was opposed by Mr Steeples in his capacities as a member of a group of objectors to the proposal, *and* as a landowner affected directly by the proposed work. He had legal standing to challenge the agreement as a landholder, part of whose land was to be taken, but it was also said his status as an adjoining landowner gave him sufficient standing to seek a declaration of illegality.[117] Additionally Webster J held Mr Steeples had a right to take action in respect of interferences with public rights provided he could show he had suffered special damage in consequence. However, in the present connection it must be remembered that loss inflicted on individual traders by competition is damage of which the law has generally taken *no* account (but see further below). Mr Steeples' special damage consisted of loss of view and damage to amenities. In such circumstances it seems the discretion of the Court is guided very much by whether the legislation in question contemplates express or implied rights for third parties to complain of alleged unlawful acts and omissions. Much will also depend on the nature of the illegality in question – a gross illegality may be a reason for allowing a person standing in a judicial review action to seek relief, whereas a minor technical breach of the law might not.[118]

Following the *Steeples* decision there were a number of cases where judicial review of decisions to grant planning permission was granted at the suit of rival retailers, especially where there was suspicion that a local planning authority favoured particular development of land they themselves owned – *R v Doncaster Metropolitan Council ex parte British Railways Board*[119] was such a case, preceded slightly earlier by *R v Sevenoaks District Council ex parte Terry*,[120] and *R v St Edmundsbury Borough Council ex parte Investors in Industry Commercial Properties Ltd.*[121] These established that irrespective of whether a local planning authority has an interest in the land in question, and despite what the authority's earlier actions may have been, a decision to grant planning permission can only be attacked if it can be shown to be unfair, or a partial and improper exercise of planning powers.[122]

Controversy over such cases is somewhat reduced by the terms of the Town and Country Planning General Regulations[123] which require a planning application to be made wherever there is a proposal for development to be undertaken by a third party on local authority owned land. This imports the need for the application to be subject to publicity, while the application itself cannot be determined by a committee, sub committee or any officer responsible for managing the land in question. Even so, it continues to be the case that disappointed commercial rivals of consented developments seek judicial review of those planning consents on the basis of allegations of improper or unfair determination by an authority 'swayed' by consideration of planning benefits offered by a rival or a desire to see the authority's own land developed.[124] Such challenges do not have a great history of success. Nevertheless it appears to be well established that a commercial undertaking likely to be affected by a particular development will have a 'sufficient interest' in the matter to be able to seek judicial review of a relevant planning decision. Equally such an undertaking could seek to become involved in any planning inquiry into a refusal of a planning permission and that would then give them the status of 'person aggrieved' under ss 284 and 288 of the Town and Country Planning Act 1990 to seek to challenge any unwelcome decision on the appeal – though, of course, as with judicial review, only on a point of law.

The issue was considered in *R v Wakefield Metropolitan District Council ex parte Pearl Assurance*.[125] Here an authority granted permission for the redevelopment of a large area of derelict and contaminated land. One part was to be used for a factory outlet centre (FOC), which, by condition, was to be limited to selling only discounted seconds, 'end-of-lines' and surplus stock. Pearl Assurance were, however, concerned about the impact of the FOC on their shopping development one mile away, and sought judicial review alleging that the authority had failed to identify and consider those material considerations listed in PPG 6. It was further alleged that the condition imposed on the FOC was unenforceable as being too wide, and thus unreasonable. It was also alleged that Pearl Assurance had a legitimate expectation that their interests would be considered following the local authority's agreement to meet with them and discuss the issue. In the High Court the application failed.

- Allegations that PPG 6 had not been 'followed' foundered on the basis that PPGs are only guidance not 'tramlines'.
- Whether in any given case a particular part of a PPG is a material consideration must be judged by reference to the particular facts of any given case, but there was no proof that the authority had failed to consider PPG 6.
- The fact that the FOC would have an impact on Pearl's development had been a central issue in the determination process, and the fact that the planning authority had made no reference in specific terms to Pearl's turnover figures did not alter that. They had carried out an exercise based on turnover figures and this had been a proper method of assessing impact.
- The authority had considered the effect of the development on future private sector investment in the area.
- An assessment of the economic impact of the development on existing

centres had been made, and this had not been shown by Pearl to be unreasonable, nor had they been able to substantiate allegations that the development would result in changes in travel patterns.

- The restrictive conditions on the FOC were not unreasonable; they might be hard to enforce but were not unreasonable *per se*.
- The fact that the authority had agreed to meet Pearl to discuss issues conferred no legitimate expectation on the company that its interests would be in any way protected.

It would thus seem clear that the ability of a third party successfully to challenge a planning decision to grant permission for a retail development is extremely limited. That third party must have a 'sufficient interest' in the matter – and that will be very hard to establish unless the party's commercial interests are threatened. It will not be possible for a group of concerned local people to 'give themselves' a sufficient interest simply by banding together to oppose a development,[126] something more, such as residence in the area likely to be affected by the development, is at least needed. Once a 'sufficient interest' exists, however, the challenger needs to be able to show some illegality in the decision making process. This, as the history of the case law shows, is hard to achieve. The discretion to grant planning permission is so apparently wide, and the willingness of the courts to recognise a wide range of matters as being perfectly proper material considerations so great, that it is hard to see how a third party could upset a grant of permission. The *Plymouth* decision is surely the *locus classicus* on this issue. Only if it can be shown that an authority has made an utterly insupportable factual conclusion or has totally misdirected itself in law, or has set out to mislead third parties, or to behave in a gratuitously oppressive way towards their interests would a challenge stand much chance of success. Such circumstances are likely to be rare.

This is well illustrated by the decision in *R v Fenland District Council ex parte Sylvia Madden*. Here planning permission had been granted to Sainsbury in 1996 to erect a food store in March. The applicant, with 2,000 others, opposed this and sought judicial review of the decision to grant permission arguing that the planning authority had not given proper regard to either the additional volume of traffic the store would generate, or the amount of support she had generated for a petition against the store. She also alleged that the car parking provision for the store was less than that required by the local plan. The court dismissed the application on the basis that it could only intervene if the planning authority could be shown to have erred in law or to have failed to discharge its duties. The court may not intervene merely because it is alleged insufficient weight has been given to a particular consideration, and in the instant case there was no impropriety or bias on the part of the planning authority.[127]

The situation is otherwise, however, where it can be shown that a planning authority has misdirected itself in law. Thus in *R v Teesside Development Corporation ex parte William Morrison plc and Redcar and Cleveland Borough Council*[128] a development corporation (TDC), which was also the local planning authority, owned an area of land they wished to see developed for residential and commercial purposes, including a major food store. This, however, was contrary to the Structure Plan for the area which favoured other locations and was averse to large scale retailing. Asda were keen to develop the food superstore and offered to purchase the site and provide car parking and ancillary facilities. TDC gave outline planning permission for this proposal, subject to an impact study and to gaining the support of the relevant borough council (Middlesbrough), which, in due course, was forthcoming. TDC also commissioned an impact study from L, a planning consultant, which concluded the new store would have at least 25 per cent impact on Morrisons' existing store, but nevertheless recommended granting permission. Then the 1996 revision of PPG 6 took place, and Morrisons informed Middlesbrough Borough Council of their objections to Asda's proposed development. Middlesbrough obtained a critique of L's assessment from P, another consultant, but nevertheless determined to support the development. Redcar and Cleveland Borough Council decided then to oppose the development because they feared an Asda store in their area would close, despite assurances to the contrary from Asda, and because of the conflict with the Structure Plan. TDC nevertheless pressed ahead with its support for the proposal, on the basis of evidence from its chief planning officer that despite the conflict with national and local policies the benefits of the proposal outweighed its disbenefits, and a conclusion that the new store would not harm the vitality of any existing centre. Middlesbrough Borough Council then changed its stance, following an intimation by Morrisons that they would pull out of a scheme in Middlesbrough if the borough continued to support Asda's proposal. Even so TDC gave formal planning permission for the development.

That decision was quashed on the basis that TDC had misdirected itself in law. It had placed over-much reliance on L's report on the proposal which was couched in terms as if L was advising the developer not the decision taker. Clearly the factual determination process here was flawed. Secondly TDC had allowed its function of securing the regeneration of urban land to dictate the performance of its planning functions. They had not evaluated the proposal objectively and without prejudgement, which is required of all planning authorities. TDC had weighted the entire exercise too much towards justifying a major departure from local planning policy, and indeed they had adopted so inflexible a line on this that they had surrendered their proper discretion on the issue. That constituted illegality as a fetter on discretion. Planning authorities must always undertake a genuine exercise of planning judgement, which must follow an impartial assessment and determination of the relevant facts and arguments.

The interesting points about this case are not the statements made by the judge, Sedley J, about the exercise of planning functions by Urban Development Corporations, for they are in reality no more than an application of well established principles. What is interesting is the identity of the third party who succeeded in upsetting the planning decision. Morrisons not only have the commercial interest to challenge grants of permission to other foodstore developers, but the resources to do so, and the expression of an intention to reconsider participation in the Middlesbrough scheme may also be noted. The intense nature of competition to develop foodstores and other similar retail outlets has been mentioned before, it is interesting to see it result in this particular challenge by one developer in the guise of a third party.

However, even a well resourced third party objector must act promptly if a challenge is to be made. Where an objector has become involved at the appellate stage of a planning application so as to have the status of a 'person aggrieved' under ss 284 and 288 of the Town and Country Planning Act 1990, there are six weeks in which to make the application to the court, which run from the day on which the decision letter is signed and date stamped. Where judicial review is sought, for example to challenge a consented planning application, there is a three month period running from the date of the illegality under s 31 of the Supreme Court Act 1981. This requirement is in addition to that of having to show a 'sufficient interest'. Furthermore, the application for review must be made promptly within the three month period. Thus in *R v Breckland District Council ex parte Budgens Stores Ltd*,[129] it was held that waiting for seven weeks before challenging a grant of permission was too long. Moreover, it was established that time for this purpose ran from the date of the authority's resolution to grant permission rather than the date of the permission itself. A major factor influencing the outcome in this case appears to have been that Budgens' decision to apply for judicial review was a purely commercial one. The authority would have expected a prompt challenge, bearing in mind the fact that preparatory works needed to be carried out on the site within a short period of time of the grant of permission. These were prejudiced by the substantial delay in making the application. A commercial objector should be aware of the possibility of challenging a grant of permission by means of judicial review well in advance of any grant, and may therefore be expected to make a challenge within a week or so of the allegedly illegal decision. Similarly in *R v Tendring District Council ex parte Freeport Village (Braintree) Ltd.*[130] despite allegations by a rival developer that there had been serious mishandling of an application to develop a factory outlet centre, the claim was struck out on the basis that the challenge had been left for far too long.

Epilogue

The initial presumption in favour of development (a feature of planning for many years), historic weak central guidance in relation to major retail development proposals, and utilisation of planning agreement/obligation procedures as outlined above, have ensured that planning law has contributed to the growth of a retail revolution. This view was confirmed by the Lee Donaldson *Superstore Appeals Review 1988*, which, in its introduction, pointed out that superstore developments are intrinsically inimical to the basic notions of planning practice which depend upon the containment of urban growth, protection of the countryside, and the fostering of balanced, self-contained communities with healthy, vigorous town centres. Planning has not been able to prevent growth of superstores and other off-centre development. At best it has managed to 'conduct' it to compromise locations such as edge of town centre or as a core for new district centres. The Lee Donaldson conclusion was

> ...despite the conflict between planning conventions and superstore operations the planning system has not necessarily proved to be a major inhibition to this form of retailing. It has at most borne most heavily upon the form and location of such stores.[131]

A telling statement from the 1988 Lee Donaldson survey concerned government policy as then represented by PPG 6 whose:

> ...publication...may be seen as an official acknowledgement or acceptance of superstores as a significant feature of the shopping hierarchy. The need for such shopping features is now explicit. The planning constraints governing their development are the proper questions of land use and environment.

> Superstore development has adapted to planning's land use requirements. Shopping planning has in turn adapted to superstores' needs.[132]

Central policy historically was apparently little concerned that the law should be so supportive of initiatives capable of drawing ever more trade towards locations virtually exclusively suitable for the car borne. That policy has now changed, and may have to develop further if the present government's ambitious targets for reducing 'greenhouse gas' and other damaging emissions from motor vehicles are to be implemented. With changes in policy may come changes in the substantive law which, as has been seen, has grown up in such a way that it has been hard for local planning authorities to resist proposals for off-centre development. It should not, however, be supposed that a simply more negative attitude on the part of law and policy towards off-centre development will have much effect on what is a very well established economic and social trend. We have lived through a retail revolution in how and where we do our shopping, and so far as shopping for food is concerned that revolution may now have gone too far to be reversed. The '*Ancien Régime*' of small independent traders has largely been lost and cannot be restored. As was stated in the previous chapter this has largely mirrored the flight of the affluent to the suburbs and the growth in car ownership. We now, however, stand in need of yet another revolution – one which sees all sectors of the community, commerce, industry and government determined to make town centres pleasant and safe places to be at all times in which to shop, and, even more importantly, to live. For if a sufficiently large number of people return to live in town centres they will bring with them new life, new resources, and new opportunities for central areas. The high street cannot be restored, it can be reinvented.

Notes

1. Contrast *IPC Developments Ltd v Secretary of State for the Environment and Salisbury District Council* [1997] JPL 930 with *R v Derbyshire County Council ex parte Woods* [1997] JPL 958.
2. *Braintree District Council v Secretary of State for the Environment and Bovis Homes Ltd*; *Carter Commercial Developments Ltd v Secretary of State for the Environment and Braintree District Council*; *Ashfield Land Ltd v Secretary of State for the Environment and Braintree District Council* [1997] JPL 217

3. *IPC Developments Ltd v Secretary of State for the Environment and Salisbury District Council* [1997] JPL 930.
4. Guy C, *The Retail Development Process*, London, Routledge, 1989, p. 72.
5. Guy C, *op. cit.* p. 73.
6. Guy C, *op. cit.* p. 76.
7. *ICP Development v Secretary of State for the Environment and Salisbury District Council* [1997] JPL 930.
8. Guy C, *op. cit.* pp. 86-89.
9. See also Department of the Environmental Circular 25/87 and Planning Policy Guidance Note (PPG) 5.
10. *Op. cit.* p. 80.
11. *Loc. cit.*
12. *St Albans District Council v Secretary of State for the Environment* [1993] JPL 374, *Sainsbury plc v Secretary of State for the Environment* [1993] JPL 651, *Gateshead Borough Council v Secretary of State for the Environment* [1994] JPL 55, *Bylander Waddell Partnership v Secretary of State for the Environment* [1994] JPL 440.
13. *Loup v Secretary of State for the Environment and Salisbury District Council* [1996] JPL 22.
14. In its first version PPG 6 added that where there were floorspace limits in existing plans these should be revised to fall into line with central guidance, see para. 8.
15. Lee Donaldson, London 1988, *Superstore Appeals Review 1988*, p. 14
16. [1985] AC 661.
17. Grant M, *Urban Planning Law*, London, Sweet & Maxwell, 1982, p. 292.
18. See Allana C F, 'Planning Inquiry Practice' as cited in Lee Donaldson, *Superstore Appeals Review 1986*.
19. [1983] JPL 812.
20. [1982] JPL 575.
21. Lee Donaldson, London 1986, *Superstore Appeals Review 1986*, para. 3.15 *et seq.* and 2.48.
22. [1998] JPL 983.
23. [1998] JPL 983 at 995.
24. Lee Donaldson, London 1986, *Superstore Appeals Review 1986*, para. 2.37 *et seq*, and especially 2.45 to 2.48.
25. Guy C, *op. cit.* pp. 80-81.
26. *West Midlands Probation Committee v Secretary of State for the Environment* [1998] 10 Environmental Law and Management 14.
27. *R v Sevenoaks District Council ex parte Terry* [1985] 3 All ER 226; *R v St Edmundsbury Borough Council ex parte Investors in Industry Commercial Properties Ltd* [1985] 3 All ER 234.
28. *The Times*, 25th October 1997.
29. [1986] JPL 914.
30. *Collis Radio v Secretary of State for the Environment* [1975] 221, *Anglia Building Society v Secretary of State for the Environment* [1984] JPL 185

and *Poundstretcher v Secretary of State for the Environment* [1988] 3 Planning Law Reports 69.

31. See *Solihull Metropolitan Borough Council v Secretary of State for the Environment* [1987] JPL 208.
32. *Asda Stores Limited v Secretary of State for Scotland and Stannifer Developments Limited and J Sainsbury plc* [1998] Planning Law Case Reports (PLCR) 233.
33. *Lakin v Secretary of State for Scotland* 1988 SLT 780 and see ' "To each his proper place" considering *Asda Stores Ltd v Secretary of State for Scotland, Stirling Council and Stannifer Developments*' R Craig Connal, [1998] JPL 849. Note also *South Northamptonshire Council v Secretary of State for the Environment; Morbaine Ltd. v Secretary of State for the Environment* [1996] JPL 135.
34. [1999] PLCR 125.
35. [1987] JPL 444.
36. [1987] JPL 444 at 445.
37. London, Construction Press, 1985 pp. 151-152.
38. Keeble L, *op. cit.* p. 152
39. [1987] JPL 444 at 445.
40. (1988) *Planning*, 23rd September, p. 16.
41. (1988-1992) *3 Digest of Environmental Statements*, London, Sweet & Maxwell, p. 90.
42. (1993) *4 Digest of Environmental Statements*, London, Sweet & Maxwell, p. 187.
43. (1994) *5 Digest of Environmental Statements*, London, Sweet & Maxwell, p. 146.
44. *Supra*, p. 171.
45. See 'Measuring the impact of the big schemes', Howard E, (1986) 55 *Town & Country Planning*, no. 10, pp. 282-284.
46. Lee Donaldson, London 1986, *Superstore Appeals Review 1986*, para. 2.2 *et seq*.
47. *Supra*, para. 2.80 *et seq*.
48. Lee Donaldson, London 1988, *Superstore Appeals Review 1988*, p. 7.
49. *Supra*, pp. 8-9.
50. *Supra*, pp. 7-8.
51. Sainsbury Superstore, Cobham, App/K3605/A186/046061, February 1987, referred to in Lee Donaldson, London, 1988, *Superstore Appeals Review 1988*, p. 11.
52. Lee Donaldson, London 1988, *Superstore Appeals Review 1988*, p. 8.
53. *The Times*, 16th December 1996.
54. Goodall M H, 'Applying the "Sequential Test" following the Trowbridge decision' [1996] JPL 913 to 915.
55. [1998] JPL B74, [1999] JPL 599, the learned commentator's views are helpful here.
56. [1998] PLCR 1.

57. [1998] PLCR 70.
58. [1991]1 WLR 153.
59. [1995] 71 P & CR 309.
60. [1998] PLCR 393.
61. [1996] 72 P & CR 342.
62. [1998] JPL 38.
63. [1999] PLCR 236.
64. *Michael Stanley Group Limited v Secretary of State for the Environment, Transport and the Regions and Royal Borough Council of Windsor and Maidenhead* [1999] 1 PLCR 188.
65. *The Times*, 7th November 1997, [1999] PLCR 1.
66. *Braintree District Council v Secretary of State for the Environment and Bovis Homes Ltd, Carter Commercial Developments Ltd v Secretary of State for the Environment and Braintree District Council, Ashfield Land Ltd v Secretary of State for the Environment and Braintree District Council* [1997] JPL 217.
67. *Pyx Granite Co. Ltd v Minister of Housing and Local Government* [1958] 1 QB 554 and *Newbury District Council v Secretary of State for the Environment* [1981] AC 578.
68. *Fawcett Properties Ltd v Buckinghamshire County Council* [1961] AC 636.
69. *R v Hillingdon London Borough Council ex parte Royco Homes Ltd* [1974] QB 720 and *Hall & Co. Ltd v Shoreham-by-Sea Urban District Council* [1964] 1 WLR 240 and *City of Bradford Metropolitan Borough Council v Secretary of State for the Environment* [1986] JPL 598.
70. *Alderson v Secretary of State for the Environment* [1984] JPL 429.
71. *British Airports Authority v Secretary of State for Scotland* [1980] JPL 260.
72. *R v London Borough of Ealing ex parte Zainuddin* [1995] JPL 925.
73. Town & Country Planning (Use Classes) Order SI 1987 No 764.
74. PPG 6 (June 1996) para. 3.11.
75. [1997] JPL 930.
76. See 'Superstores Unlimited' an interview with Giles Shaw, then Under Secretary of State for the Environment, Toft A, (1983) *Independent Grocer*, vol. III, no. 10, p. 34; the question of 'purchase' was directly raised and *indirectly* not answered.
77. Grant M, *Urban Planning Law*, pp. 292-293.
78. (1983) vol. 80, p. 2190.
79. *Hall & Co. Ltd v Shoreham-by-Sea Urban District Council* [1964] 1 WLR 240, *R v Hillingdon London Borough Council ex parte Royco Homes Ltd* [1974] QB 720 and *Westminster Renslade Ltd v Secretary of State for the Environment* [1983] JPL 454.
80. 'Planning Gain', London HMSO, 1981, para. 7.06; also 7.02, 7.04 and 7.07.
81. DoE Circular 22/83 paras 4 to 8.
82. DoE Circular 22/83, para. 2.
83. [1986] JPL 292.
84. (1986) 278 EG 1249.

85. 1988 Edition, para. 14.
86. [1988] JPL 336.
87. [1989] JPL 837.
88. 'Planning Obligations'.
89. DoE Circular 16/91 para. B7.
90. DoE Circular 16/91 para. B8.
91. DoE Circular 16/91 para. B9.
92. [1993] JPL 1099.
93. [1994] JPL 372.
94. [1994] JPL 919 and [1995] 1 WLR 759 and see Moore V M, *A Practical Approach to Planning Law*, 6th Edition, London, Blackstone 1997 pp. 301-303 to which indebtedness is acknowledged.
95. See also *Barber v Secretary of State for the Environment* [1991] JPL 559.
96. 'Planning Obligations'.
97. 'Planning Obligations' paras B2 to B4.
98. 'Planning Obligations' paras B7 to B11.
99. 'Planning Obligations' paras B12 to B15.
100. 'Planning Obligations' paras B16 to B18.
101. 'Planning Obligations' para. B19.
102. Cm 3729, 'Shopping Centres', London, HMSO, 1997 paras 28-29.
103. 'Planning Obligations' para. B28.
104. [1995] 1 WLR 759.
105. Moore V M, *op. cit.* pp. 302-303.
106. Moore V M, *loc. cit.*
107. See further the Nolan Committee Report on 'Standards of Conduct in England, Wales and Scotland', Cm 3702, R.36, London, HMSO, 1997.
108. DETR Consultation Paper 'Modernising Local Government - A New Ethical Framework' London, DETR, April 1998.
109. 'The Future of the Planning System', London, ADC, 10th July 1996.
110. *The Times*, 4th July 1997.
111. *The Independent*, 25th November 1997.
112. 'What Price Development?' Denton Hall, *Property Brief*, London, February 1997, Issue 4, pp. 5 to 6.
113. *Ibid.*
114. *The Times*, 5th August 1999.
115. *R v Torfaen Borough Council ex parte Jones* [1986] JPL 686, *R v Great Yarmouth Borough Council ex parte Botton Bros Ltd* [1988] JPL 18, and *Wilson v Secretary of State for the Environment* [1988] JPL 540.
116. [1985] 1 WLR 256.
117. Following *R v Hendon Rural District Council ex parte Chorley* [1933] 2 KB 696 and *R v North Hertfordshire District Council ex parte Sullivan* [1981] JPL 752.
118. *IRC v National Federation of Self Employed and Small Businesses Ltd* [1981] 2 ALL ER 65.
119. [1987] JPL 444.

120. [1985] 3 All ER 226.
121. [1985] 1 WLR 1168.
122. *R v London Borough of Merton ex parte Barnett* [1990] JPL 354.
123. SI 1992/1492.
124. *R v Canterbury City Council ex parte Springimage Ltd* [1994] JPL 4227, and *R v Plymouth City Council ex parte Plymouth and South Devon Co-operative Society* [1993] JPL 1099.
125. [1997] Lawtel, 5th March.
126. *R v Secretary of State for the Environment ex parte Rose Theatre Co.* [1990] 1 QB 504.
127. [1997] JPL B 138.
128. [1998] JPL 23.
129. [1999] JPL 85.
130. (Unreported) Denton Hall *Property Brief*, London, 1998, issue 7, p. 10.
131. Lee Donaldson, London 1988 *Superstore Appeals Review 1988*, p. 2.
132. Lee Donaldson, London 1988 *Superstore Appeals Review 1988*, p. 15.

PART III

COMPETITION LAW AND POLICY AND RETAILING

7 Preliminary observations

In this part of the book we move on from planning to competition law. Given our context, there is a need to approach the subject from various aspects, and also to make preliminary observations.

To begin with, it has to be explained that the burden carried by the chapters immediately following is to sketch the basic domestic and European principles of the UK's competition régime, and that in relation to this exercise a number of points arise:–

First, the régime does not of course focus on retailing in particular. Its remit is the far broader one of furthering competition in trade and industry generally. Indeed, although this may change in the future, the law has been primarily interested and involved in challenging the practices and abuses emanating from the industrial sector.

Secondly, the sketch is provided with twin aims. One is to outline the framework in which business (including retailers) have had, and will have, to operate. The other is to provide the necessary setting for the treatment which follows of certain particular issues.

Thirdly, while no area of law stands still, competition law is, at present, in a particular state of flux. With the enactment of the Competition Act 1998, the greater portion of the law which has controlled the competitive process for decades, and which has been for some time considered in many respects defective, is gradually being replaced by a fundamentally new régime. Completely different in style from its predecessor, and with its central pillars taking effect from 1st March 2000, it is modelled, for a number of reasons, on the competition provisions of European Community law.

This being the situation, it has been thought best to start with a review of the domestic law up to the Competition Act 1998, and to follow this with an account of the basic thrust of the new Act. It has to be emphasised, however, that this approach is for ease of exposition only, and is in a strict sense 'artificial'. One reason for the artificiality is that it is only (as just noted) the greater portion of the law which is being replaced – parts are retained (with some partial amendments). And another is that parts of the earlier law will continue for some years to have significance for transitional reasons.

With the fundamentals of the domestic scene painted, we turn to a résumé of the key principles of the EC law. While it might have been helpful to gain an insight into the European elements before moving on to the domestic reforms, this possible advantage was dismissed because it was felt on balance to be outweighed by two matters. There was the fact that parts of the 'old' law are retained and not 'Europeanised', and the further fact that there was a need to adopt an order which accommodated and reflected the gradual flow of one régime into another. Accordingly, the 'old' and 'new' domestic systems have been dealt with in sequence before addressing the European components.

The overview having been put in place, we then allocate two chapters to a range of specific matters which require 'highlighting'. In the first of these chapters we discuss the approach taken by the law to price discrimination and to mergers. This we believe is called for inasmuch as the practice of discrimination and the pursuit of mergers, together with the legal stance adopted in respect of them, have been amongst the principal 'drivers' of the retail revolution.

In the second, and final, chapter we concentrate on certain further major issues. These are the discrete but overlapping matters of 'vertical issues' and 'the aggrandisement of the retailer'. Being matters which (along with the impact of the far-reaching law reforms) have risen to the top of the competition 'agenda' in the retailing arena, they invite our attention.

There remains one last point to be made by way of introduction to this part of the book. This is that reference will frequently be made to the European competition provisions, *i.e.* the well known Articles 85 and 86 of the Treaty of Rome. Due to a re-numbering exercise necessitated by the Treaty on European Union (TEU) which came into force in May 1999, they are now in fact Articles 81 and 82. However, to avoid confusion to those readers unaccustomed to the new numbering (and for the nostalgic amongst us!) the 'old' Articles are referred to throughout the text.

8 The domestic law ~ up to the Competition Act 1998

By way of introduction to a résumé of law which has long been familiar to competition lawyers, the already noted consequence of the gradual establishment of a new régime merits repetition. This is that with the coming into force on 1st March 2000 of the régime's pivotal measures, even so the earlier provisions to some considerable extent retain significance, albeit in a variety of ways. This is an important fact, and reference will be made to it as and where appropriate.

Also, by way of preliminary it should be explained that the outline which follows is arranged by reference to the conduct and structures over which the law (through years of piecemeal growth) has developed an array of controls. So, we shall consider in turn restrictive trading agreements, monopolies, mergers, anti-competitive practices ('a.c.ps'), and resale price maintenance.

Restrictive trading agreements

For the final quarter of the century it was to fall to the Restrictive Trade Practices Act 1976[1] to regulate restrictive trading agreements and arrangements, and to do so by means of a system comprising registration, reference to the Restrictive Practices Court, and adjudication in the light of the public interest.[2]

Section 6 of the Act required, subject to exceptions, the registration with the Director General of Fair Trading of any agreements made between two or more persons carrying on business in the United Kingdom in the production or supply of goods, being an agreement under which restrictions are accepted in respect of such matters as the prices to be charged for goods, the quantities of goods to be supplied, and the persons to whom or the areas in which goods are to be supplied.[3] While the Act was designed to catch both 'horizontal' agreements (*i.e.* those entered into by firms operating at the same level of the market, and including agreements such as price fixing, market sharing and quota schemes), and 'vertical' agreements (*i.e.* those entered into by firms operating at different levels of the market, and including such agreements as those involving exclusive distribution, exclusive purchasing and selective distribution),[4] its prime target would be the horizontal cartel. It has been far more tolerant of vertical agreements, which, if carefully drafted, have escaped its clutches.[5]

When an agreement has been registered in accordance with the Act's requirements, the Director General has then (generally speaking) fallen under a duty to refer it to the Restrictive Practices Court, where the parties to the agreement have been given an opportunity to seek to defend its restrictions. Most importantly, however, he has not had to do so if discharged from the duty by a direction of the Secretary of State where the latter is satisfied that the agreement is not sufficiently 'significant' to require the court's investigation.[6]

Under the equally pivotal provisions of s 10, a restriction has been deemed contrary to the public interest unless the court should be satisfied of the existence of one or more of a series of specified circumstances, and further satisfied that the restriction was not unreasonable having regard to the balance between any such specified circumstance and any detriment to the public resulting from the restriction's operation, (the so called 'balancing tailpiece'). The circumstances have been set out in a series of paragraphs generally referred to as 'gateways', through one of which a restriction has had to be steered, and all but one 'gateway' have contemplated a situation in which the restriction provided some positively advantageous effect for the public. With the successful negotiation of a 'gateway' and the successful surmounting of the 'balancing tailpiece', the restrictions in question have been able to continue to operate, but if the court has concluded that the restrictions in issue were contrary to the public interest, then the agreement would be void in respect of them.

To the central question of the ease or otherwise of successfully defending a restrictive agreement, the simple answer is that it has always been difficult, because *inter alia* of the approach of the court. Not long after the enactment of the predecessor to s 10, it became plain to the business community that the stance of the then newly established court would be almost implacably 'pro free competition'. So for instance, until the addition of an extra 'gateway', it was for years plain that even harmless restrictions would be found contrary to the public interest – a matter illustrated by the well known *Doncaster and Retford Co-op* case in which an innocuous market sharing agreement between two small retail Co-op societies fell foul of the court.[7]

Of the numerous cases which the court heard in its early days there were very few in which the hurdles to the continuing in existence of any restriction were overcome. For the court to be satisfied that a particular restrictive agreement was not against the public interest it was soon realised that there would need to be proved the presence of some highly advantageous feature or some particularly unusual conditions. Indeed, just how exceptional were the successfully defended cases and how rigorous was the court in its 'pro free competition' attitude is reflected in the observation made by Whish in *Competition Law* that '...[In] practice out of nearly 10,000 goods and services agreements entered on the register between 1956 and the end of 1991 only 11 successfully penetrated one of the gateways',[8] and his further comment that '...the passage of the 1956 Act [led] to widespread abandonment of restrictive trade practices throughout British industry...'.[9]

For almost half a century, the signal sent to retailers (as to other firms) by the interpretation of the restrictive trade practices legislation has been plain, namely that forays made into *explicit* horizontal collusion would be too fraught with danger to be worthy of pursuit.[10] In one important respect, therefore, the law has presented to business a forceful image, but hidden, secret cartels have been a pressing and continuing problem,[11] and further, there are weaknesses in the approach of the law which have served seriously to blunt its edge as a tool for the promotion of competition. For a long time the focus of criticism, the 1976 Act is described in an Office of Fair Trading guideline accompanying the Competition Act 1998 as '...unduly technical ...and...[failing to]...contain sufficient sanctions against genuinely harmful anti-competitive conduct, while unnecessarily catching many innocuous agreements...'.[12] Given such inadequacies, the operation of an updated system will be welcomed by many, but the gradual character of the change needs emphasis. The transitional arrangements are such that it will be a long time before the 1976 Act fades completely from sight.[13]

Monopolies

For the control of monopolies over a similar period we have had to look to the Fair Trading Act 1973, (as amended). Never assuming that monopoly in itself is bad, but rather seeking to challenge the abuse of the power which monopoly can bring, it established a régime which relies on referral, investigation, report and (if necessary) remedial action. Involving the Director General of Fair Trading, the Secretary of State, and the Monopolies and Mergers Commission (now the Competition Commission), the machinery has worked as follows:–

Where it has appeared that there exists (or may exist) what the Act refers to as a 'monopoly situation', either the Secretary of State or, in most instances, the Director General of Fair Trading, has been empowered to refer it to the Commission for that body to carry out an investigation and make a report. A 'monopoly situation' being capable of existing under the Act with reference to the supply either of goods or of services, it may exist in relation to the supply of goods if *inter alia* at least one quarter of all goods of the relevant description supplied in the United Kingdom are *inter alia* supplied by or to one person, or a group of connected companies, or two or more persons who so conduct their respective affairs as to prevent, restrict or distort competition.

It will be noted that a 'monopoly situation' can exist by reference not only to circumstances involving one or a group of connected companies, but also to those involving two or more companies who so conduct their respective affairs as to impede competition. Thus it embraces not only 'scale monopolies' (based on 'structure'), but also 'complex monopolies' (based on 'behaviour'). The inclusion of the latter has proved of considerable practical significance, it facilitating, if the 25 per cent threshold is met, the investigation of parallel but uncoordinated behaviour of firms the non-collusive character of which would put it outwith the restrictive trade practices legislation.

When a monopoly reference has been made to the Commission, the Act has required that it should specify the description of the goods or services in issue and also the questions on which the Commission should investigate and report. It may be the Commission has been requested to confine itself to the exploration of facts (*i.e.* to establish for example in whose favour a monopoly situation exists and whether it is being in any way kept in existence), or, and far more usefully, to report also on whether the matter investigated operates (or may operate) against the public interest. And in the latter case the Commission has been required both to take into account all relevant matters, and to have regard to a list of *desiderata* including, for example, the maintenance of effective competition, the promotion of consumers' interests, the facilitation of new entrants into the market and the maintenance of the balanced distribution of industry and employment.

Where, upon the completion of inquiries, the conclusion has been that the public interest would be unharmed, it would follow that no further action was called for, but for situations of identifiable harm the Act has made provision for 'follow up' action of two varieties: 'informal follow up' action, involving the giving of appropriate undertakings by the party or parties in question, and 'formal follow up action', involving the making by the Secretary of State of remedial orders.[14]

In some five decades of activity the Commission has conducted numerous investigations, and its Reports cover areas of utmost diversity. As there is no application of the concept of binding precedent, and as the body of cases is so large, to give an overall picture is not easy. It must suffice here simply to note certain of the kinds of possible abuse of monopoly power which have arisen for consideration.[15]

Pricing policy has been naturally prominent, with the charging of high prices a focal point. Thus, for example, in the case of *Contact Lens Solutions*,[16] the Commission found *inter alia* that Boots enjoyed a scale monopoly at retail level, had been selling at recommended resale prices and achieving substantial margins, and that this was against the public interest. Similarly, discriminatory pricing has proved a further focus, as, for example, in the case of the *Supply of Beer* in 1989 where the Commission perceived considerable differences in the prices charged for beer in different areas of the country and concluded that this practice conflicted with the public interest.[17]

The level of profits has been another major issue. In the *Contact Lens Solutions* case mentioned above, for instance, the Commission was as much concerned with the supplying as the retailing of the product, and found amongst the suppliers the making of high profits contrary to the public interest.[18] However, it should be added that high levels of profit may not necessarily be considered harmful to that interest, as is illustrated by the *Soluble Coffee* case.[19]

Of the many and varied issues which have come before the Commission some have been very broad. For example, in an early investigation into *Beer*,[20] consideration was being given to efficiency and whether conduct was wasteful. Here the Commission concluded the system of tying public houses maintained in existence excessive brewing capacity and recommended the lifting of legal constraints so that other retail outlets might compete. More specific was the issue, for instance, in the *Wallpaper* case where conditions imposed upon retailers by the dominant supplier that they should buy their paper exclusively from the latter failed to find favour with the Commission.[21] From the aspect of breadth of issues it is not, though, without interest that whereas the questions for the Commission have almost inevitably been of a commercial character, the law has been able to accommodate the legitimate consideration of non-commercial issues. So, in the fairly recent case of *Contraceptive Sheaths*, the Commission took into account, in deliberating upon whether or not to lift certain earlier imposed price controls, the chance of enhanced competition leading to more intensive advertising, and the fact that public health would benefit from the greater promotion of the product's use.[22]

A final and important point on the 'case law' is the way in which it has revealed the utility of the Act's embrace of complex monopolies. Because the statute has extended to behavioural as well as structural monopolies, it has been possible to enquire into situations where competition appeared threatened because of the simultaneous operation of rigid distribution networks. From many instances, there may be cited the investigations into the exclusivity of purchasing required of *Petrol Retailers*,[23] selective distribution systems operated by the fragrance houses in *Fine Fragrances*[24] and the selective and exclusive distribution systems pursued by car manufacturers in *New Motor Cars*.[25] Indeed, so useful has the Act proved in connection with complex monopolies that, in order the better to control them, the monopolies régime has been retained. So far as concerns this and another purpose (see later) the law reformers decided it should not be superseded.

Mergers

Subject to certain fundamental distinctions, the control exercised by the Fair Trading Act 1973 over mergers has been similar to that controlling monopolies. Again, its essential components have been referral to the Monopolies and Mergers Commission, investigation in the light of the public interest, report and, if necessary, 'follow up' action. In outline, the system operates in the following way:-

The Act provides for the Secretary of State to refer to the Commission for investigation certain merger situations.[26] In broad terms, these are situations in which it appears that two or more enterprises have ceased to be distinct,[27] and either the value of the assets taken over exceeds £70mn[28] or else a monopoly situation in goods or services is created or intensified by the merger.

In the case of mergers, the timing of a reference is most important. A reference may be made either before or after a merger takes place. Section 75 makes provision for the reference of mergers in anticipation of their taking place and such is the usual practice. Where, though, a merger has taken place, any reference has to be made within four months of its completion.[29] Again, in the context of the machinery of reference, provision is made both for the pre-notification of mergers[30] and also for the giving of undertakings as an alternative to reference.[31]

When the Commission receives a reference, which, in the case of mergers, is always a public interest reference, it is assisted in its task of considering whether or not the situation might have consequences harmful to that interest by there being set out in the Act the matters which the Commission shall take into account.[32] If the Commission comes to the conclusion that there is no adverse impact upon the public interest, then the merger, if completed, may stand, and, if not completed, may go ahead. Should it be, though, that the Commission thinks the public interest would suffer, then 'follow up' action may follow, and the Act provides both for the giving of undertakings[33] and the imposition of remedial orders by the Secretary of State.[34]

So far as the approach of the Commission to its task is concerned, the system being discretionary and free from any doctrine of binding precedent, it is again hard to give a coherent overview. Some insight can be gained, however, from reference to certain aspects of the work involved.

To begin with, we may note that while the Commission can be concerned with horizontal, vertical or conglomerate mergers,[35] it is the horizontal which come naturally to the forefront because they impinge *directly* upon competition. The loss of competition inherent in a horizontal merger can result in a range of harmful consequences, amongst them the raising of prices, the lowering of quality and the lessening of consumer choice. So, for instance, in *GUS/Empire Stores*[36] both an existing and a proposed merger were viewed unfavourably because of the consequential weakening of competition and ability to influence prices. And similarly, the proposed merger between *Kingfisher plc and Dixons Group plc*[37] was found against the public interest on grounds of a significant weakening of competition and resultant higher prices. Even so, and for a variety of reasons, very many horizontal mergers do not find disfavour with the Commission. It may be, for instance, that the Commission believes that even after a merger sufficient competition remains for there to be little danger of significant market power ensuing,[38] or that the threat of such power emerging is averted by the presence of countervailing power.[39]

The history of the Commission's concern with mergers is not as long as that with monopolies, but nevertheless the span of its involvement is wide. In its delicate task of balancing benefits and detriments to the public interest, richly assorted issues have emerged for consideration.[40] Amongst them are, for instance, consideration of impact upon employment, upon the balance of payments and upon research and development.[41] Again, the prime focus may be upon the target itself, with questions raised as to its post-merger efficiency[42] or whether indeed, without a merger, it would simply fail to survive at all.[43] And again, such apparently nebulous but nevertheless important matters for scrutiny may be those of the impact of the merger upon management and morale,[44] or even of the very character of the bidder himself.[45]

Over the years of its operation, the mergers régime has not escaped questioning. One matter has been the grounds upon which it might be expected that a merger could be referred to the Commission for inquiry. Throughout its lengthy period of office the Conservative government from time to time emphasised that the prime consideration in determining whether to refer was competition. Another critical issue has been the perceived need for the Commission, via its Reports, to lay down coherent principles. Plainly, the business community suffers if there is impredictability, and efforts have been made to establish some consistency. Of its very nature, however, it is not an area which lends itself to a strict doctrine of precedent.

For some, the major criticism has perhaps been that the regulatory system has been too benign. Only a small number of mergers are actually referred to the Commission. Before the Secretary of State can prohibit a merger, a two thirds majority of the Commission have to take the view that it will work against the public interest, and even if that view is taken the Secretary of State can still decide the merger should not be condemned. When all these considerations are taken together, and then linked to the fact that a merger is presumed not to operate against the public interest but actually has to be shown as likely to do so,[46] then the conclusion is surely drawn that the régime errs on the side of tolerance.

Criticism apart, however, the system is seen as having distinct value, and testimony to that perception is found in the fact that the régime is not the subject of reform under the new legislation, but being retained.

Anti-competitive practices ('a.c.ps')

With *inter alia* the aim of filling a gap in the control network, the Competition Act 1980 was enacted to govern anti-competitive practices, *i.e.* courses of conduct having or likely to have the effect of restricting, distorting or preventing competition ('a.c.ps').[47] Designed for expedition, it put in place a 'two tier' régime, providing for preliminary investigations by the Director General of Fair Trading with the possibility of further investigation by the Commission.

Through the years of the Act's operation a variety of matters would come before the authorities. One to arise quite early was selective dealing, *i.e.* the pursuit by a supplier of a distribution policy under which supplies are limited to a chosen class of distributor, and hence a practice which implicitly involves a refusal to deal with those outside that class. In such a case concern is aroused by the distortion of competition at retail level, and too by the extent to which a supplier should be allowed to control the route via which his product is made available to the consumer.[48] The authorities' attention was also soon to be taken by arrangements conferring exclusivity, *i.e.* with situations in which an enterprise chooses to conduct certain trade only with one other enterprise. A situation of this kind can pose a query for competition policy in that on the one hand it may promote efficiency, but on the other hand foreclose opportunities of entry to the market.[49]

Predatory conduct also proved a focus of concern, *i.e.* the adoption of a very low pricing policy aimed at ousting from the market a particular competitor or competitors. So, for instance, in the *London Electricity Board* case investigations were made into the Board's long standing practice or retailing electrical appliances at a loss by subsidising its prices from other activities where it enjoyed a statutory monopoly. The Director General thought the practice anti-competitive, and the Commission agreed. However, it was not felt that the distortion of competition was sufficiently substantial to harm the market.[50] It might be added that because a very fine line exists between unacceptable, predatory behaviour and vigorous, healthy competition, predation is notoriously difficult to control, and the cases reveal an earnest, continuing search for workable regulatory principles.[51]

Yet a further activity to exercise the Director General and the Commission was refusal to supply goods on the ground of their use as 'loss-leaders'. When *Black and Decker* so refused, inquiries were instituted and the public interest found to be harmed. The argument that loss leading leads to lowering of brand image was rejected, and while the concept of a refusal was thought legitimate in principle, Black and Decker's *general* rule to refuse to supply any retailers with a gross margin of less than 12.5 per cent was considered unacceptable.[52]

When the Act was passed, it was thought it would be a valuable adjunct to the array of controls already then existing, but it was to prove disappointing. There were fewer and less speedy investigations than were hoped for, and not only that, the tendency was for its operation to focus on rather narrow, sometimes local, issues. Under the reforms, the régime undergoes a demise, and is replaced by provisions challenging the 'abuse of a dominant position'. There are few perhaps to mourn its passing, the replacement being in the view of Singleton in *Blackstone's Guide to the Competition Act 1998*, a 'much improved device in the hands of the OFT'.[53]

Resale price maintenance (r.p.m.)

Whereas no separate controlling system is created by the 'new' régimes, r.p.m. has for long been the subject of special provisions, these being contained in the Resale Prices Act 1976 and the Restrictive Trade Practices Act 1976.

Simple vertical r.p.m. agreements have been the subject of the former Act, with a minimum r.p.m. condition being rendered void, and it being made unlawful to include such a condition in an agreement. However, the *mere* recommending of a resale price has not been prohibited, and neither was the imposition of maximum resale prices to be challenged. Furthermore, the Act provided a route by which exemption from its prohibition might be sought for classes of goods.

Despite the law having provided an escape route, it has to be said, however, that the chance of any successful application for exemption ever being made was always to prove virtually nil. There has already been mentioned the failure in the mid-'60s of the chocolate and sweets manufacturers to ride free of the prohibition, and this high profile failure signalled to the business community the generally dismal prospects for any such venture.[54] True, success attended an application for an exemption to allow the price maintenance of proprietary medicines,[55] but it was exceptional. In due course (as has been explained) a question mark began to hover over this particular 'permissibility'. At the beginning of 1998 the Director General, being of the view that circumstances had greatly changed,[56] announced that he was seeking leave to apply to the Restrictive Practices Court for a reconsideration of the exemption Order. Signalling a successful 'first round' for the Office of Fair Trading in its attempt to have the exemption overturned, the court granted the Director General leave to apply for an order removing the exemption. The view was taken that there was *prima facie* evidence of a material change in the retailing of pharmaceuticals, and hence the question whether r.p.m. is in the public interest in this section of the market will be fully explored again.[57]

Moving from the vertical to the horizontal plane, the approach has been to make horizontal agreements with 'built in' enforcement provisions unlawful *per se*, an approach illustrating the extreme disfavour which attends tactics of this kind. Again, while they would never become the target of the draconian '*per se* illegality' approach, horizontal agreements lacking 'built in' enforcement provisions would not escape the law, and became subject to successive Restrictive Trade Practices Acts. In fact, the *Net Book Agreement* was successfully defended under the Restrictive Trade Practices

Act 1956,[58] and for years thereafter the resale prices of books were lawfully maintained, but (as earlier observed), this agreement eventually collapsed, and the Court then concluded that r.p.m. for books could no longer be sustained.[59]

Finally, it should be explained that the Competition Act 1998 brings about the demise of the separate régime of the Resale Prices Act, and the bringing of r.p.m. within provisions designed to control anti-competitive agreements generally. How the practice will fare under the new system only time will tell, but any change of attitude such as to engender less hostility seems, in the prevailing climate, most unlikely.

Notes

1. – as amended by the De-regulation and Contracting Out Act 1994.
2. While the 1976 Act has applied to restrictive agreements and exchange of information agreements involving goods or services, for the purpose of this sketch we confine ourselves to its application to restrictive agreements relating to goods.
3. By virtue of s 27A and the Restrictive Trade Practices (non-notifiable Agreements) (Turnover Threshold) Order 1996, (SI 1996 No 348) agreements the parties to which are persons whose aggregate annual turnover in the UK does not exceed £20mn have not, unless involving price fixing, had to be notified.
4. An exclusive distribution agreement is one in which a producer agrees with a distributor that he will sell only to that distributor in a specified area; an exclusive purchasing agreement is one in which a purchaser has to agree with his supplier that he will purchase his requirements of certain goods only from that supplier, and a selective dealing agreement is one in which the producer imposes upon a distributor of his goods terms as to the kinds of outlet through which the latter may resell them.
5. Vertical agreements such as those mentioned have found their escape from the Act in a variety of ways.
6. See s 21(2).
7. *Re Doncaster & Retford Co-op Societies Agreement* (1960) LR 1RP 105.
8. 3rd. Edn. Butterworths, p. 161.
9. *Ibid.* at pp. 122-3.
10. In 'Competition in Retailing' (Research paper, 13th September 1997, prepared for the Office of Fair Trading by London Economics) the authors noted that '...[T]here have been few retailing cases in recent decades in which explicit collusion was even suspected, let alone found...' (p. 92). Even, it has long appeared, the Act might have stood in the way of small and

medium sized wholesalers and retailers who could have otherwise pursued collective exclusive dealing or collective refusals to deal as a fully effective means of counteracting the impact of multiple buying power. Despite the promising wording of one of the 'gateways', there has had to be added to the high cost and burden of defending a case the very slim chance of success. (See *Discounts to Retailers*, (1981) HC 311, paras 8.26 and 8.27.) (By virtue of the mechanism contained in s 21(2) of the 1976 Act for the exemption from court proceedings of insignificant agreements, certain agreements necessary for the operating of such 'voluntary groups' have been allowed to exist – but they are necessarily limited.)

11. – leading to the creation by the Office of Fair Trading of a special 'cartels task force'. The work of this body was highlighted recently with the uncovering of a secret price fixing agreement in a section of the car industry and the consequential giving of assurances to the Director General of Fair Trading. (See Office of Fair Trading Press Release PN 24/99, 9th July 1999, 'Volvo involved in price fixing cartels'.)
12. The guideline entitled 'The Major Provisions', at para. 1.2.
13. For transitional arrangements see Schedule 13 to the Competition Act 1998 and the Office of Fair Trading's guideline bearing that title.
14. The powers are extensive – from the prohibition of harmful conduct to the imposition of obligations to divest.
15. To the basic question if, should the existence of dominance over a particular market be established, there is any opportunity for its exploitation, the answer may, of course, be 'no'. It may be, for example, that there is sufficient competition about of some variety to prevent it, (as, for instance, in the case of the *Supply of Cinema Advertising Services* Cm 1080 (1990), where a monopoly position could not be exploited because advertisers could use other forms of display advertising).
16. Cm 2242 (1993).
17. Cm 651. Just as discriminatory pricing might be frowned upon, so too might predatory pricing, *i.e.* very low pricing designed to oust a particular competitor from the market. Following the de-regulation of certain bus services under the Transport Act 1985, allegations of predation considerably exercised the competition authorities. (See by way of illustration *The Supply of Bus Services in Mid and West Kent* Cm 2309 (1993), and *The Supply of Bus Services in the North East of England* Cm 2933 (1995).)
18. Cm 2242 (1993).
19. Cm 1459 (1991).
20. HCP (1969-70).
21. HCP (1963-64) – the practice led to the eventual emergence of more retail outlets than demand justified.
22. Cm 2529 (1994).
23. *The Supply of Petrol* Cm 972 (1990); (a number of investigations have been carried out in this area).
24. Cm 2380 (1993).

25. Cm 1808 (1992).
26. See s 64. In the case of merger situations only the Secretary of State may refer.
27. The concept of 'ceasing to be distinct' is actually highly complex: see s 65.
28. The figure became £70mn by the Monopolies and Mergers (Merger References, Increase in Value of Assets) Order 1994, SI 1994 No 72.
29. See s 64(4) as amended by the De-regulation (Fair Trading Act 1973) (Amendment) (Merger Reference Time Limits) Order 1996, (SI 1996 No 345).
30. See ss 75A and B. Notification is non-mandatory.
31. See s 75G (as amended by s 9 of the De-regulation and Contracting Out Act 1994).
32. Section 84 provides that the Commission shall take into account all relevant matters and have regard to *desiderata* including the maintenance of effective competition, the promotion of consumer interests and the maintenance of the balanced distribution of industry and employment.
33. See s 88.
34. See s 73.
35. 'Horizontal' mergers involve firms at the same level of distribution, 'vertical' firms at different levels, and 'conglomerate' firms with disparate interests.
36. Cmnd 8777 (1983).
37. Cm 1079 (1990).
38. See, for instance, *Trusthouse Forte plc/Hanson Trust plc* Cm 96 (1987) in the arena of roadside catering outlets.
39. So, for example, in *The Gillette Company/Parker Pens Holdings Ltd* Cm 2221 (1993) a proposed merger between these manufacturers of pens was not considered harmful because *inter alia* the great bargaining power of the large retailers meant there would be little chance of the merged group exploiting its position.
40. A particularly interesting 'balancing' exercise arose in *Prosper De Mulder Ltd/Croda International plc* Cm 1611 (1991) where competition issues had to be balanced against environmental issues – a matter perhaps likely to emerge with more frequency in the coming years.
41. See, for instance, in these contexts respectively, *Euro-Canadian Shipholdings/Furness Withy/Manchester Liners* HCP (1971-76) 639; *Babcock & Wilcox/Herbert Morris* HCP (1976-77) 175; and *Alcatel Cable SA/STC Ltd* Cm 2477 (1994).
42. See, for example, *Lonrho/House of Fraser* HCP (1979) 175, where the Commission considered that the bidder's interests being diversified might mean harm could befall the specialised retailing methods of the target.
43. See, for example, *Hillsdown Holdings plc/Enterprises belonging to Associated British Foods plc* Cm 2004 (1992).
44. See, for example, *Rank Organisation/De La Rue* HCP (1968-69) 298.

45. See, for example, *Amalgamated Industries/Herbert-Morris* HCP (1975-76) 434.
46. As to the strength of the evidence needed to overcome the beneficial presumption see *British Sugar/Berisford* HCP (1980) 241 at para. 9.40. The Commission want evidence raising a real expectation of harm to the public interest.
47. See s 2.
48. By way of illustration of the issues see, for instance, the *Raleigh Bicycles* case [*TI Raleigh Industries Ltd* (OFT 27/2/81); *Bicycles* HCP (1981-82) 67].
49. See, for instance, *British Railways Board/Brighton Taxis* (OFT 24th November 1982).
50. OFT 29th April 1982; Cmnd 8812 (1983).
51. Particularly illuminating are the investigations into allegations of predation in bus services following the de-regulation achieved by the Transport Act 1985. (See, especially, *South Yorkshire Transport Ltd* (OFT 13th October 1989).)
52. OFT 8th March 1989; Cm 805 (1989).
53. – at p. 39.
54. *Re Chocolate and Sugar Confectionery Resale Price Reference* [1967] LR 6RP 338, RPC.
55. *Re Medicaments Reference (No 2)* (1970) LR 7RP 267.
56. – changed circumstances including numbers of chemists shops no longer declining, 'protected' income from dispensing NHS prescriptions accounting for a large proportion of chemist's turnover, and growth in chains of chemists shops enabling them to withstand competition. (See Office of Fair Trading, Press Release 1/98, 8th January 1998.)
57. See Office of Fair Trading Press Release 7/99, 11th March 1999.
58. *Re Net Book Agreement* (1962) LR 3RP 246.
59. *In re Net Book Agreement* 1957 (No 4) [1998] ICR 753.

9 Domestic law reform ~ the new Act

Behind the enactment of the Competition Act 1998[1] lies a decade of reform proposals which eventually expanded to meet the more extensive reformatory zeal displayed by this present Government than that of its predecessor.[2] As has been noted, the Act brings in fundamental (albeit in certain respects gradual) change over the greater portion of the earlier law – the most significant retention of the 'old' provisions being those relating to mergers.[3]

Set within the context of a general desire to encourage competitiveness, growth and consumer welfare, a range of specific objectives suffuses the new system. Already mentioned is the concern to modernise the unwieldy and in many ways ineffective regulation of restrictive trade agreements, and the keenness to control not only these phenomena but also monopolies and a.c.ps *via* measures fashioned in the European mould is distinct. It may be added that the eagerness of the reformers to introduce a domestic régime 'mirroring' that emanating from the Treaty of Rome stems from three perceptions: the forcefulness of the régime, the convenience for business of harmonious régimes, and the need to be seen as positioned 'at the heart of Europe'.

In the effort to meet the many and interlinked *desiderata*, the régime which the Act puts in place is naturally both extensive and intricate. Its main thrust, however, may be outlined thus:–

At its heart are the two pivotal sets of provisions, known as the 'Chapter I and Chapter II prohibitions'. Respectively, they challenge concerted anti-competitive activity and the anti-competitive conduct of firms enjoying some power over a market, (*i.e.* 'abuse of a dominant position').

Beginning with the former, s 2 prohibits agreements and concerted practices having as their object or effect the prevention, restriction or distortion of competition within the UK. Based on Article 85 of the Treaty of Rome, it renders infringing practices void, and sets out an illustrative list of infringing practices such as price fixing, market sharing, limiting production, discrimination and 'tying'. An agreement will only infringe the provision, however, if it appreciably prevents, restricts or distorts competition.[4]

Further, the Act makes provision for exclusions from the prohibition. Numerous categories of agreement are specifically excluded by certain schedules, and one such category must be mentioned. Schedule 3 excludes agreements which, as 'insignificant', are the subject of a direction under s 21(2) of the Restrictive Trade Practices Act 1976. There being in excess of 10,000 agreements falling into this category, this is a most important exclusion. Again, s 50 of the 1998 Act provides for the special treatment under the Chapter I of prohibition of *inter alia* vertical agreements, including provision for their exclusion. Economics analysts suggesting that they do not generally raise competition concerns, the reformers thought it appropriate to provide in many instances for their exclusion (though with provision for a 'clawback') and, as will emerge in a later, more detailed discussion of vertical issues, such treatment is in progress.

Recognising that concerted activity which infringes the prohibition can nevertheless exhibit countervailing beneficial attributes, the Act provides also for exemptions. Section 9 provides the exemption criteria. Echoing Article 85(3) of the Treaty of Rome, it embraces agreements which contribute to improving production or distribution or to promoting technical or economic progress, while allowing consumers a fair share of the resulting benefit, and which do not impose restrictions which are not indispensable to the attainment of those objectives or afford the possibility of eliminating competition.

The Director General of Fair Trading is given power by s 4 to grant individual exemptions, and measures are also included for the creation of 'bloc' exemptions.[5] If an agreement is exempt it will not be void.

Procedures are made available for parties to an agreement they think *may* infringe the prohibition to seek from the Director General either informal guidance or a formal decision. As to the former, upon an application being made under s 13, the Director General may give guidance to the applicant as to whether or not the agreement is likely to infringe the prohibition and, if he thinks it is likely to do so, whether there is a likelihood of its benefiting from an exemption. And as to the latter, upon an application being made under s 14, the Director General may make a decision as to whether the prohibition has been infringed and, if not, whether that is due to the effect of an exclusion or because the agreement is exempt. Furthermore, in an application made under s 14, a request may be included for the granting of an exemption.

At this point we turn from the Chapter I to the Chapter II prohibition, dealing with abuse of a dominant position. Echoing, though with a national slant, the European Article 86, s 18 prohibits conduct which amounts to such abuse if it may affect trade within the UK. Like its EC counterpart, it then sets out an illustrative list of conduct which may constitute an abuse, the list including such conduct as the imposition of unfair prices, the limitation of production, the pursuit of discrimination and of 'tying'.[6]

Again, the Act affords opportunity for those believing their conduct might infringe the prohibition to seek its consideration by the Director General. Facility is given for application to be made either for informal guidance or a formal decision.[7]

Moving on, we find Chapter III concerning itself with investigation and enforcement. In this chapter the Act makes provisions for the new régime to be applied and enforced by the Director General. Amongst the many powers given to him are powers to require the termination of agreements and conduct which infringe the prohibitions, to award significant penalties in respect of the same,[8] and to impose interim measures. Moreover, there are bestowed upon him extensive investigatory powers including those of entry and search.

As part of the system the Act also establishes a new body called the 'Competition Commission', which has a dual rôle. One of its functions will be to hear appeals made against decisions of the Director General regarding the prohibitions, the other is to assume the earlier functions of the Monopolies and Mergers Commission (which is dissolved).[9]

With the basics noted, certain further matters must be mentioned. The first relates to monopolies, an important point being that the monopoly framework provided by the Fair Trading Act 1973, is (as earlier mentioned) retained. This is to meet concerns regarding both complex and scale monopolies. As to the former, because they raise issues of market structure and operation, it was felt that the two prohibitions would not readily deal with the matter. And as to the latter, it was believed that the powers of the 1973 régime should be kept to deal with the situation where, a company having infringed the prohibitions and appearing likely to commit further abuses, the only effective way of preventing such abuses might be to have resort to the structural remedies available under the earlier system. However, the particularity of the purposes for which the régime is kept must be underscored. The Office of Fair Trading makes it clear that '...it is not intended that the prohibitions contained in the Competition Act and the retained...monopoly provisions in the Fair Trading Act should be used in parallel to investigate the same matter'.[10] The new Act is clearly seen as pre-eminent.

Secondly, there is the matter of timing, which, given the extensive scope of the Act, and the seriousness of the ultimate penalties, is obviously a crucial issue for business in general – whether in retail or otherwise. The Act provides for the coming into force of many of its provisions on appointed days, one of the reasons for the delaying of the coming into effect of the central prohibitions being the giving to business of time to prepare for compliance. Furthermore, the Act contains special transitional arrangements with respect to the prohibition of anti-competitive agreements[11] – although for the prohibition of abuse of a dominant position it was not thought that any special transitional provisions were needed, beyond, that was, with respect to the initial period prior to the prohibition's coming into effect.

The third (and broader) issue is raised by the modelling of the law on Articles 85 and 86, and relates to the degree to which the interpretation of its provisions will be influenced by the European jurisprudence. So, for instance, when the need arises for the UK competition authorities under the Chapter II prohibition to clarify the kinds of competitive activity to be deemed abusive and unlawful, to what extent will they adopt the broad pro-competitive approach of the European Court of Justice and condemn '...methods of competition which in practice could be exclusionary but which many critics would argue were 'normal' in competition situations'?[12] And on a similarly critical question, when considering the matters to be taken into account for the purpose of granting an exemption from the Chapter I prohibition, to what extent will the authorities follow those used for the purpose of giving exemptions under Article 85(3)?[13]

Although the Government did not envisage an identicality of approach, they believed that the '...objectives of effectiveness and minimum burden in operation...[would be]...best served by ensuring that the domestic prohibition [was] interpreted in such a way as to avoid inconsistency with the way Articles 85 and 86...are interpreted by the European Court'.[14] Accordingly, s 60 of the Act contains measures designed to ensure that, so far as is possible, questions relating to competition in the United Kingdom '...are dealt with in a manner which is consistent with the treatment of corresponding questions arising in Community law in relation to competition within the Community'.[15]

In consequence, as the Office of Fair Trading's guideline on 'The Major Provisions' advises:– 'The Act...places a dual obligation on the United Kingdom authorities in considering and dealing with the application of the Chapter I and Chapter II prohibitions. First, they must ensure that there is no inconsistency with either the principles laid down by the EC Treaty and the European Court or any relevant decision of the European Court. Secondly, the United Kingdom authorities must have regard to any relevant decision or statement of the European Commission...'[16]

It should be emphasised, however, that the search to ensure consistency is only (as s 60(1) puts it) 'so far as possible...having regard to any relevant differences between the provisions concerned...'. A note of caution is thus introduced, caution which may be prudent, for the EC provisions are infused with policies additional to the objective of promoting competition. A pivotal objective is, for instance, that of market integration, a goal which can conflict with that of competition, and the resulting tension between which may, in the view of one author, '...prove one of the principal difficulties in transferring [European] principles into UK law...'.[17] Similarly, a desire to protect the weaker of the parties to a bargain has coloured European thinking, and it has been asked whether the domestic law should share such a concern.[18] Indeed, the problem of the need for consistency of interpretation but of the extent of the materiality of the European jurisdiction may be basic, but perhaps still more basic is that of the very desirability of so closely mirroring the European law in the first place.[19]

The fourth matter is the need to keep in mind the distance which the reformers have put between the earlier law and the new. So, for instance, while the 'form based' Restrictive Trade Practices Act 1976 was apt to catch harmless agreements and at the same time could be avoided by cleverly drafted agreements, this issue is overcome by the new Act in that it is not concerned with the form of an agreement but with its effects upon competition. Again, whereas under the 'old' competition régime restrictive agreements needed to be challenged in court before their restrictions could be struck down,[20] and conduct abusive of a dominant position could only be halted after lengthy investigation, the new legislation works on the principle of the prohibition at the outset of the abuse of a dominant position and (unless benefiting from an exemption)[21] of anti-competitive agreements and concerted practices. And again, while the 'old' law was for long regarded as seriously deficient in sanctions, this situation is remedied by the creation of a system including provision for the imposition of heavy penalties on firms found to be in breach of the prohibitions.[22] And yet again, whereas grave inadequacies were perceived in the area of investigatory powers, those have been met with a set of significantly strengthening measures, amongst which is a power to enter premises, even, in some circumstances, unannounced.[23]

This distancing between the old and the new was recently highlighted by the Director General of Fair Trading in the context of certain secret price fixing activity which the Cartels Task Force had uncovered in a section of the car industry. Having accepted assurances about future behaviour, the Director General emphasised the weakness of the existing law (in the shape here of aspects of the Restrictive Practices Act 1976 and the Resale Prices Act 1976) and also emphasised the difference of the position which would pertain under the new law.[24] This, he explained, would provide him with considerably improved powers of investigation and the ability to order the immediate cessation of anti-competitive activities. 'Furthermore', he continued, 'I will be able to fine companies up to ten per cent of their UK turnover for infringement of the prohibition on price-fixing agreements'.[25]

For retailers (as for other sectors of business) the implications of the 1998 Act are indeed far-reaching and will surely extend the practice of the creation and implementation of 'compliance programmes'. Singleton in *Blackstone's Guide to the Competition Act 1998* speaks of the improvement wrought by the new law, but refers also to the 'rude awakening' which lies in wait for some. Further, in an article for the food sector entitled 'Brakes on Power', the author describes the change as 'radical', and as involving a cracking down on anti-competitive practices as never before, but points out that the Act is '...certainly not intended to inhibit the use of normal marketing techniques'.[26] It remains to say that it will obviously be some considerable time before any 'working picture' emerges and even longer before its operation can be in any way usefully assessed. (The great length of the list of guidelines issued by the Office of Fair Trading is evidence of the complexity of the reform. Particular mention may be made here of the guidelines entitled respectively 'The Major Provisions', 'The Chapter I Prohibition' and 'The Chapter II Prohibition'.)

Notes

1. The Act was given the Royal Assent on 9th November 1998.
2. While the present administration favoured wholesale overhaul (with the exception of mergers control) the predecessors had favoured reform of the restrictive trade practices legislation but only a strengthening of the law on monopolies and anti-competitive practices. The reform papers culminated with the Consultation Document entitled 'A prohibition approach to anti-competitive agreements and abuse of dominant position: draft Bill' DTI, August, 1997.
3. – *i.e.* under the Fair Trading Act 1973. Although the Secretary of State for Trade and Industry has spoken of the exploration of a reformed system, aimed at removing any political slant on the decision making process. (See *Hansard*, 10th March 1999, Column 369.)
4. The desire that only agreements *significantly* affecting competition should be caught is achieved obliquely. Article 85(1) of the Treaty of Rome is

interpreted in such a way as to require an *appreciable* effect on competition, and by s 60 the Act requires the prohibition it contains to be interpreted consistently therewith. (Further detail is given on 'appreciable effect' in the Office of Fair Trading's guideline on 'The Major Provisions', at paras 3.4 - 3.8.)

5. See s 6.
6. The Act also provides for exclusions.
7. See ss 21 and 22.
8. It is worthy of note that, with the exception of price fixing agreements, immunity from penalties is afforded 'small agreements' and 'conduct of minor significance'; see respectively ss 39 and 40.
9. In its latter rôle it will, of course, embrace mergers.
10. Office of Fair Trading guideline 'The Major Provisions', para. 13.3.
11. See Schedule 13. The arrangements are extremely intricate, though assistance is forthcoming from the guideline entitled 'Transitional Arrangements' published by the Office of Fair Trading. (In the context of transitional arrangements particular mention should be made of resale price maintenance. As has been noted, the Director General of Fair Trading has been granted leave to apply to the Restrictive Practices Court for a full reconsideration of the exemption Order under which resale price maintenance is lawful for 'over the counter' medicines. If, at the end of proceedings, it were held it should still remain lawful, the need would arise for the new prohibition to be disapplied for a period. Schedule 13 provides for such a situation.)
12. See Barry J. Rodger's Annotations to the Act in Current Law Statutes, where he notes that 'common types of exclusionary abuses include export bans, price discrimination, predatory pricing and refusals to supply'. (In the Office of Fair Trading's guideline 'The Chapter II Prohibition' there is considerable advice on what constitutes abuse of dominance, as too on dominance itself (see parts 3 and 4).)
13. It is of interest to add that in a commissioned study on the scope of the exemption criteria, in which the question was particularly raised as to whether environmental, health and social benefits were within the sphere of legitimate appraisal, the author (Whish) concluded that to a considerable extent environmental and social benefits were material circumstances. In *Competition Law*, 3rd Edn. Butterworths, the same author expresses the view that Article 85(3) 'is a very flexible provision' (see p. 228), whereas the structure of the Restrictive Trade Practices Act 1976 has actually been '...a disincentive to *beneficial* collaboration' (see p. 162).
14. The DTI's Consultation Document, August 1997, para. 1.3.
15. Section 60 is a 'key' section, which, it has been observed, '...takes EC law right into the heart of domestic legislation'. 'Has the UK Gone European: Is the European Approach to the Competition Bill more than an Illusion?' Frances Barr, [1998] ECLR 139 at p. 140.
16. Para. 6.2 of the guideline.

17. Barry J. Rodger – Annotations to the Act in Current Law Statutes.
18. See Whish, *Competition Law*, 3rd Edn. Butterworths, p. 735.
19. A letter written to *The Times* on 13th February 1998 by certain members of the European Business School who had served on the Monopolies and Mergers Commission questioned the wisdom of a shift in competition policy which involved the abolition of the 'public interest' as its 'cornerstone', and its replacement with 'interpretations of Articles 85 and 86 of the Treaty of Rome'. These authors were convinced '...that the principle of the public interest [had] been a shining beacon in the fog of competition policy', and that it should '...not be snuffed out'.
20. Though note that under the Resale Prices Act 1976, resale price maintenance agreements have been rendered void without a prior ruling.
21. – or unless excluded, see s 3.
22. – up to 10 per cent of UK turnover. (See s 36. The imposition of penalties is dependent upon the infringement being committed intentionally or negligently.) Further, in the context of sanctions, a particularly difficult problem was the protection of victims of anti-competitive activity during protracted investigations. This has been addressed by the provision of interim measures for the halting of abuse.
23. For years, the European Commission has had power to enter premises in the conducting of competition investigations; (power authorising so called 'dawn raids').
24. See the Office of Fair Trading Press Release PN 24/99, 9th July 1999, entitled 'Volvo involved in car pricing cartels'. The situation involved the pursuit by dealers of price-fixing and collusion therein by the UK manufacturer.
25. *Ibid.*
26. Richard Taylor, *The Grocer*, 5th December 1998. On the note of 'radical change' he points out that 'new provisions prohibiting abuse of market power will, unlike the corresponding EU rules, apply not only to firms with a national or international dimension but to any business which has a dominant position in a particular geographic market'. And he goes on to warn that '...a shop dominant in a region or town could be found to be abusing that position by conduct hitherto perfectly lawful'.

10 The European law

Introduction

Preliminaries

As has implicitly emerged from earlier chapters, the United Kingdom's membership of the European Community means that competition law has two branches. Proceeding alongside the national system, which is concerned with conduct distorting the national market, the competition régime of the Community is concerned with conduct affecting trade between member States. It has grown, over a comparatively short period, into a large and intricate body of law, and we can but note its leading features.

From its inception to the present day, the promotion of free competition has been one of the main pillars of the Community. The founding Treaty, the Treaty of Rome,[1] listed amongst tasks set for the furtherance of Community aims the institution of a system ensuring the prevention of the distortion of competition, and, with the integration of the European Community since greatly advanced and its objectives broadened, the Treaty in its current terms still speaks expressly of the institution of a system designed to this end.[2]

The fundamental nature of the impact of the system is revealed in the fact that its provisions are both 'directly applicable' and 'directly effective'. Because they are 'directly applicable', the Community enforcing authority can inquire into, and take action against, practices of UK firms which are in breach of them.[3] Because they are 'directly effective',[4] it means that they can be deployed in private litigation in this country's courts. So, for example, if the provisions are infringed, and the infringing conduct causes injury or loss, the injured person can seek damages or an injunction, doing so on the basis that the infringement constitutes a breach of statutory duty.[5]

When, as a result of the doctrine of 'direct effect', a national court which is engaged in the determination of private rights and duties becomes involved in the enforcement of Community competition laws, it shoulders a burdensome task. However, assistance is forthcoming in guidance which has been issued by the European Commission in a Notice. This is the 'Notice on Co-operation between National Courts and the Commission in Applying

Articles 85 and 86 of the EEC Treaty'.[6] Furthermore, it is worthy of mention that this guidance is of considerable importance, inasmuch as the authorities are keen to heighten the rôle of the national courts and themselves to concentrate on cases which are legally, politically or economically significant for the EC as a whole.

So far as problems of 'overlap' between the two régimes are concerned, it is naturally the case that where any two systems of law function side by side, the question inevitably arises of potential conflict. With the UK national law addressing the hindering of competition in the national market, and Community law dealing with activity affecting trade between member States, it might *prima facie* appear that there would be little room for a clash, but, because it is possible for purely domestic conduct to have a consequential impact on inter-state trade, situations can arise in which the jurisdiction may overlap, and hence a chance for conflict to emerge. Whereas the resolution of this aspect of the interface proceeds from the simple principle that in the event of conflict Community law prevails,[7] it is nevertheless a matter of on-going and particular complexity.

Lastly, by way of a further and equally brief preliminary point, it should be explained that there is an important respect in which the competition régime of the EC distinguishes itself from other such régimes. This concerns a special dimension in the application of the rules by the Community's competition authorities. They espouse the widely held view that competition has inherent worth inasmuch as it assures the benefits which flow from an unhindered vying for custom, but at the same time they have kept to the forefront of their thinking the Community's integrationary aim of creating a single market, and in consequence they have dealt especially vigorously with any such anti-competitive conduct as might tend to compartmentalisation.

Institutions involved

The EC Institutions include the Council of Ministers (the supreme legislative body); the Commission (the executive arm of the EC); the European Parliament (which has developed from a body of originally few powers to a rôle of increasing significance including powers of co-decision in many areas);[8] the European Court of Justice (whose purpose is to ensure the law in the Treaties is observed); and the Court of First Instance (which has jurisdiction in certain classes of case including competition matters).

In the working of the competition régime three of these institutions are principally involved. To the Commission of the EC is given the central rôle. Blessed with ample powers, there falls to it the tasks of '...developing competition policy, fact finding, taking action against infringement of the law, imposing penalties and granting exemptions'.[9] Responsible for ensuring the application of the competition provisions, its relevant procedures, duties and powers are set out in a Council Regulation.[10] From its decisions, appeals may be made to the Court of First Instance, and there is a right of appeal therefrom on certain specified grounds to the Court of Justice of the European Community.[11] (And as has been noted, in addition to these Community institutions, the national courts of this country also have a part to play).

Sources of Community competition law

The fundamental provisions are to be found in Articles 85 and 86 of the Treaty of Rome.[12] To Article 85 falls the task of dealing with agreements and concerted practices, while Article 86 deals with abuse of a dominant position. In addition to these basic provisions, however, heed has also to be paid to regulations promulgated by Community authorities, judgements and rulings of the European Court of Justice and the Court of First Instance, and decisions and notices issued by Community authorities.

The basic principles

Control over agreements and concerted practices: Article 85

Article 85(1) Article 85(1) is concerned with the distortion of competition by agreement. It prohibits, as being incompatible with the Common Market, all agreements between undertakings, decisions by associations of undertakings and concerted practices which may affect trade between member States and which have as their object or effect the prevention, restriction or distortion of competition within the common market. In particular, it prohibits those which *inter alia* fix purchase or selling prices; limit or control production; share markets or sources of supply; apply dissimilar conditions to equivalent transactions with other trading parties (placing them at a competitive disadvantage); and make the conclusion of contracts subject to the acceptance of supplementary, unconnected obligations.

In less than half a century, case law has cloaked this structure in elaborate and extensive attire. Of the innumerable matters which the provision has raised, we may note the following:–

The concept of an 'undertaking' (undefined by the Article) has been given the most flexible interpretation, to embrace the spectrum ranging from an individual at one end to a state-owned enterprise at the other. As was observed by the Commission in the *Polypropylene* case, the notion of an 'undertaking' could refer '...to any entity engaged in commercial activities',[13] and indeed, it does not matter that there is no profit motive.[14] Given the aims of the Article, it is no surprise, moreover, to find that the liberality of interpretation extends to the inclusion, to an extent, of non-EC based parties.[15] By contrast, however, if an agreement is formed between parties who have a close relationship (such as that between a parent company and its subsidiary where the latter enjoys no real freedom of action), then it is not caught by the Article, because the parties are regarded as an 'economic entity'.[16]

The understandable desire for wide interpretation is further revealed in the fact that the list of restrictive practices which follows the general words is not regarded as exhaustive, as also in the fact that the understanding of both 'agreements' and 'concerted practices' is broad. Regarding the former, 'agreements', the Article embraces not only legally enforceable agreements, but also informal, 'gentlemen's agreements'.[17] As to the latter, 'concerted practices', any form of co-operation which falls short of an agreement, lessens competition, and affects normal market conditions, is included,[18] and the firms under scrutiny need not have formulated any 'plan'. Businesses are not prohibited from taking into account the likely conduct of their competitors, but the view is that their strategies should be worked out independently.[19] Obviously, it is no easy task for the authorities to separate parallel conduct which is the result of collusion from that which is the consequence of the character of the market, and parallel conduct cannot necessarily raise a presumption of collusion if there are other reasonable explanations for it.

From the few observations so far made on Article 85(1), it will be seen that the controlling net is extensive – it is not, however, without some bounds. If the Article is to bite, the agreement must affect interstate trade, and have as its object or effect the prevention, restriction or distortion of competition within the common market.

Starting with the former (the need to affect interstate trade), the rules do not accordingly catch an agreement whose working is limited to one member State. On the other hand, the notion of the affecting of interstate trade is again given a very broad construction – and it is so given because of the Treaty's desire to challenge attempts at national isolation, and to create a single market by the encouragement of free movement of goods and services and the elimination of trade barriers.[20] In *Société Technique Minière v Maschinenbau Ulm*, the European Court of Justice provided a test for the defining of circumstances in which an agreement might be caught in terms that it had to be possible to foresee '...with a sufficient degree of probability...that [it might] have influence direct or indirect, actual or potential, on the pattern of trade between member States'.[21] So expansive an interpretation can capture agreements which *prima facie* one might imagine would not be covered, and so, for instance, may catch agreements which cover the entire territory of a member State '...because they tend to reinforce national boundaries and hinder the economic inter-penetration which the Treaty is designed to realise'.[22] As Whish observes, 'the fact that the parties to an agreement are from the same member State does not mean that there can be no effect on inter-state trade'.[23]

Turning to the latter, the need for an agreement to have as its object or effect the prevention, restriction or distortion of competition within the common market, we find an approach to interpretation which testifies to a keenness for wide application but which is also practical, and, furthermore, is one which reflects the twin aims of promoting competition for its inherent benefits and of creating a single market. Over the years, cases have covered the Article's phraseology with an elaborate gloss, but of its highlights we may note the following:–

First, as the *Technique Minière* case[24] makes clear, for an agreement to be caught, it does not have to have both the object and the effect of harming competition, and, as that case also explains, if an agreement does not have the object of restraining competition,[25] then a market analysis has to be undertaken to determine whether its effects are anti-competitive. In the enquiry into the economic context of the agreement there are taken into account such elements as the situation of the parties in the market, the nature and quantity of the products in question and whether the agreement is isolated or part of a network of agreements.[26]

Secondly, it has for long been established that the competition which the Article contemplates as being affected includes not only that between the parties to an agreement (and so embraces horizontal agreements) but also that between a party to an agreement and third parties (and so also covers vertical agreements).[27]

This fundamental fact was established by the early leading case of *Consten and Grundig*,[28] which concerned an agreement entered into between Grundig (a German manufacturer) and Consten (a French distributor). The agreement in question was one by means of which Grundig appointed Consten its exclusive distributor of radios and television sets in France, and further, was one of a series of such agreements through which Grundig established a distributor network in the various member States. Under the terms of the agreement between Grundig and Consten, the former undertook not to deliver goods of the kind in question to anyone in France other than the latter, and the latter undertook not to sell any competitor's products and not to re-export the products bought into any other member State. Further, Grundig undertook to ensure that its other distributors in the other member States be required to enter into similar undertakings to refrain from re-exporting the products which they respectively bought from Grundig. Thus, Consten (along with the other distributors) had conferred upon it absolute territorial protection from the competition of so called 'parallel imports'.[29] Moreover, this elaborate scheme of protection was fortified by the grant to Consten of the exclusive use in France of the Grundig trademark 'GINT'.

Despite the intricacy of the system, a French firm UNEF became able to import Grundig products into France and sold them at prices undercutting Consten. It also used the GINT mark. Various proceedings followed which had their seeds in a claim of 'unfair competition' being met by a contention that the restrictions in the distribution agreement infringed the Treaty of Rome. Ultimately it was concluded that inter-state trade was clearly affected, in that Consten might not export from France nor other firms import thereto, and that competition was plainly impeded in that the agreement furthered the artificial maintenance of separate markets. That the competition which the agreement harmed was that between one of the parties to the agreement and 'outside' firms did not matter, Article 85 was just as capable of catching such an agreement as one in which the competition harmed was that between the parties to the agreement themselves.[30]

The third point which needs to be made on the matter of the affecting of competition relates to the *significance* of the effect. If an agreement has no appreciable effect on competition Article 85(1) is not thereby infringed. The point was made early on in *Volk v Vervaecke*.[31] Here an agreement was made between a German manufacturer of washing machines and a Belgian distributor, the latter to be the exclusive distributor of the machines in Belgium and Luxembourg and to enjoy territorial protection. Inasmuch as the manufacturer had less than 0.5 per cent of the German market, the European Court of Justice concluded that the effect on competition was insignificant and that Article 85(1) was not contravened.[32]

The *Volk* case reflected an enduring desire to further co-operation between small and medium sized enterprises. This desire became enshrined in successive Notices issued by the Commission on 'Agreements of Minor Importance'. (Briefly, the thrust of these is (at present) to the effect that Article 85(1) is not normally infringed by agreements in which the aggregate market shares held by all the participants do not exceed, on any of the relevant markets, 5 per cent in the case of horizontal agreements and 10 per cent in the case of vertical agreements.)[33]

Article 85(2) If an agreement is prohibited by Article 85(1), then it is automatically (*i.e.* without further ado) made void by Article 85(2). Such, however, may not necessarily be its fate, inasmuch as the Treaty recognises the fact that an agreement with anti-competitive influences may nevertheless have outweighing, advantageous consequences. *Via* Article 85(3) provision is made for exemption from the basic prohibition to be granted in such circumstances, and to the fundamentals of that provision we turn next.

Article 85(3) Under the terms of Article 85(3), the prohibition contained in Article 85(1) can be declared inapplicable in the case of any

> ...agreement...decision...or...concerted practice which contributes to improving the production or distribution of goods or to promoting technical or economic progress, while allowing consumers a fair share of the resulting benefit, and which does not a) impose upon the undertakings concerned restrictions which are not indispensable to the attainment of these objectives, b) afford such undertakings the possibility of eliminating competition in respect of a substantial part of the products in question.

Article 85(3) thus contains four elements, two positive and two negative, all of which have to be satisfied if exemption is to be secured. It has, however, been observed that

> ...the provisions are drafted liberally and the Commission has not found it difficult to apply them in a way which promotes those types of agreement which it considers desirable... [It] has encouraged [*inter alia*] research and development, specialisation in production, licensing of intellectual property and know-how...and even crisis cartels.[34]

As may be imagined, Article 85(3) has spawned a considerable body of case law, and one or two instances must suffice. By way of illustration of the first requirement (*i.e.* contribution to the improvement of the production or distribution of goods or to the promotion of technical or economic progress), one may cite *Ford/Volkswagen*.[35] Here, improvement in production was perceived to flow from the pooling of resources facilitated by a certain joint venture in vehicle manufacture, and an exemption was granted. Similarly, reference may be made to the grant of exemption in *Re Vacuum Interrupters*,[36] where technical progress was seen to result from the research and development facilitated by a joint venture agreement in the manufacture of switchgear.

In the same context, we may note too the case of *Prym/Beka*,[37] where exemption was given to a specialisation agreement under which production arrangements led to a reduction in the price of needles. And equally well known is another comparatively early case, *Fine Papers*,[38] where a specialisation agreement enabled the participant manufacturers to cope with significant competition and the pressure of powerful buyers. Again, if we focus on distribution as distinct from production, we may note the exemption given in the famous *Transocean Marine Paint* case,[39] where a group of small and medium sized manufacturers of marine paint together established *inter alia* a global and streamlined distribution system, and so produced a situation in which '...the gain in international competition outweighed the reduction in competition between [them]'.[40]

From cases relating to the second requirement (*i.e.* that consumers be allowed a fair share of resultant benefit), two observations may be made which testify to a practicality of approach. First, 'consumers' are broadly defined to include not only ultimate purchasers but also persons acquiring goods in the course of a business,[41] and secondly, no effort is made precisely to pin down what constitutes 'fairness' for the purpose of 'fair share'.[42]

So far as the third requirement is concerned (*i.e.* that the agreement should contain no restrictions which are not indispensable to the attainment of the positive objectives), the need is to distinguish between restrictions which are necessary to such attainment and those which go further than is needed to secure them. So for instance in *Clima Chappée/Buderus*,[43] exemption was given to a specialisation and reciprocal exclusive supply agreement entered into by Clima Chappée and Buderus,[44] one of the grounds for its grant being that the agreement did not import any non-indispensable restrictions. If the prices of the product in question were not competitive, neither concern was obliged under the agreement to purchase them from the other.

Lastly, regarding the fourth requirement (*i.e.* that the agreement must not afford the undertakings involved the possibility of eliminating competition), it has been noted that '...[in] all the cases in which exemption has been granted, the parties have been subject to substantial inter-brand competition, whether from producers inside the common market or from outside'.[45] And the example is cited of *Re Vacuum Interrupters*,[46] in which the parties to the agreement were facing competition from both the Americans and the Japanese.

An important feature of the system is that the power to grant exemptions lies solely with the Commission. This is a situation which led to an unduly heavy workload accruing to that body, and, in consequence, to inevitable delays. One of the solutions to what became a very real problem was found in the establishment of a series of so called 'block exemptions', which would operate alongside the granting of individual exemptions.[47]

Block exemptions are created by Regulations, and embrace several categories of restrictive agreement which are generally considered to be advantageous and no real threat to the competitive process. The agreements are made valid without individual authorisation, the Regulations identifying '...the contractual obligations which fulfil the criteria set out in Article 85(3) and which are therefore entitled to the benefit of exemption'.[48] The Regulations are valuable not only for the lessening of the Commission's workload but also for the certainty which they afford business, and it has become widespread, standard practice to draft agreements so as to conform to the relevant Regulation. Should, though, the parties to an agreement wish to go further with their restrictions than the particular block exemption permits, then they lose its protection and, importantly, the protection is lost for the agreement as a whole.[49]

Of the categories of agreement involved in the block exemption régime, three have particular significance for retailing. These are exclusive distribution agreements, which are covered by Regulation 1983/83,[50] exclusive purchasing agreements, which are covered by Regulation 1984/83,[51] and franchising agreements, which are covered by Regulation 4087/88.[52] The Regulations exhibit a similar pattern in that *inter alia* they open with an explanation of the Commission's policy, move to a list of restrictions on competition which are 'permissible' and thus exempted (the so called 'white' list), and from there turn to a list of restrictions on competition which are 'prohibited' and the inclusion of which in an agreement will mean the loss of the advantage of exemption – (this last feature being known as the 'black list').

Let us take first the basics of the exemption of exclusive distribution agreements, *i.e.* of bipartite agreements for the supply of goods for resale, in which the one party undertakes not to supply in a defined area of the common market anyone other than the other party. Under Regulation 1983/83 permissible restrictions in addition to the principal restriction imposed upon the supplier include, for instance, an obligation upon him that he will not himself sell to users in the dealer's area, and upon the dealer that he will take all he needs of such goods only from the supplier, that he will not deal in competing goods, and that he will not actively seek out customers outside his area. However, the advantage of the Regulation would be lost if, as part of a policy of attempting to confer absolute territorial protection upon each of his dealers, a supplier tried to restrict a dealer not only from seeking actively to sell outside his allotted area, but also from making passive sales outwith his territory. In other words, if an effort were made to achieve for each dealer absolute territorial protection from parallel imports, the benefit of the protective umbrella would be forsaken.[53]

An exclusive distribution agreement has to be distinguished from an exclusive purchasing agreement. The idea of the latter is that the dealer agrees to secure his supplies only from the supplier who is the other party to the agreement, thus denying competitors of the supplier the opportunity of supplying the particular dealer in question. Unlike the case of exclusive distribution, the dealer is not afforded an exclusive territory. Regulation 1984/83, provides a block exemption for exclusive purchasing agreements by declaring Article 85(1) inapplicable to bipartite agreements under the terms of which the one party (the reseller) agrees with the other party (the supplier) to purchase certain goods only from that other. No restrictive obligation may be imposed upon the supplier other than one to refrain from distributing either contract or competing goods in the reseller's prime sales area, and no restrictive obligation may be imposed upon the reseller other than one not to manufacture or distribute goods which compete with the contract goods. The protection of the Regulation is not lost if the reseller agrees to restrictive terms including obligations to take complete ranges or minimum quantities of goods, but it is lost if, for instance, the agreement imports 'tying' terms, or is concluded for an indefinite duration, or for a period of more than five years. It should also be noted that the Regulation contains special provisions which cover exclusive purchasing agreements in the arenas of beer and petrol supplies.[54]

The third kind of agreement under discussion, franchise agreements, are those in which 'the franchisee pays for the right to use the franchisor's know-how in return for the right to sell goods or services according to a standard business format (or marketing style and premises)'.[55] The boundaries set by the relevant Regulation (4087/88) if a franchise agreement is to gain the benefit of block exemption are intricate. Very briefly, it contains a list of primary restrictions which may permissibly be placed on the franchisor (such as not to grant the right to exploit the franchise to others in the franchisee's area), and on the franchisee, (such as to exploit the franchise only on specified premises). It also contains a 'white list' of permitted ancillary restrictions, covering matters such as quality control, which may be inserted without sacrificing the exemption. Further, and by contrast, it provides a 'black list' of terms, such as terms imposing resale price maintenance or leading to territorial division, the inclusion of which results in the removal of the protective exemption.

Before leaving these sets of Regulations it should be added that in 1996 the European Commission issued a Green Paper on vertical restraints, in which observations were sought on what shape the legal control of them should take.[56] In due course, a Communication was adopted and circulated containing proposals for a new régime.[57] These Regulations therefore have to be approached against a background of future change.

So much, then, for the essence of Article 85; we turn now to Article 86.

Control of the abuse of a dominant position: Article 86

While Article 85 is concerned with the distortion of competition by means of concerted activity, Article 86 deals with its distortion *via* concentrated economic power. It prohibits, as being incompatible with the common market in so far as it may affect trade between member States, any abuse of a dominant position by one or more undertakings. In particular, it says, abuse may consist in *inter alia* imposing unfair prices or trading conditions, limiting production, markets or technical development, applying dissimilar conditions to equivalent transactions, and making the conclusion of contracts subject to acceptance by the other parties of unconnected supplementary obligations.

Certain basic, significant points may at once be made. First, the particular matters listed are not exhaustive. Secondly, a condition for the applicability of the Article is the affecting of inter-state trade, so that if an abuse impinges only within a single member State, there is no violation of the prohibition.[58] Thirdly, the law is concerned to challenge not the dominant position in itself, but the abuse of that position.

These preliminary points made, we have now to consider the concepts of 'dominance' and of 'abuse'.

In *United Brands v Commission* 'dominance' was understood to be a

> ...position of economic strength enjoyed by an undertaking which enables it to prevent effective competition being maintained on the relevant market by giving it the power to behave to an appreciable effect independently of its competitors and ultimately of its consumers.[59]

This is a much used definition, and so succinct as perhaps to belie the fact that the establishment, in any given instance, of whether or not a firm occupies a dominant position on a particular market, is not an easy process.

Because dominance cannot exist in a vacuum, the very first need is precisely to identify the market, and in this exercise three aspects may be involved. The 'product market' has to be identified – the general idea here being 'substitutability', *i.e.* if one product can be directly substituted for another they belong to the same market.[60] The 'geographical market' also requires definition, it being necessary, in deciding whether a firm has market power, to consider the extent of its area of operation to see with which other firms it is competing.[61] And it can be that 'temporal elements' are germane, with the need arising to consider the market from the angle of the impact on competition of periodic variations in conditions.[62]

With the object of providing guidance as to how the concept of the relevant product and geographical market is applied in the enforcement of Community competition law, the Commission issued in 1997 a Notice on the Definition of the Relevant Market.[63] In the Notice it is explained that the main purpose of market definition is to identify in a systematic fashion the competitive constraints which the undertakings involved encounter.

Once the initial issues of the relevant markets in terms of product, geography and time have been established, the next question is then to see whether the firm which is the subject of challenge is *indeed* dominant within it. This in itself is a complex matter, and involves consideration of issues including the market share of the undertaking itself,[64] the market shares of its competitors, what access it enjoys to financial and technical resources, what barriers to entry there are, and what countervailing power exists.

Once the actual existence of dominance has been detected, then the next step is to consider whether that dominance has been abused, for, as noted, it is with abuse and not with the dominant position *per se* that the Article is concerned. As to what may constitute abuse, we have seen that Article 86 itself provides instances (*i.e.* the charging of unfair prices, and the limitation of production, *etc.*), but in fact it embraces an array of exploitative and/or anti-competitive kinds of conduct. It has been used, for example, to challenge the imposition of unfair trading terms, discrimination and refusals to supply.[65] It has extended, too, to 'requirements contracts',[66] and predatory pricing.[67] And, as might well be imagined, it has been exercised in relation to import and export bans.[68]

Upon the impact of Article 86 an interesting question has arisen as to whether it might be used to control the conduct of independent undertakings and so regulate oligopolies. Whereas for a long time it had been thought the Article was not an apt tool for this purpose, doubt was cast a few years ago upon this negative view in the famous case of *Re Italian Flat Glass*.[69]

To conclude this thumbnail sketch of Article 86, an important dissimilarity from Article 85 must be noted. Unlike with anti-competitive agreements, there is no provision for the seeking for, and granting of, an exemption from the Article's impact.

Taken together, the measures of Article 86 governing abuse of dominance and those of Article 85 governing cartels provide the two fundamental pillars of EC antitrust. Mergers are controlled by means of a separate régime of which mention has already been made and to which further attention will be paid shortly. But first, a note is needed on the enforcement of Articles 85 and 86.

Articles 85 and 86: enforcement

Introduction By way of introduction to this topic, two preliminary observations must be made, the first regarding the prominent position of the Commission, the second regarding the base line from which the enforcement machinery proceeds.

First, as to the prominence of the Commission:- While Article 89 of the Treaty clothes the Commission with the general responsibility for administering the Competition rules, Regulation 17[70] sets out at length its powers, duties and responsibilities, and the briefest summary of their extent underscores the fact that the Commission has the central enforcement rôle. It is able to investigate agreements and practices, to direct the termination of those which contravene the rules, and to impose fines for breaches of the rules. Further, it can declare that agreements and practices do not fall within either Article 85(1) or Article 86, and can grant exemptions to individual agreements or classes of agreement under Article 85(3).

Secondly, as to the basis of the machinery:- It has been seen that Article 85 prohibits concerted anti-competitive activities, rendering them 'absolutely void', and that Article 86 prohibits abuse of dominance. This situation is re-affirmed by the fundamental Article of Regulation 17 (Article 1) which states that concerted anti-competitive activity and abuse of dominance is prohibited, and further, makes clear that the prohibition is automatic in that no prior decision to that effect is required. Even so, compliance with the Articles is a matter which needs ensuring, and Regulation 17 provides the necessary machinery. Very briefly, we may consider it under three headings – investigation and termination of infringements, (so called) 'negative clearance', and exemptions.

Investigation and termination of infringements Along with the power given to the Commission to apply Articles 85 and 86[71] comes, of course, the need to acquire information. This need may arise in the context of investigating suspected infringements of the prohibitions, or in the contexts (shortly to be discussed) of determining whether any particular activities fall outside Articles 85 and 86, or whether, though they fall inside Article 85, they merit exemption.

To meet this need Regulation 17 bestows extensive powers upon the Commission. It is able to request and ultimately require all necessary information,[72] and in the pursuit thereof it is empowered *inter alia* to enter premises and carry out 'on the spot' inquiries.[73]

Investigation of suspected infringements can be carried out either upon the initiative of the Commission or upon applications made to it,[74] and if an infringement is found to exist two routes are available. Either the Commission can make informal recommendations as to termination or, by formal decision, can require termination.[75] Furthermore, under Article 15 of the Regulation the Commission is given power to impose upon undertakings very steep fines, a power which has been used 'to the full'.[76]

'Negative clearance' By Article 2 of the Regulation provision is made for undertakings to seek from the Commission certification that, on the basis of facts in its possession, there are no grounds under Articles 85 and 86 of the Treaty for action to be taken in respect of particular conduct. Such certification is known as 'negative clearance'. In fact, the Commission is not bound thereby, but, given the fact that it is not always clear whether any particular conduct is caught or not, and the further fact of the heavy penalties for infringement, it is a useful procedure.[77]

Exemptions Mention has already been made of the fact that Article 85, though not 86, makes provision for exemption from its prohibitions, and that the sole power to grant exemptions resides with the Commission.[78] Unlike a 'negative clearance' which, as seen, does not bind, an exemption is valid for a specified period and indeed, is susceptible of renewal.[79]

Subject to certain and increasingly important exceptions, if an undertaking seeks an individual exemption, it must formally notify the Commission,[80] and notification for exemption is usually accompanied by a request for 'negative clearance'. It should be explained that, unlike the position which has pertained under the Restrictive Trade Practices Act 1976, there is no basic *duty* to notify agreements to the Commission, but there are certain incentives so to do. In addition to the point just noted (*i.e.* that, subject to certain and increasingly important exceptions, only a notified agreement qualifies for exemption), there is also the fact that if an agreement has been notified, should it then fail eventually to gain an individual exemption, the parties to it gain an immunity from the imposition of fines.[81] (It should be pointed out, however, that other than in the case of certain 'old' agreements, if a notified agreement fails to merit exemption and is thus caught by the prohibition its notification will not have conferred upon it provisional validity during the notification period.)[82]

To conclude the matter of dispensations reference may be briefly made to what are known as 'comfort letters'. Because of the considerable analysis required, scarcity of resources and heavy workloads, negative clearance or exemption can take a very long time. Amongst the short cuts devised is the 'comfort letter'. As Steiner and Woods explain, these '...may be issued giving soft clearance or exemption, after only brief investigation and enquiry, following which the Commission will close the file'.[83] Again, however, as these authors observe, while the process has afforded parties a measure of security and served to reduce a backlog, '...they have been criticised as lacking the essential safeguards of the prescribed procedures'.[84]

So, with this brief glimpse of the machinery we move on from cartels and abuse of dominance, and turn to mergers.

Merger control

After a long period of gestation, and the emergence of the limited and imperfect utility of Articles 85 and 86 as means of challenging mergers,[85] there arrived (as has been intimated) a specific instrument of control in the shape of the Merger Regulation.[86]

It has been noted that the intention of the Regulation is to regulate only those concentrations which have 'a Community dimension', and that the criteria by reference to which that crucial quality is determined set very high quantitive thresholds. Thus, Article 1(2) of the Regulation provides that a concentration has a Community dimension where:

(a) the aggregate world-wide turnover of all the undertakings concerned is more that 5,000mn ECUs and (b) the aggregate Community-wide turnover of each of at least two of the undertakings concerned is more than 250mn ECUs...

And the article further constrains the concept of a concentration having a 'Community dimension', by adding '...unless each of the undertakings concerned achieves more than two thirds of its aggregate Community-wide turnover within one and the same member State'.[87]

It will be appreciated that with so circumscribed a set of criteria relatively few concentrations will be caught, and if one falls below the 'Community threshold' then, generally speaking, it falls for investigation by the relevant domestic authorities. A concentration caught by the Regulation has to be formally notified to the Commission,[88] and those involved may be fined for failure to notify.[89]

Under Article 2(1) of the Regulation a concentration falling within the Regulation's scope is appraised with a view to establishing whether or not it is compatible with the common market. Article 2(2) provides that a concentration which does not create or strengthen a dominant position as a result of which competition would be significantly impeded in the common market or in a substantial part of it shall be declared compatible with the common market. By contrast Article 2(3) provides that a concentration which does so impinge is to be declared incompatible therewith.[90] Again, the same Article requires the Commission, in making the appraisal, to take into account matters including the need to maintain and develop effective competition,[91] the market position of the undertakings involved, alternatives available to suppliers and users, barriers to entry, the interests of consumers and the development of technical and economic progress.[92]

At the heart of the régime, and in the interests of certainty and clarity for business, is the principle of 'one-stop merger control'. This principle enshrines the idea that mergers with a Community dimension shall be investigated only by the Commission, and mergers lacking such a dimension shall be investigated only (if at all) by the relevant national authorities. To this end, Article 21(1) provides that only the Commission may take decisions regarding mergers having a Community dimension, and Article 21(2) complements this rule by refusing any member State the ability to apply to such concentrations any national competition law.

The singularity of purpose behind the 'one-stop' system has not, however, met with entire success. Certain concerns of member States dictated otherwise. For instance, they feared that a concentration with a

Community dimension might be acceptable at Community level and yet even so be harmful at the domestic level. Article 9 allayed this fear by providing a means whereby the Commission can be requested to take action, or to allow domestic action, where competition conditions are threatened within a 'distinct market' in a member State.[93] And conversely, Article 22(3) provides a mechanism whereby a member State can request the Commission to investigate a concentration, even though it does not have a Community dimension, if it would create or strengthen a dominant position and impede competition within the territory of the State.[94]

The examination of a concentration takes place in two phases. In the initial, one month phase, the Commission considers whether serious doubts are raised as to compatibility with the common market. If it is concluded that they are indeed so raised, then the procedure is extended into a second phase, in-depth investigation, lasting a further four months or so whereupon the Commission may either clear the deal (often subject to conditions) or prohibit it.

Lastly, on the subject of mergers, it should be noted that aspects of the régime, in particular the 'thresholds' in Article 1 of the Regulation, became the subject of a Review, and the scope of the 'Community dimension' concept saw some amendment. In order to meet the problem where certain mergers with significant cross-border effect but without a 'Community dimension' had to be notified to numerous member States, a further combination of criteria was added to those by reference to which the existence or not of a 'Community dimension' is determined. The addition was made to simplify the task of notification in such cases, and in furtherance of the 'one-stop' principle.[95]

The impairment of free trade by administrative controls

Before we leave the EC component a *caveat* is in order. The theme of this book being the impact of competition and planning law on retailing, and this Part of the work being devoted to the former, we have concentrated (in the EC context) on Articles 85 and 86 and the Merger Regulation. It should not be thought, however, that these measures alone constitute the Community's effort to further free trade, for such is far from the truth. Reference must also be made, for instance, to Articles 30 to 36 of the Treaty which are designed to further the free movement of goods throughout the common market.[96] While Articles 85 and 86 and the Merger Regulation deal with the anti-competitive activity of private undertakings and are strictly 'competition measures', Articles 30 to 36 form the other side of the coin in that they are concerned to regulate 'administrative controls' which can preclude or hamper access to a particular market. Such 'administrative controls' cover an enormous trading and marketing spectrum, and include, for instance, licensing controls and the regulation of standards.

Of the relevant Articles, Article 30 carries the principal burden, prohibiting quantitative restrictions and all measures having equivalent effect on imports.[97] Over the years, this Article has spawned a body of jurisprudence which is both extensive and of central importance to the Community. While its exploration is not within the scope of this book, certain fundamental matters may be briefly addressed.[98]

To begin with, it should be noted that a broad interpretation has been given to the notion contained in the Article of 'measures having equivalent effect'. The concept has been construed so as to apply not just to national measures which apply only to imports and so are overtly protective of the domestic market, but also to measures (such as for instance standards regulation) which apply alike to imports *and* domestic goods. While the former are known as 'distinctly applicable measures', the latter are described as 'indistinctly applicable measures', and the reason for the inclusion of the latter is that such measures, while their imposition may not have carried any protectionist intent, may nevertheless result in the exclusion of goods from a market or the making of access thereto more burdensome. As will be appreciated, the taking of so broad an approach to the interpretation of the clutch of Article 30 has greatly contributed to the furtherance of the cause of market integration.[99]

The wide scope afforded to Article 30 by virtue of construction is, however, in a certain sense offset by the further fact that its ambit has been constrained (in the context at least of its coverage of indistinctly applicable measures) through the introduction of a so called 'rule of reason'. In the seminal *Cassis de Dijon* case, the European Court of Justice established two fundamental principles of interpretation, the first of which gained the 'rule of reason' appellation. Under this principle, national restrictive measures should be acceptable in so far as they might be recognised as necessary to satisfy '...mandatory requirements relating in particular to the effectiveness of fiscal supervision, the protection of public health, the fairness of commercial transactions and the defence of the consumer'.[100]

In this case the European Court of Justice was called upon to consider whether a German national measure requiring certain spirits to have a minimum alcohol content of 25 per cent (an 'indistinctly applicable measure') was or was not prohibited by Article 30. While it could be contended that the law sought both to promote public health and to further fair trade, the view was taken that such ends could be achieved by more proportionate, less hampering means (such as labelling) and hence the measure was not 'necessary' to satisfy those requirements.

Although the prohibition in Article 30 is addressed primarily to member States, resort has frequently been had to it as a means of defence by persons prosecuted for breach of national provisions relating to trade. In this context, the Article achieved a considerable prominence in this country in a series of cases arising out of the Shops Act 1950, prior to the reforms wrought by the Sunday Trading Act 1994 and the Deregulation and Contracting Out Act 1994. To the forefront of the series was *Torfaen Borough Council v B & Q plc.*[101]

Here, B & Q (a DIY retailer) was prosecuted for trading on a Sunday in contravention of the provisions of the Shops Act 1950. The company argued that 10 per cent of its goods were sourced from other member States of the EC, that the Shops Act limited its sales and hence its importing, that the provisions in the Act thus amounted to a restriction on imports, that they were accordingly prohibited by Article 30, that Article 30 had direct effect in the UK, and that it (the company) could not be convicted of an offence under national provisions which were incompatible therewith.

To enable the reaching of a decision on the matter the magistrates hearing the case sought a preliminary ruling from the European Court of Justice.[102] The Court held that the measures in the Shops Act were *prima facie* contrary to Article 30, but that, even so, they might be recognised as measures satisfying mandatory requirements relating to the protection of national or regional socio-cultural characteristics, *i.e.* that they were to ensure the ordering of working hours in accordance therewith. However, in order to be justified, the measures had also to be no more than was necessary to satisfy such requirements, *i.e.* not to be excessive means to their end, and the magistrates were directed to examine the provisions to decide whether or not they were in that sense, 'proportionate'.

The upshot was that it was for the national courts ultimately to decide whether the provisions of the Shops Act were indeed 'proportionate', and subsequent case law was to reveal just how difficult was the task. According to the view reached as to the ends intended to be served by the provisions, so the provisions might or might not be considered excessive and 'disproportionate'.[103] Eventually, the European Court of Justice itself held that the Sunday trading provisions were not disproportionate to the purpose which they sought to meet.[104]

For the retailers challenged in the 'Sunday trading' cases, Article 30 would not have appeared as a particularly obvious refuge. Indistinctly applicable measures limiting opening days would not have seemed *readily* to lend themselves to characterisation as measures having an equivalent effect to a quantitative restriction on imports, as would by contrast, for instance, the rule as to alcohol level in the *Cassis de Dijon*[105] case or (as in the equally famous *Dassonville* case)[106] a requirement that goods bearing a designation of origin be accompanied by a certificate of entitlement thereto. But Article 30 was to be deployed by traders as a 'Euro-defence' across a broad span of charges, and the increase in the practice was followed by different approaches being made by the European Court of Justice to the subject. Thus, for instance, in *Keck and Mithuard*[107] which involved the legality of a French provision outlawing below cost selling, the Court decided to distinguish between rules 'setting requirements' for goods (such as regarding composition, weight, labelling, *etc.*) and rules concerning 'selling arrangements'. For the former (*i.e.* rules setting requirements to be met), it was explained that the position remained thus:– They might escape the prohibition on measures with equivalent effect to restrictions on quantities if they met the first principle in *Cassis* (*i.e.* they fulfilled mandatory requirements on matters such as public health or fair trade and were not 'disproportionate'). Regarding the latter (*i.e.* rules concerning selling arrangements), however, the position was thence changed, as follows:– Provided they affected in the same manner the marketing of domestic products and of those from other member States, and provided they applied to all affected traders within the national territory, such rules were to be regarded as falling outside the sphere of Article 30 in the first place, and without resort to the 'rule of reason'.

Some little while later, in the *DIP SpA* case,[108] the Court again came to the view that a certain national law altogether lay outside the prohibition contained in Article 30, but the Court arrived at its destination by another route. In this instance, the Court had to consider whether an Italian law requiring new development in certain areas to be licensed was caught by the Article 30 prohibition or was in conformity with Community law. Examining what the effects were of this licensing requirement, the line was taken that its consequences were 'too uncertain and too indirect' for the conclusion to be drawn that it hampered trade between member States, and that accordingly it did not fall foul of Article 30.

With the reference to the *DIP SpA* case immediately above we conclude this *excurcus*. Though necessarily brief, its relevance will be apparent and the reader may wish to pursue the subject further. In our context it remains to reiterate the importance of noting that in no sense is it solely in the sphere of acts or agreements of private undertakings that the Community's influence over the retail environment is exerted.

Notes

1. – establishing the European Economic Community in 1957. The United Kingdom became a member in 1973.
2. The original aims of the EEC, as articulated in the Treaty of Rome, included (*via* the establishment *inter alia* of a common market) such *desiderata* as harmonious economic development, expansion and increased stability. To these ends the Community set itself tasks including, in addition to the preservation of competition, the elimination of customs duties and of quantitative restrictions on imports and exports, and the abolition of obstacles to the free movement of goods, persons, services and capital. Now, many years on, with the purpose of the Community having both widened and deepened, the amended Treaty of Rome articulates a yet greater vision. According to its terms, the EC also aspires, *via, inter alia,* the establishment of a common market and an economic and monetary union, to goals which include high levels of employment, economic and social cohesion, and respect for the environment. To these ends the Community sets itself revised and extended activities including an internal market, consumer protection, and the promotion of research and technological development, but even so, there still remains high on the list the preservation of competition.
3. It may be observed here that the sanctions are onerous.
4. See *Belgische Radio en Televisie, (BRT) v Société Belge des Auteurs, Compositeurs, et Editeurs (SABAM)* Case 127/73 [1974] 2 CMLR 238.
5. See *Garden Cottage Foods v Milk Marketing Board* [1984] AC 130. It may be noted that the doctrine of 'direct effects' may lead not only to the utilisation of the competition provisions as a cause of action, but also as a defence.
6. [1993] OJ C39/6.
7. See Case 106/77 *Amministrazione delle Finanze dello Stato v Simmenthal* [1978] ECR 629; Case C-213/89 *R v Secretary of State for Transport, ex p Factortame Ltd (nos. 2 & 3)* [1990] 3 CMLR 1, [1991] 1 AC 603; Case C-221/89 *R v Secretary of State ex parte Factortame Ltd (nos. 2 & 3)* [1991] 3 CMLR 589, [1992] 1 QB 680.
8. See Article 189 (Article 249 Treaty on European Union).
9. Whish *Competition Law*, 3rd Edn. Butterworths, p. 32. The criticism has been made that this formidable body acts as '...a policeman, prosecutor, judge and jury...'. (*Ibid.* p. 286). Though for an acclamatory approach to its efforts see 'European Competition Policy - Keeping the Playing-Field Level', Sir Leon Brittan, Brassey's (UK) for CEPS (1992)

10. Regulation 17/62. (JO 1959 - 62/87)
11. In all cases, it is possible for the Court of Justice to review the decisions of the Court of First Instance on points of law. Furthermore, the Court of Justice may also hear references on points of law made to it by national courts. Article 177 of the Treaty gives the Court jurisdiction to provide preliminary rulings on *inter alia* the interpretation of the Treaty.
12. Though, as earlier noted, the Treaty on European Union has necessitated a re-numbering exercise from which they have emerged as Articles 81 and 82, throughout this text the 'old' numbers have been retained.
13. [1988] 4 CMLR 347 para. 99.
14. *P and I Clubs* OJ [1985] L 376/2.
15. *Ahlstrom v Commission (Wood Pulp)* [1988] ECR 5193. (The jurisdiction extended only over parties who operated or implemented their agreement within the EC.)
16. See, for instance, *Re Kodak* [1970] CMLR D19.
17. *Re Quinine Cartel* [1969] CMLR D41.
18. *ICI v Commission* [1972] ECR 619 (The 'dyestuffs' case).
19. *Suiker Unie v Commission* [1975] ECR 1663 (The 'sugar cartel').
20. In the light of these aims, plain candidates for the clutch of Article 85(1) are agreements which restrict exports between member States and confer geographical exclusivity upon distributors in the various states.
21. [1966] ECR 235, 249 and 251.
22. *Chitty on Contracts*, vol. II, (27th Edn. Sweet & Maxwell), para. 40-302. See *Cementhandelaren v Commission* [1972] ECR 977, 991.
23. *Competition Law* (3rd Edn. Butterworths) p. 218.
24. *Supra.*
25. Horizontal agreements involving price fixing or market sharing of their very character have an anti-competitive object, as do similar vertical agreements which contain prohibitions on exporting.
26. See, for example, *Brasserie De Haecht v Wilkin* [1967] ECR 407 and *De Limitis v Henniger Bräu* [1991] 1 ECR 935.
27. In the context of the application of Article 85 commonly met agreements of the horizontal kind include price fixing, geographical market sharing and quota schemes, and of the vertical kind include exclusive distribution, exclusive purchasing and selective distribution.
28. *Consten and Grundig v Commission* [1966] ECR 299.
29. The simple phrase 'parallel imports' is commonly used to describe the practice of traders other than the concessionaire independently importing goods of the variety which are the subject of the exclusive distribution agreement and selling them alongside (or in parallel with) the concessionaire. Protection from such imports would obviously provide a concessionaire with a high degree of advantageous exclusivity, and also reflect the supplier's desire to keep out of one market goods he might have circulating in another. The mutual benefit stems, of course, from the conferment of greater freedom in the prices which can be charged.

30. Since the 'landmark' case of *Consten v Grundig* numerous efforts to prevent 'parallel imports' have fallen foul of Article 85(1): absolute territorial protection, with its capacity to fragment the market, would necessarily become a particular target for challenge by EC competition law.
31. [1969] CMLR 273.
32. – the effect on inter-state trade was likewise insignificant.
33. [1997] OJ C372/1. The applicability of Article 85(1) cannot be ruled out with regard to horizontal agreements involving *inter alia* price fixing or market sharing or to vertical agreements involving resale price maintenance or conferring territorial protection.
34. Whish, *Competition Law*, 3rd Edn. p. 235.
35. [1993] 5 CMLR 617.
36. [1977] 1 CMLR D67.
37. *Re William Prym-Werke KG and Beka Agreement* [1973] CMLR D250.
38. *Agreement of Papeteries Bollore SA and Branstein Frères SA* [1972] CMLR D94.
39. *Transocean Marine Paint Association* [1967] CMLR D9.
40. *Law of the European Union*, Penelope Kent, (2nd Edn. M & E Pitman Publishing) p. 188.
41. See *Re ACEC/Berliet Agreements* [1968] CMLR D35.
42. By way of an instance of the working of the requirement, we may take *Re VBBB and VBVB Agreement* [1982] 2 CMLR 344, [1985] 1 CMLR 27, in which a resale price maintenance agreement was considered not to allow a fair share, in that it denied consumers choice and the chance of finding lower prices.
43. [1970] CMLR D7.
44. These companies manufactured air-conditioning, ventilation and central heating equipment.
45. *Textbook on EC Law*, Josephine Steiner and Lorna Woods, (6th Edn. Blackstone Press Ltd) p. 219.
46. [1977] 1 CMLR D67.
47. Another possible way round the difficulty was to emerge from the way in which the European Court of Justice has on a number of occasions and over a lengthy period taken the view that in certain circumstances restrictions fall outside Article 85(1) *altogether*. So for instance in the leading case of *Metro SB - Grossmärkte v Commission* [1977] ECR 1875, [1978] 2 CMLR 1, it was held that a selective distribution system might escape the clutch of the Article if dealers were chosen in a non-discriminatory fashion according to objective criteria. And in *Delimitis v Henninger Bräu AG* [1991] ECR I–935, [1992] 5 CMLR 1 the court took the line that a certain exclusive purchasing undertaking would only be caught by the Article if it contributed to the intensification of any access difficulty already experienced by competitors.
48. *Chitty on Contracts*, vol. II, 27th Edn. para. 40-304.

49. If in agreement there are restrictions outside the protection of the relevant Regulation, it can still be granted an individual exemption.
50. OJ L173/1.
51. OJ L173/5.
52. OJ L359/46.
53. Whish observes (in *Competition Law*, 3rd Edn. p. 573) that the Commission is determined '...to ensure that exclusive agreements do not totally eliminate intra-brand competition'. Accordingly, the '...exclusivity permitted under the block exemption is a qualified exclusivity', and there '...must always be the possibility of parallel importing of the contract goods...'.
54. Titles II and III.
55. *Law of the European Union*, Penelope Kent, 2nd Edn. p. 190.
56. 'Green Paper on Vertical Restraints in EC Competition Policy' [1997] 4 CMLR 519.
57. 'Communication on the application of the Community competition rules to vertical restraints' [1998] OJ C365/3 [1999] 4 CMLR 281.
58. See, for example, *Hugin v Commission* [1979] 3 CMLR 345.
59. *United Brands v Commission* Case 27/76, [1978] 1 CMLR 429.
60. So, for example, in the *United Brands* case, bananas were deemed to form a distinct market by virtue of their particular suitability for children and the infirm, and their continuous availability.
61. In *United Brands* it was explained that competition opportunities had to be considered

    > ...with reference to a clearly defined geographical area in which (the product) is marketed and where the conditions are sufficiently homogenous for the effect of the economic power of the undertaking concerned to be able to be evaluated.

62. In *United Brands*, despite argument to the contrary, only one temporal market was identified.
63. OJ [1997] C 372/3.
64. This is a key issue and a starting point. While a very large share may evidence dominance, it does not inevitably lead to that conclusion.
65. All these three activities were revealed in the leading *United Brands* case. Particular mention must be made of refusals to supply, which raise sensitive issues about commercial freedom, and which arise in different contexts so far as competition law is concerned. One such context is selective distribution, *i.e.* the adoption of systems in which a producer seeks to ensure that his goods reach the consumer only through limited outlets, thus involving a denial of supplies to unfavoured retailers. Such systems may find themselves the subject of attention under both Article 85 and 86 of the Treaty, as was the case in *Metro v Commission (No 2)*, (Case 75/84 [1986] ECR 3021, [1987] 1 CMLR 118). Metro, unable to gain access to SABA products, had resort *inter alia* to Article 86, but was unable to establish that SABA was dominant, the latter having less than a 10 per cent share of what was a competitive market for colour television sets.

66. See *e.g. Hoffman - La Roche & Co. AG v Commission* (case 85/76) [1979] 3 CMLR 211.
67. See *e.g. AKZO v Commission* [1993] 5 CMLR 215.
68. See *e.g. Suiker Unie v Commission* [1976] 1 CMLR 295.
69. [1992] 5 CMLR 302. Furthermore, while *Italian Flat Glass* was a Court of First Instance case, it appears from the *IJM* case that the European Court of Justice is also prepared to have resort to the notion that collective dominance can be the subject of Article 86; (see *Gemeente Almelo and others v Energiebedrijt Ijsselmij NV* Case C-392/92 [1994] ECR I-1477).
70. Council Regulation 17/62.
71. Given by Article 9 of the Regulation.
72. See Article 11.
73. See Article 14.
74. See Article 3.
75. See Article 3. (Before taking a formal 'decision', the Commission must give to those concerned opportunity to be heard – and may hear other interested persons. See Article 19.)
76. See further re sanctions, Steiner and Woods *Textbook on EC Law* (6th Edn. Blackstone) pp. 250-253.
77. In this context, it is worthwhile to refer also to the way in which the Commission has issued 'Notices' in relation to various categories of concerted activity, such as its 'Notice on Agreements of Minor Importance' ([1997] OJ C 372/1). Operating as (so to speak) 'bloc' negative clearance, they are not binding but act as helpful guides to practices which in the Commission's view do not infringe the Competition provisions.
78. See Article 9 of Regulation 17.
79. *Ibid.* Article 8.
80. It has long been the position that, under Article 4(2) of Regulation 17, a limited class of agreements perceived to be 'less harmful' have not had to be notified to qualify for exemption. However, as part of an on-going exercise to reform the treatment of vertical restraints, this measure has been considerably extended. (See Council Regulation 1216/99, replacing the relevant provision in Regulation 17.)
81. See Regulation 17, Article 15(5).
82. See *Brasserie de Haecht v Wilkin (No 2)* (Case 48/72) [1973] CMLR 287.
83. *Textbook on EC Law* (6th Edn. Blackstone), p. 246.
84. *Ibid.*
85. See, for example, *Continental Can v Commission* [1973] CMLR 199, and *BAT & Reynolds v Commission* [1988] 4 CMLR 24.
86. Regulation 4064/89 OJ [1989] L 395/1, which came into force in 1990.
87. The reader may find of interest two relatively new Commission Notices on the interpretation of 'concentration' and calculation of turnover. They are, respectively, OJ 98/C 66/02 p. 5 and OJ 98/C 66/04 p. 25.
88. See Article 4.
89. See Article 14.

90. In providing a test of compatibility with the common market which involves the question of whether or not the merger creates or intensifies a dominant position, a further important question has arisen as to whether or not this provision extended to the creation of oligopolistic dominance. In the view of the Commission in *Nestlé/Perrier* ([1992] OJ L 356/1, [1993] 4 CMLR M17) the provision does so extend.
91. See Article 2(1)(a).
92. See Article 2(1)(b).
93. Article 9 (the so called 'German clause') is for exceptional cases, and was seen at work, for instance, in the context of the pharmaceuticals sector. When GEHE AG sought a merger with Lloyds Chemists plc the matter fell for consideration under the Regulation, but it was agreed that it should be considered by the UK competition authorities. (See, *Unichem plc/Lloyds Chemists plc* and *GEHE AG/Lloyds Chemists plc* Cm 3344 (1996).)
94. The Commission can take action only in so far as there is an effect on inter-state trade.
95. See Regulation 1310/97 (OJ L 180/1).
96. Again, there is re-numbering, but throughout this text the 'old' have been retained.
97. Article 34 contains a similar prohibition with regard to exports. Further, the Treaty provides (in Article 36) for the prohibitions not to apply to restrictions justified on certain specified grounds, including for example public morality, public health and the protection of national treasures. However, such a restriction may not constitute a means of arbitrary discrimination or a disguised restriction on trade between member States.
98. For a succinct account of Articles 30 - 36 see chapters 9 and 10 of *Textbook on EC Law*, Josephine Steiner & Lorna Woods (6th Edn. Blackstone).
99. In the leading case of *Procureur du Roi v Dassonville* [1974] ECR 837, [1974] 2 CMLR 436 the European Court of Justice provided the following wide definition of measures having equivalent effect to quantitative restrictions:– 'All trading rules enacted by member States which are capable of hindering directly or indirectly, actually or potentially, intra-Community trade'. This was furthered a few years later in the equally well known case *Rewe Zentrale AG v Bundesmonopolverwaltung für Branntwein* [1979] ECR 649, [1979] 3 CMLR 494, – the *Cassis de Dijon* case, in which it was formally decided by the European Court of Justice that Article 30 could catch measures which were not *in themselves* of a discriminatory character.
100. *Rewe Zentrale AG v Bundesmonopolverwaltung für Branntwein* [1979] ECR 649, [1979] 3 CMLR 494. Before this case, it had been thought that justification for a measure violating Article 30 could be sought only in Article 36.
101. [1989] ECR 3851, [1990] 1 CMLR 337.
102. – by means of a mechanism provided for such a purpose in Article 177 of the Treaty of Rome.

103. See for example *B & Q Ltd v Shrewsbury & Atcham Borough Council* [1990] 3 CMLR 535 and *Wellingborough Borough Council v Payless DIY Ltd* [1990] 1 CMLR 773.
104. See *Stoke on Trent City Council v B & Q plc* [1992] ECR I-6457, 6493, 6635, [1993] 1 CMLR 426.
105. See note 102 *supra*.
106. *Ibid.*
107. [1993] ECR I-6097.
108. *DIP SpA v Commune di Bassano del Grappa* [1995] ECR I-3257.

11 The approach to price discrimination and mergers

With the process of 'concentration' going to the roots of the retail 'revolution', price discrimination and mergers featuring amongst the prime contributors to that process, and the benign approach of competition law to those contributors helping to fuel the fire of the revolution, the need arises – as earlier mentioned – to consider further their treatment, and they are now taken in turn.

Price discrimination

The practice of discrimination has been generally described as one involving the supplying of goods of like grade and quality to customers of similar standing at different prices, where the difference in price does not correspond with differences in the supplier's costs. The term embraces, however, numerous practices, 'price' including any kind of preferential treatment which can be translated into a price advantage, and includes, for instance, volume discounts, over-riders,[1] and the provision of favourable credit terms. To constitute discrimination, the difference in the treatment of customers of similar standing for the supplying of similar goods must not correspond with differences in the supplier's costs. If the difference does so correspond, then it is said to be 'cost justified', and does not constitute discrimination. It is when the difference goes further than reflecting savings in the supplier's costs that it becomes discriminatory.

As has been observed, the practice can be initiated on either the selling or the buying side, and, when initiated on the buying side, may be backed by either threatened or actual 'de-listing' – involving the removal (or threatened removal) from the buyer's shelves of the relevant products. Further, when discrimination is so initiated, it can be accompanied by exclusionary practices such as loss-leading and below cost selling. In the years following the virtual outlawing of r.p.m, and with (as noted) no specific regulation of price discrimination, the practice became so rife in a number of mass markets and in grocery particularly as to arouse concern. In 1977, amidst disquiet about the developing buying power of the multiple retailers, and the disappearance of small traders from the market, the subject was referred to the Monopolies and Mergers Commission. The Secretary of State asked the Commission to inquire into the impact upon the public interest of the practice of granting and acquiring non cost-related preferences. After four years' labour, a Report entitled *Discounts to Retailers* emerged, the findings and recommendations of which were entirely to colour the subsequent legal approach to the matter.[2]

Having investigated the nature and extent of the practice and its effects on suppliers, retailers and consumers, the Commission found its extent, both in prevalence and degree was considerable, but concluded that it did not in general operate against the public interest.[3] They believed that it was '...widely associated with enhanced price competition amongst manufacturers', and that vigorous competition amongst retailers had ensured that '... the benefits of this competition [had] been in the main passed on to the consumer...'.[4]

Although the view was formed that discriminatory conduct did not generally harm the public interest, it was thought that there were circumstances in which the practice could adversely impinge. Moreover, it was believed that the practice might unduly encourage concentration. Following these conclusions certain recommendations were made. First, no overall prohibition or regulation was called for. Secondly, as there were, nevertheless, circumstances in which discrimination might adversely impinge, provision for selective investigation was needed. Thirdly, to meet fears of the practice fostering undue concentration a close watch should be kept on mergers in the distributive trades. And with regard to the second recommendation, the members thought that the need for selective investigation was already met in the provisions contained in the Fair Trading Act 1973 and the Competition Act 1980.

At the outset of the investigation, the market was already so concentrated as to warrant a widely held conviction that specific control should be introduced, and numerous suggestions were put forward as to possible measures of regulation, but each was rejected.

Varied proposals were advanced for the *comprehensive* regulation of discrimination. To the forefront was a proposal that the practice be prohibited as it is under the USA's Robinson-Patman Act 1936,[5] but it was dismissed.[6] Other variants of comprehensive regulation likewise met with a chill reception, concerns being voiced of impracticability, reduced competition, and the ease of circumvention. Suggestions were also made for less dramatic measures, such as altering the Restrictive Trade Practices Act 1976, so that firms with less power than the major multiples might, without fear of flouting its strictures, strengthen their commercial muscle by competition, but these also found no favour.[7]

A notable feature of the *Discounts* Report was the consistency with which the members of the Commission largely maintained their unwillingness to consider tightening control over discrimination. Material to their consideration were fears of throwing out the bath water of free competition with the baby of discrimination, anxieties relating to the importing into the UK the problematic US experience with discounts legislation, and the perception of already extant law as adequate for the mounting of selective investigations. But regarding the last mentioned consideration, it is wondered whether the members' contentment had sufficient foundation. Both the Fair Trading Act 1973 and the Competition Act 1980 had their limitations, including (regarding the former) the limiting aspect of the need to meet a 25 per cent threshold before the Act would bite, and the inequity resulting if certain companies were denied recourse to discrimination while others were left free to pursue it, and (regarding the latter) the similar problem of inequity, and the difficulty, were a coercive purchaser challenged thereunder, of how to frame an effectual, remedial order.

Furthermore, there was a significant restraint upon the utility of both Acts in the content of the *Discounts* Report itself. In advocating a system of selective investigation, the members of the Commission intimated the view that the existence of price discrimination was not *per se* a sufficient ground for investigation, but refrained from precise identification of the nature of the 'plus factors' implicitly requisite to support an investigation, and merely listed a number of circumstantial features which they described as 'significant questions'.[8]

The negative approach adopted by the Commission to the introduction of any specific regulation of discrimination, coupled with the weakness of the existing law, resulted in the practice continuing unabated and the Report remaining a focus of critical attention. There followed an investigation by the Director General of Fair Trading into the information which had led the Commission to the view that discrimination in general benefited the public, and in 1985 the emergence of a Report 'Competition and Retailing'. It updated the information upon which the Commission had based its conclusions, and interpreted the newly found facts in such a way as to conclude that no material change had taken place.[9]

This implicit 'acceptance' of discrimination by the Office of Fair

Trading ensured the maintenance of a climate conducive to the granting and inducing of non cost justified preferences, and the practice continued to be strenuously pursued. Equally vigorous and unremitting was, for a time, the opposition from those in the market place who had most to lose, *i.e.* the small, independent retailers, and amongst the challenges they made was a complaint to the Commission of the EC. This, however, did not prosper.

In its prohibition of agreements which impede competition Article 85 of the Treaty of Rome particularly mentions agreements in which there are applied '... dissimilar conditions to equivalent transactions with other trading parties, thereby placing them at a competitive disadvantage', and likewise, in its prohibition of abuse of dominance, Article 86 particularly refers to the application of '... dissimilar conditions to equivalent transactions with other trading parties, thereby placing them at a competitive disadvantage'. At first sight this wording appears particularly promising as a means of challenging discrimination. However, Articles 85 and 86 being international in character, it is crucial for an effect to be shown on trade *between* member states, and the essentially domestic nature of the issue meant that the need to prove an impact on inter-state trade was an insurmountable hurdle. Accordingly, they did not come to the aid of the beleaguered independents.

With this closure of the EC avenue, the independents' endeavours to achieve some overall regulation of discrimination faded, and for the rest of the '80s and beyond there was to exist not only a legal but also a political climate in which the practice flourished. Indeed, so long as discrimination continued to enhance competition amongst suppliers and further, competition amongst retailers was such as to ensure the passing on of the benefit to consumers, in official eyes the practice would be regarded not merely as causing no harm to the public interest, but rather as positively promoting it.

Mergers

In the course of the description earlier given of the control exercised by the Fair Trading Act 1973 over mergers, it will be recalled that the régime was regarded as tolerant. Indeed, it was (and still is) essentially predisposed in their favour,[10] and in a climate of such legal 'warmth', mergers can be energetically and frequently pursued.

During the '80s, when the acceleration of the revolution was at its greatest, there was such a wave of merger activity as to be dubbed 'merger mania', and a considerable number came from retailing.[11] Although only a tiny percentage of mergers are referred for investigation, this period witnessed a clutch of merger references in the area of distribution.

The first to mention is *Great Universal Stores/Empire Stores*,[12] in which it was argued that the merger would result in greater efficiency. The Commission was, however, sceptical, and took the view that the social costs from a resultant lessening of competition mattered more. By contrast, the next three mergers of special interest to the distributive trade fared well before the Commission. In 1983, the *Linfood/Fitch Lovell*[13] bid was found not to be against the public interest, the view being that, as regards retailing, there was no adverse impact in the sense of the combined group being enabled to exploit the market, and that, as regards impact on suppliers, the combined buying power was not great. Not long afterwards, the bid by *Dee* for *Booker*[14] was found not to harm the public interest. From the wholesaling aspect, the Commission did not think there would be a potential for abuse of the consequential increase in strength, and on the retailing side the Commission believed that the combined market share would not appreciably affect competition.

At the same time the Commission again became concerned with *House of Fraser* and a proposal by *Lonrho* for its acquisition,[15] and on this occasion concluded that the proposal might not be expected to operate against the public interest. The prevailing philosophy of minimal intervention in the market place was amply reflected in the Commission's rejection of House of Fraser's arguments that the policies of Lonrho would result in a weakening of the former's competitiveness.

Reference has earlier been made to the fact that the prime consideration in determining whether or not to refer a merger is the effect upon competition, and, faithful to this approach, the mid-'80s saw a number of significant mergers in the distributive trades escaping reference to the Commission. They included those involving such household names as *Dixons/Currys*, *Woolworth Holdings/Comet*, and *Habitat/Mothercare/ British Home Stores*. Individually they appeared to give rise to no serious issue relating to competition, and a similarly happy fate attended a series of bids in food distribution, including those of *Dee* for *Fine Fare*, of *Argyll* for *Safeway* and of *Tesco* for *Hillards*. If however, competition was felt to be threatened, then, as a reference at the turn of the decade shows, a reference would follow. Such was the position with the proposed merger between *Kingfisher* and *Dixons* which was found (as earlier noted) to be potentially harmful to the public, as leading in all likelihood to a significant weakening of competition in the retailing of electrical appliances.[16]

Although only briefly outlined, it is hoped this sketch of the 'cases' illuminates the 'light touch' of the Competition authorities in merger control.

Commenting in 1987 on the restrained approach to the actual making of a reference in the first place, Dr. Martin Howe of the Office of Fair Trading noted that:–

> There [had] been considerable merger activity in the distribution sector...with many bids involving large acquisitions which [had] easily met the assets criterion, even after its increase to £30mn in July 1984. Major mergers in the department and variety stores, DIY, electrical and clothing retailing sectors [had] been scrutinised by the Office of Fair Trading but not referred by the Secretary of State for investigation by the Commission.[17]

Taken together, the general 'hands off' approach of the authorities and the 'neutral' character of the régime itself served to fan the flames of the retail revolution. But the concentration of the retail sector which it facilitated was a subject which, in terms of impact upon the needs of society, was one that gave (to some) cause for concern. In a paper entitled 'Mergers and Acquisitions: issues for UK Competition Policy', Dr Howe also observed during the same period: 'There may be fears that the concentration now taking place in retailing will, at least at some stage in the future, work against the public interest...'.[18]

To complete this outline of the contribution of merger control to the great changes of the period it must be noted that, because the matters in issue were of an essentially national character, it is on the quality of the domestic régime that we have needed to dwell. Had there taken place mergers with effect on inter-state trade which were significant in the transformation of the retail scene there would have been a need to explore the relevant EC component of the UK's competition law. Reference would have had to be made to those leading features of EC mergers control earlier described, *i.e.* to the inappropriateness of Articles 85 and 86 as control 'tools' and to its later remedying via the coming into force of the EC Merger Regulation.[19] In the circumstances however, this was not to arise.

More recent times

In the foregoing paragraphs there has been outlined the considerable contribution made by the law on price discrimination and mergers to the shape of our retail heritage. So influential has it been, the question arises as to the more recent incidence of these features of the market place and of the attitudes shown to them.

Taking first price discrimination: although the practice continued and buying power grew, for a long time they remained out of the spotlight. In the latter part of the '90s, however, the pricing policies of major retailers began to attract closer attention. In 1998 there appeared an Office of Fair Trading commissioned paper entitled 'The Welfare Consequence of the Exercise of Buying Power',[20] the conclusion drawn in which cast doubt upon the continuing wisdom of the support which the authorities had given to the exercise of such power. Further, against a backdrop of growing criticism of retailer power, the Director General launched an inquiry into competition amongst supermarkets,[21] looking into profit levels and a number of competition issues. At the end of some eight months' investigation, he referred grocery retailing to the newly named Competition Commission.[22]

In making this reference, Mr Bridgeman noted that his Office's inquiry had raised an array of matters including the intensity of competition, the relationship between multiples and suppliers and the exercise of buying power, barriers to entry, and the impact of land on the cost structure of competitors. He acknowledged the vital rôle in the economy played by the supermarkets, and the benefits they afforded to consumers in terms of convenience and choice, but, he explained, he was interested in the exploration of whether excessive profits were being made, whether buying power was being exploited, and whether there was effective competition between retailers or simply a matching of prices. This last question, he felt, was made more imperative by reason of the significant barriers to entry created by the planning system.

While for years it had remained fallow, the subject of price discrimination and the exercise of buying power thus resurfaced. With a Commission inquiry focusing upon it as one of a number of intertwined competition and planning issues, it has once again come to the forefront.

Secondly, as to mergers... Again, the spotlight which shone so briefly for a while upon mergers in the distributive trades and upon the official approach thereto moved away, and, other than in the very specialised fields of 'agency mail order'[23] and betting offices,[24] the Commission was not to be burdened with mergers involving leading retailers. Early in 1998 there took place the merger of Somerfield and Kwik Save which, while it would create a powerful high street presence and a 7 per cent overall market share, was evidently thought not to raise any public interest issues and was not referred to the Commission. Indeed, the lack of any heavy inquisitorial burden for that body reflects (in grocery retailing at least) the simple fact that for some considerable while the sector saw relatively few take-overs.

As with buying power, however, the scene would eventually alter.

Amidst an intensification of merger enthusiasm, the early spring of 1999 saw the pursuit of a union to overshadow Somerfield/Kwik Save with Kingfisher and Asda proposing a marriage which would produce Europe's fifth largest retailer.[25] It was, though, to come to naught, and be itself eclipsed. Only a few weeks later Kingfisher bowed out, and the announcement appeared of an offer made for Asda by the giant US retailer, Wal-Mart. Notified to the European Commission in June 1999,[26] the merger was cleared a few weeks later, the view being taken that the operation did not raise competition concerns. According to the European Commission, as '...both companies [had] no overlapping activities, the concentration on the retail side [did] not result in any increment of market shares'.[27] Furthermore, there would neither be any adverse impact on the procurement side, because there were '...very few overlaps and suppliers [tended] to be multinational companies of significant bargaining power'.[28]

The profusion of features in the press accompanying the making of the offer by Wal-Mart not only emphasised the inherent 'drama' of the venture, but speculated also upon its ability to trigger other partnerships.[29] Of the increasing 'urge to merge' there is no doubt, from which increase must surely follow an increase in regulatory attentions,[30] with all the potential for the shaping of the retail landscape which that implies.

Notes

1. *i.e.* a variety of retrospective discount, given on the fulfilment of a condition.
2. HC 311 (1981).
3. *Ibid.* para. 9.23.
4. *Ibid.* para. 9.22. The value to the community of the 'passing on' of the benefits extracted appears to be the whole crux of the matter. A few years later, in the report on the *Dee/Booker* merger the Commission expressed its confidence that the proposed merged concern would pass on to its customers most of the advantages which would flow from the exercise of its enhanced buying power (Cmnd 9429 (1985) para. 8.45).
5. This Act makes it illegal to discriminate in price between different purchasers of commodities of like grade and quality where the effect of such discrimination may be to lessen competition. Having challenged the discriminating supplier, the Act affords him two defences, cost justification, and *bona fide* meeting competition. If the supplier can show that the differences in price make only due allowance for differences in costs, then he may be saved. Likewise, if he can show that the lower of his prices was made

in good faith to meet an equally low price of a competitor then, again, he may escape. Furthermore, the Act recognises that it is by no means always the supplier who initiates the discrimination. *Via* a provision designed to catch the coercive purchaser, it outlaws also the knowing inducement or receipt of a prohibited discrimination in price.

6. – on grounds of intricacy and the burden of compliance.
7. Though the Commission did not *fully* close the door to the possibility of so amending the 1976 Act as to allow for the development of co-ordinated buying power; (see HC 311 para. 9.33).
8. These included the possession of exceptional market power by either of the parties, a serious threatening of the viability of efficient traders, and exceptionally great differentiation in pricing. (HC 311 para. 9.27).
9. For a detailed criticism see 'Competition Policies for the Food Industry', J.Burns, *Food Marketing*, vol. 3, no. 1 1987 p. 7.
10. See Whish, *Competition Law*, 3rd Edn. Butterworths, at p. 679.
11. The high street was by that time no stranger to them. In a late '80s report there were listed over 250 key mergers, take-over and investment deals in UK retailing between the years 1961 to 1987. (See The Scottish Council Development and Industry Report 'Retailing in Scotland 2005'.)
12. Cmnd 8777 (1983).
13. Cmnd 8874 (1983).
14. *The Dee Corporation plc/Booker McConnell plc* Cmnd 9429 (1985).
15. Cmnd 9458 (1985).
16. *Kingfisher plc/Dixons Group plc* Cm 1079 (1990).
17. 'UK Competition Policy and the Food Sector', at p. 10. (Paper given by Dr Howe, Director of Competition Policy, at a conference on 'Competition Policy in the Food Industries', at the University of Reading, September 1987.)
18. Spring, 1986.
19. Regulation 4064/89, OJ [1989] L 395/1.
20. – by Dobson, Waterson & Chu (September 1998).
21. – See Office of Fair Trading Press Release No 33/98 (30th July 1998).
22. – See Office of Fair Trading Press Release No PN 11/99 (8th April 1999).
23. In *The Littlewoods Organisation plc/Freemans plc* Cm 3761 (1997), the Commission was concerned with a proposed union in a small but nevertheless significant sphere of non-food retailing. With five firms operating in agency mail order, and with the market leader (GUS) enjoying a nearly 41 per cent share, a merger between Littlewoods and Freemans would have resulted in the merged company and GUS accounting between them for over 80 per cent of agency sales. Coming to the conclusion that the proposed merger would yet further concentrate an already highly concentrated market, that less competition could be to the detriment of choice, efficiency and prices, and that the potential harm was not outweighed by possible benefits such as the passing on to customers of any derivative savings, the

Commission recommended that the merger should be prohibited.

24. In *Ladbroke Group plc/the Coral Betting Business* Cm 4030 (1998), the Commission had to consider the impact of the acquisition by Ladbroke (the largest firm in the UK off-course betting industry) of Coral, bringing together numerous licensed betting offices. The view was taken that the public interest was harmed, for reasons including the significant reduction of local choice. It was pointed out that '...as in much of retailing the preservation of consumer choice at the local level was important' (para. 1.10).
25. See *The Financial Times*, 17th/18th April 1999.
26. OJ C 181/16, 26th June 1999, Case No IV/M.1612.
27. IP/99/561, Brussels 26th July 1999, 'Commission clears the merger between Wal-Mart (USA) and Asda (UK)'.
28. *Ibid.*
29. See *The Times*, 15th June 1999.
30. Though academic, it is interesting to note that the proposed merger between Kingfisher and Asda was not opposed by the European Commission (Case No IV/M.1541). It was declared compatible with the common market on the ground of a modest resultant market share increment and the presence of significant competitors together meaning the absence of competition concerns (IP/99/397, Brussels 16th June 1999).

12 A consideration of certain further major issues

Vertical issues

In recent times, considerable attention has been paid to what may be broadly categorised as 'vertical issues', *i.e.* those arising from behaviour which involves firms at different levels of the market and which may display 'competition threatening' features.

In *Competition Law* Whish provides an excellent theoretical introduction to his treatment of 'vertical restraints', which he describes as a restraint '...accepted between firms which operate at different levels of the market'.[1] Noting their great range and scope and the complex problems they pose, he speaks of the need to decide which provisions actually raise restrictions on competition, and the need to distinguish between beneficial and harmless restraints. He points out that a vertical agreement may restrict 'intra-brand' but enhance 'inter-brand' competition,[2] or that, by contrast, it may indeed reduce the latter.[3] Moving then to methods of distribution, included in which are distribution agreements, he provides a list of types of such agreement, a list embracing *inter alia* exclusive distribution, exclusive purchasing and selective distribution systems.

The basics complete, the author turns to distribution agreements and competition policy. He explains in general that whereas '...both UK and EEC law are relatively sympathetic towards vertical restraints in distribution agreements...',[4] neither system '...has succeeded in developing a policy towards restraints in distribution agreements which has a unifying doctrinal consistency'.[5] And thence, proceeding from the general to the particular, he deals with an array of specific issues. First, he considers the potential which different kinds of restraint have to foreclose competition at different levels of the market – instancing the harmful potential of an exclusive purchasing agreement for competition at primary level,[6] and of a selective dealing system for competition at secondary level.[7] Secondly, he contemplates the harm which vertical restraints may do to consumers, noting the tendency to higher prices and the reduction in consumer choice. A third issue is the way in which vertical restraints may 'themselves be the product of, or the cause of, cartels between producers or distributors...',[8] while a fourth is their capacity '...which is crucial as far as EEC law is concerned, to seal off one geographical market from another'.[9] Fifth and last is the issue as to who should decide the manner in which goods are to be distributed. Some would argue, we are told, that the vested interest of the producer suffices to ensure a striving for the most efficient system, whereas others contend that the possible disadvantages to consumers are such that '...decision-making power is best taken away from individual producers and vested in some public body'.[10]

Such then are the highlights of a particularly illuminating account. Although necessarily very brief, it serves, it is hoped, both to indicate the intricacy of the topic and to provide the background for a consideration of some recent inquiries involving vertical issues.

An inquiry conducted in the mid '90s by the Monopolies and Mergers Commission into *Ice Cream*, involved a restraint aimed at attaining a measure of exclusivity. The Commission investigated the impact of the practice of the leading ice cream manufacturers to supply retailers with refrigerated cabinets on terms that they might not use them to stock ice cream from other suppliers. It was concluded that this practice (so called 'freezer exclusivity') did not operate against the public interest. The Commission noted *inter alia* that retailers could secure their own freezers or add second freezers, and the members came to the view that in the circumstances prevailing the practice neither seriously deterred other suppliers from entering the market nor limited consumer choice.[11]

Some little while earlier the Commission had been called upon to explore the effect of restraints aspiring both to exclusivity and selectivity. The investigation in question was into the supply of *New Motor Cars*, where the Commission found *inter alia* that a complex monopoly situation existed with regard to a number of car suppliers in the UK. Virtually all of them selected their dealers, gave to them exclusive territories, and imposed upon them a variety of restraints. These included (in addition to restraints upon selling outside the allocated territory) restraints such as those involving the setting of sales ceilings for individual dealers and the prohibition of the holding of competing dealerships. The Commission appreciated that for products like motor cars there were efficiencies to be gained from selective and exclusive distribution systems, and they came to the view that the suppliers' systems, although limiting dealers' freedom, actually enhanced inter-brand competition.

Even so, they had recommendations to make – including, for instance, that no sales ceilings should be set, that it should be possible for dealers to form within their territory outlets for other cars, and that there should be no constraint upon dealers advertising outside their own areas.[12] In the days which followed, however, it was to emerge that these recommendations would not redress the harmful nature of the situation and this fact, coupled with the use of recommended resale pricing in ways considered by the Director General to reduce competition, caused him to refer the new car industry to the Commission for re-examination.[13]

Selectivity was at the heart of a high-profile investigation into the supply of high quality perfume. In *Fine Fragrances*[14] the Commission was of the view that a complex monopoly existed in that all the leading fragrance houses supplied their products[15] only to outlets providing an ambience appropriate to luxury items, and refused to supply unauthorised retailers. The conclusion reached from the inquiry was that the market was competitive, and that the selective distribution systems in operation were not as a whole contrary to the public interest. It was not thought that the houses unfairly assessed retailers' applications for authorised status, nor that there was an attempt to use the systems as a means of maintaining resale prices. Furthermore, the Commission was prepared to accept the argument that refusal to deal with retailers having no positive impact on brand image was justified on the basis of a need to protect that image.

A common feature of the cases so far discussed, it will be noted, was the comparative leniency of the Commission's stance. The more recent reports of the enquiries into domestic electrical goods reveal a more critical approach. The supply of both 'brown' and 'white' goods became the subject of extensive investigation by the Commission, the results emerging in two lengthy reports – *Domestic Electrical Goods I and II*.[16] We begin with the former, which related to 'brown' goods.

Finding *inter alia* the existence of certain complex monopolies, the Commission explored the impact of the following:– the recommendation of resale prices by the suppliers; either the taking into account of those prices by retailers or the setting by the same of prices coinciding therewith;[17] the operation by many large suppliers of selective distribution systems, and, in connection with those systems, the withholding of supplies from certain retailers.

The conclusion was reached that these forms of behaviour were contrary to the public interest. It was thought that, the relationship between suppliers and retailers being strong, the recommended resale prices were very influential. They were seen to lead to higher prices and less choice than would otherwise have prevailed and to the discouragement of innovation.

Again, it was believed that the criteria used to found the selective distribution systems were applied discriminatorily, and resulted in similarly disadvantageous consequences.

The findings culminated in a series of recommendations. Regarding the price restraint, it was recommended that suppliers should be prohibited both from recommending resale prices and influencing dealers to sell at higher prices than they themselves would choose. And it was also recommended that dealers should be prohibited from persuading suppliers to recommend prices. Regarding the selective dealing and withholding of supplies, it was recommended that suppliers should be prohibited from applying the selective dealing criteria discriminatorily, and should only withhold supplies if able to satisfy the Director General that a refusal to supply was neither anti-competitive nor discriminatory. The recommendations so made were, furthermore, seen as complementary, and as tending together to reduce the suppliers' influence on retail prices.

It should be added that from the inquiries made into the behaviour surrounding the provision of 'white' goods a similar picture emerged. The findings were similar and so were the recommendations.

Following the findings and recommendations of the Commission, and in order to remedy the adverse impact upon consumers, undertakings were sought and an Order made.[18] *Via* the Order, a package of remedies was put in place. It prohibits, for instance, recommending of resale prices, withholding of supplies, (other than on certain grounds)[19] and discriminating between dealers on the ground of the prices at which the latter supply the goods in question.

It will be noticed that while the inquiries under discussion reveal the Commission's considerable interest in vertical issues, they have not yielded any overarching principles. It has been very much a case by case approach, the Commission guided in each instance by the individual circumstances prevailing. Indeed, this point is underscored by, for instance, the *Contact Lens Solutions* inquiry[20] which featured recommended resale prices in a market controlled by Government regulation at both the supply and retail stage. Having discerned *inter alia* the setting of retail prices both at and just below recommended levels, and having found this conduct to be against the public interest, the Commission also found the adverse effects of the industry's general pricing behaviour to be much influenced by the regulatory régime and recommended that it be altered.

The interest which the Commission has for some time been taking in vertical restraints has been responsible in part for their achieving a certain prominence.[21] However, they were also to receive considerable attention in the arena of law reform.

So far as concerns the domestic component of the law, it has already been explained that in the 'sea-changes' brought about by the Competition Act 1998 vertical agreements were given special consideration, the reason being that they posed a particular problem for the reformers. Their regulation under the 'old' domestic law was elaborate, but basically might be expressed thus:– If (and only if) vertical restrictive agreements were appropriately drawn, they by and large escaped the clutches of the Restrictive Trade Practices Act 1976. They could, however, be challenged, in certain conditions, on a case by case basis under the Fair Trading Act 1973 and the Competition Act 1980. Further, if they took the form of a vertical resale price maintenance system, they were all but outlawed under the Resale Prices Act 1976.

The issue for the reformers concerned the regulation of non price fixing vertical agreements in circumstances where there was neither the market power to make them susceptible of challenge under abuse of dominance provisions, nor the presence of an entire network of similar parallel agreements such as to invite challenge under complex monopoly provisions. When introducing provisions prohibiting concerted activity with competition threatening effects, the reformers questioned whether there should be exempt therefrom non price vertical agreements lacking the attendant circumstances identified.[22]

Aware that '...arguments [could] be advanced both for and against the exclusion of vertical agreements', the reformers took the view that '...on balance...there [were] potentially significant benefits in excluding vertical agreements, so long as they [were] not price-fixing agreements, from the scope of the prohibition of anti-competitive agreements',[23] and that if vertical agreements were subjected only to '...the prohibition of abuse of dominant position and the complex monopoly provisions of the Fair Trading Act 1973', regulatory attention could be focussed on cases of market power or series of parallel vertical agreements '...which [were] most likely to operate anti-competitively...'.[24]

The treatment of vertical restraints was in fact delayed by the yet on-going European reformatory deliberations on the same subject, but a draft Order has been made under s 50 of the Act, a section enabling the Secretary of State to exclude *inter alia* vertical agreements from the Chapter I prohibition.[25]

In the accompanying Consultation Document,[26] it was explained that because first, vertical agreements did not generally raise competition concerns in the absence of market power or a network of agreements;

secondly, it was desirable for competition authorities to concentrate energy on significant issues rather than 'becoming bogged down in the detailed scrutiny of benign agreements'; and thirdly, unnecessary regulatory burdens on business should be avoided, there existed a sound argument for disapplying the Chapter I prohibition to vertical agreements – other that was, than to those fixing prices. Furthermore, it was pointed out that a) inasmuch as it was possible to provide for the 'clawing back' of particular agreements, b) the Fair Trading Act 1973 could deal with situations in which vertical agreements were prevalent in a market, and c) the Chapter II prohibition was available where concerns arose involving abuse of dominance, there were in place sufficiently 'powerful safeguards' to permit of the proposed exclusion.

In general terms, vertical agreements are defined for the purpose of the Order as agreements between two or more undertakings operating at a different stage of the economic process in respect of the supply or purchase of goods or both.[27] The Order provides that the Chapter I prohibition shall not apply to vertical agreements. However, it also goes on to provide that the exclusion shall not avail agreements whose object or effect is resale price fixing, neither shall it apply to any particular agreement if the Director General has so directed.

As has been observed, the treatment of vertical agreements is also the subject of continuing scrutiny at the European level. That it has been equally problematic is reflected in the extensive review undertaken by the EC Commission. According to the Green Paper published,[28] the review has covered four major varieties of vertical restraint, exclusive distribution, exclusive purchasing, franchising and selective distribution. Such restraints it was said could, on the one hand, further competition, promote efficient distribution and encourage market integration, or, on the other hand, block integration and harm competition. And it was explained that because of the Union's commitment to integration, and the strong positive and negative links thereto of vertical restraints, they '...[had] been of particular importance to the Union's competition policy'.[29]

The Commission went on to advise that they believed their policy on vertical relationships over the last thirty years had been successful, in that its approach accommodated the ambiguous nature of their impact on competition and promoted market integration. However, for reasons including the temporal character of the relevant exempting regulations, and shifts in patterns of commercial conduct, it was thought that the time for a review had come.

The Paper reflected the pursuit of considerable research, the subject having been explored from a number of aspects and in varied ways. For instance, research was conducted into the structure of distribution, and revealed far reaching changes with implications for vertical restraints.[30] In this context, an important issue arose regarding 'parallel trade' – insistence upon freedom to engage in which had always been a cornerstone of Commission policy for ensuring that distribution agreements should have an integrating rather than a partitioning effect. It arose from the fact that information technology facilitated the espousal of 'Just in Time' techniques,[31] that this espousal meant a decline in traditional channels in which independent operators dealt at arm's length in favour of channels involving co-operative relationships, that such systems reduced the scope for the 'parallel trade' mechanism to operate,[32] and that it might thus be asked in consequence whether insistence on freedom to engage in parallel trade no longer sufficed '...to ensure a positive outcome for restraints on competition and market integration...'.[33]

The Commission also made inquiries into the economic analysis of vertical restraints and the single market, and gained a number of insights. They noted *inter alia* that the modern approach to vertical restraints was individual analysis rather than generalised approbation or condemnation, and further, that the effects of such restraints upon competition related to the strength or weakness of inter-brand competition.[34] Again, they observed that analysis '...should concentrate on the impact on the market rather than the form of the agreement',[35] and, too, they perceived a need for more favourable treatment to be afforded restraints which involved new and integrationary flows of trade. In spite, however, of the importance of economic analysis, they thought it could '...not be the only factor in the design of policy',[36] and furthermore, that '...a full evaluation of every individual case would be too costly in resource terms and [might] lead to legal insecurity'.[37]

As part of their research effort the Commission also consulted widely, and found themselves on occasion the recipients of criticism of current policy. They heard, for example, claims that 'bloc' exemptions lacked flexibility and were unduly regulatory,[38] but that legal certainty was crucial and might be forfeited by the abandonment of the 'bloc' exemption approach. Further, they were advised by some that '...too much emphasis [was] put on analysis of clauses and not enough on the economic impact of...agreements'.[39]

With their survey completed, the Commission moved to options for reform, of which they provided four. Option 1 would maintain the current system, and Option 2 would widen and make more flexible the 'bloc' exemptions. Option 3 (responding to the fact that vertical restraints could be anti-competitive when coupled with market power) would limit the exemption bestowed by 'bloc' exemption to companies with market shares below a certain threshold. Option 4 ('as a response to...criticisms that ['bloc'] exemption...had a strait-jacket effect and that Article 85(1) [had] been applied too widely to vertical restraints without reference to their economic and market context')[40] would introduce for parties with less than a certain market share a rebuttable presumption that their restraint was compatible with Article 85(1) – and for persons with a higher market share a 'bloc' exemption approach would be retained.

The Commission invited the expression of opinions on the Paper and the options it contained, so that a decision might be taken on the formulation of appropriate policy, and, in due course, adopted and circulated a Communication.

This Communication[41] contains a proposal to introduce a completely new régime replacing the existing distribution 'bloc' exemptions and including selective distribution. There would be brought in one broad umbrella 'bloc' exemption, the highlights of which would include the following:–

In the first place, it would apply not only to goods but also to services, and it would depart from the present system by defining what is not 'bloc' exempted instead of what is exempted,[42] so removing the undesirable 'straight jacket' effect. There would always fall outside the exemption what are regarded as 'hard-core' restraints, including restrictions such as those imposing resale price maintenance, and those restricting resales, imports and exports (though, regarding the latter, with exceptions – such as restrictions in exclusive distribution systems relating to 'active' sales outside or into an allocated territory, and restrictions in selective distribution systems regarding sales to unauthorised distributors).[43]

The proposed régime would also contain a cap (or caps) related to market share in order to link the exemption to market power. Were it eventually decided to adopt a system operating on one such cap, the 'threshold' might lie in the range of 25-30 per cent market share. Below this threshold, because they would not be considered to have any significant anti-competitive effects, vertical restraints without 'hard-core' restrictions would be exempt and fall into a 'safe harbour'.

In addition, it was proposed *inter alia* that vertical restraints falling outside the exemption would not be presumed to be illegal but might need individual examination to see whether they should be given a negative clearance or individual exemption, or should be prohibited. Also, there would be a power retained to withdraw the benefit of the 'bloc' exemption.

The changes envisaged would be fundamental, and overcome problems arising from the existing regulations. 'Form' rather than 'effects' based, and without any market share limit, the current régime has meant that companies without significant market power are burdened with unnecessary regulation, while companies with significant market power can even so benefit from it. Moreover, as to the critical matter of the proposed use of a market share related cap (or caps), a single threshold appears to have gained favour.[44]

To conclude, a final point relating to the reform programme needs to be made:- In order to avert certain possible adverse consequences flowing in some situations from the non-notification of a vertical agreement,[45] there has long been an incentive to notify the agreement on a precautionary basis. To lessen the various burdens falling upon business and the Commission in this context, a considerable extension has been made of the embrace of a measure (contained in Article 4(2) of Regulation 17) which has removed the need for notification from only a hitherto limited class of agreement.[46]

Retailer 'aggrandisement'

One of the principal themes of this book has been an attempt to trace the 'aggrandisement' of the retailer, together with certain of its consequences. Emerging from the limited horizon of the simple 'stockist and seller', certain retailers have, as we have seen, evolved into major contributors to the overall value chain, and have grown into firms able to trade with hitherto dominant suppliers on either at least equal or sometimes superior terms. And this translation they have achieved by a variety of means, including the amassing of large formats, the exercise of buying power, and, of course, the development of formidable expertise in that driver of the modern supply chain – information technology.[47]

Constituting a current issue of particular moment, it will be recalled that the manifestations and implications of retailer aggrandisement have become, in the grocery sector, the subject *per se* of investigation by the Competition Commission. Following, as earlier noted, a preliminary inquiry into matters including the intensity of competition, the exercise of buying power and barriers to entry,[48] the Director General referred the grocery retailing sector for fuller investigation.[49] While he was mindful of the beneficial contribution to the economy made by the large retailers, he was interested in the exploration of the possible making of excessive profits, and the possible exploitation of buying power. Again, impliedly characterising the retail grocery market as 'oligopolistic', and concerned about the barriers to entry created by planning control, he sought the further pursuit of the question of whether existing retailers did in fact compete, or whether their prices were respectively set to match those of competitors.

The inclusion of buying power among the matters for investigation must detain us. Though not lending itself to definition,[50] and best perhaps simply defined as a situation in which a firm (or group) is able, because of its market strength, to obtain from its suppliers markedly better terms than are accorded other buyers, it is a feature of retailer aggrandisement attracting increasing interest.

Reference has been made to the commissioned paper 'The Welfare Consequences of the Exercise of Buying Power',[51] whose authors sought to identify conditions in which the detrimental effects of buying power outweighed its beneficial effects and *vice versa*. They came to the view that it could yield efficiency advantages, but that welfare could be detrimentally affected if buyers were not constrained to pass on resultant benefits.[52] Further, if buyer power was (as likely) unequal among buyers, it could '...exacerbate differences in downstream competitive positions...'.[53] And further, not only were consumer welfare and downstream competition pertinent, '...the long-term viability of firms within the industry [could] also be undermined...'.[54] In all, with increasing retailer concentration and margin,[55] the authors doubted (as has been noted) whether the support of the authorities in the '80s, on the ground of countervailing power, still held.

As an issue of concern for the regulators, buying power is not confined to these shores. It was the subject of attention by the European Commission in *Kesko/Tuko*, a case involving a merger between two leading wholesaling and retailing groups of daily consumer goods in Finland,[56] and one to the broader content of which we will come shortly. Suffice to say, in the present context, that amongst the matters investigated in the appraisal of compatibility or otherwise with the common market the exercise of buying power was closely scrutinised.

The groups' strong buying position was perceived as both a contributor to the augmenting of dominance and a significant barrier to entry. Importantly, the Commission paid heed not only to the acquisition's effect on the downstream market but also on the procurement market, and in relation to the latter they raised an array of matters. For instance, they spoke of the dependency of the suppliers upon the groups, the absence, to the same extent, of any reciprocal dependency, and the restriction of any countervailing power to the positions only of large producers with highly regarded branded products. And they referred, too, to the way in which retailer negotiating power was enhanced by such recent developments as loyalty card schemes, with their conferment of access to consumer information not shared by the suppliers.[57]

In a feature entitled 'The Lessons of the Kesko/Tuko Decision'[58] Michael Hutchings ventured the suggestion that competition authorities in the EU would be '...examining how to assess the competition law implications of growing buyer power in the retail sector...'.[59] And in the same period, in an article on 'The Retail Sector and Application of Antitrust Rules',[60] Luca Sanfilippo pondered why there had been so few cases of enforcement of the European abuse provisions against buying power, and gave two reasons. The first, that small victims were too afraid of reprisals to bring an action, he dismissed inasmuch as buyer power had become a singular problem also for medium and large manufacturers. The second, that to measure the justification of particular discounts to particular buyers involved the extremely difficult exercise of apportioning distribution costs to individual products, he dismissed as surmountable with information technology.

An article by Louis Vogel appearing a little later and entitled 'Competition Law and Buying Power: The Case for a New Approach in Europe',[61] noted that buying power had contributed to a shift in the balance of power and that the '...overall effect of large retailers' conduct [was] not necessarily positive...'.[62] He considered that the relative inactivity of the authorities in the face of developing retail power might be owed to the fact that the apportionment of margin was not a matter for antitrust control, and that traditional antitrust provisions were not suitable for dealing with buying power.[63] Further, Vogel observed that because even large retailers controlled only a small portion of any particular product market, and their conduct only infrequently crossed the law's objectives (as generally defined) '...they seldom [fell] within the scope of antitrust rules'.[64]

According to this author, more effective protection against abuse of buying power was needed. He believed major social costs had accompanied its increase, the effects of which legitimately fell within the scope of European competition law – a régime which had '...never been conceived solely in terms of economic efficiency'.[65] For the more effective regulation of abuse of such power he advocated the improvement of the measurement of retailers' power on the downstream market, and the moving of control '...away from the current focus on the downstream market, in order to address the genuine problems on the upstream market'.[66]

For Luca Sanfilippo it was significant that in *Kesko/Tuko*[67] the Commission took separately the procurement market and explored therein the extent of buyer power. In his view, '...if a market [could] be construed as a separate relevant market, it [was] indeed possible to find out dominant positions held by large retailers'.[68] Whereas buyer power and dominance were not synonymous, if '...a large buyer [were] proved dominant on a procurement market, the whole of Article 86 of the Treaty [of Rome] could be read as a reversed picture'.[69] And, he continued,

> ...unfair purchase prices, refusal to buy, discrimination, and unjustified obligations on manufacturers to pay marketing fees or promotional contributions [might] be regarded as typical cases of abusive conduct within the meaning of Article 86.[70]

A rather different approach to the more effective regulation of buyer power was explored by Jean-Paul Tran Thiet in 'The Regulation of Networks and Relations between Industry and Trade: A French Perspective'.[71] First, he explained the way in which (as he perceived it) retailers had, *via* the accumulation of 'own brand', become competitors of their suppliers, suppliers had to meet ever more restrictive and discriminatory conditions to achieve the distribution of their products, and traditional competition law was inadequate to deal with the distortion. Then he pointed to the parallel which might be drawn between access to retailer shelf space and access to such networks as those of the telecommunications, energy and transport operators, and considered whether resort could be had to specific 'tools' already to hand for opening up such industries. Were it possible to deploy the techniques deployed for the regulation of 'network' industries[72] then, he submitted, there could be imposed on large scale retailing '...a significant number of obligations...like transparency, non-discrimination and third party access to the network'.[73] Whilst such an approach would raise questions, the author believed, nevertheless, it could prove 'very fruitful'. And, it might be added, it has been noted closer home that the problem for manufacturers can be seen as one of '...access to an essential facility...'. It being critical for their business that they achieve distribution through the outlets of the major chains, the position of the latter becomes that of a 'gatekeeper'.[74]

Returning to the wider context of the investigation by the UK Competition Commission into supermarkets, it is submitted that of the questions upon which their deliberations have been sought, those raised by buying power might prove the most intractable, more taxing perhaps than those involved in oligopoly and the interface of planning and competition control. The difficulty of discerning appropriate governing principles is equally matched by the highly problematic search for an appropriate remedy.

In addition to raising issues susceptible of investigation in their own right, retailer aggrandisement is a phenomenon from which considerations arise germane to other arenas of concern to competition regulators. One such is the regulation of vertical restraints, where it appears in connection with the basic question of how best to deal with them.

While it has not led to an identity of consequential articulation, we have seen how the view that market power at either retailer or manufacturer level must exist for a vertical restraint to have regulatory significance has proved central to the thinking of reformers in both the national and European spheres. In the context of the latter sphere, however, the question has been asked whether the Green Paper on Vertical Restraints sufficiently acknowledged the importance for the subject of the great shift of power from manufacturers to retailers. In the earlier mentioned article entitled 'The Retail Sector and Application of Antitrust Rules',[75] Luca Sanfilippo noted that European distribution law had developed under the influence of a perceived need generally to protect 'poor distributors', and that the Green Paper still followed the '...patterns of...traditional European distribution law reasoning...'. In his view, the fact that power in the chain had '...clearly shifted from manufacturers to retailers...' was a good reason (amongst others) '...for reconsidering from scratch European policy and antitrust legislation on vertical restraints'.[76]

A second area of regulatory involvement in which retailer aggrandisement can be a material consideration is merger control. In this context, we are taken back to the European Commission's decision in *Kesko/Tuko*[77] (involving the concluded merger between two leading wholesaling and retailing groups of daily consumer goods in Finland).

Because of a failure to meet the prescribed thresholds, this particular merger was not in fact caught by the European Merger Regulation, but it was examined by the European Commission upon a referral made by the Finnish authorities.[78] So far as scale was concerned, it was in European terms a comparatively small union, but with the groups together accounting for at least 53 per cent of all sales of daily consumer goods in Finland, it was of great social and political consequence in that country. A widespread investigation led to the conclusion that the merger was incompatible with the common market, and to the decision that appropriate measures were in need of adoption to restore effective competition.

The attention given to buying power has been noted, but here it is important to add that in reaching their adverse decision the Commission explored a range of inter-related matters. These included the groups' significant control of suitable, large retail premises, their customer loyalty schemes, their private label products, their distribution systems, and the position of their central organs as buyers of daily consumer goods. The Commission took the view that these all contributed to the strengthening of market dominance, and to the raising of significant barriers to entry – both of which consequences were unacceptably anti-competitive. It was, it must be conceded, an extreme case, and of prime direct importance to the Finnish consumer. Inasmuch, though, as the Commission were investigating conditions and conduct which are by no means the prerogative of one Member State, the insights provided on the approach to the control of retailer power are clearly of value Community-wide.[79]

The possibility of undue dominance of retailing *via* the merger process was a fear to which the UK Monopolies and Mergers Commission adverted nearly two decades ago in *Discounts to Retailers*.[80] Yet, as has emerged, that body was not to be called upon to investigate any combination of leading retail grocery chains. Indeed, union between major players would not be a feature of the retail sector until the appearance of the successive bids for Asda by Kingfisher and Wal-Mart respectively. From these recent high-profile events might eventually flow ripples which, in their turn, attract the authorities' interest, and that attraction, in its own turn, might involve the re-visiting of *Kesko/Tuko*. The least that can be said is that, amongst the big UK operators, the lengthy period of comparative merger 'calm' appears to have been broken.

From the aspect of tensions in the retailer/supplier relationship, it may be added in conclusion that they are not necessarily reflected in the mirror of competition law. Not long ago they were played out in litigation in the arena of intellectual property.

The litigation in question had as its background i) the desire of many major retailers to resell exclusive, branded goods at discount prices, ii) their inability to make direct purchases of the same by reason of their failure to meet the criteria of the producers' selective distribution systems, and iii) their consequential sourcing of them through the so called international 'grey' market.

The pursuit of this practice by an Austrian retailer, Hartlauer, led to an action being brought by an Austrian manufacturer, Silhouette International. It involved the European Court in the question whether, under European law, the producer/brand owner of certain high quality goods to which his trademark was affixed could seek an order prohibiting their resale in the European Economic Area by a retailer who, unable to purchase them directly, had imported them into the Area there to sell them under the mark at low prices. The European Court, upholding the right of the producer/brand owner, decided that he might ask a national court for such an order.[81]

While it was the case that the Court was being asked to interpret an intricate European Directive[82] and to do so in circumstances of considerable particularity, the *Silhouette* case (as it became known) even so quickly caught the general eye. That it should have achieved a high profile was owed, it is believed, to the fact that it crystallised what was described at the time as the '...diametrically opposed moral crusades...' of the retailers and the manufacturers,[83] the former keen to meet the customers' need of low prices, the latter equally eager to protect their products' reputation and image. Implicitly, the decision fortified the notion of selective distribution. Simultaneously, it evoked from retailers the renewal of their commitment to continue the furtherance of their 'cause'.[84]

Notes

1. 3rd Edn. Butterworths, at p. 536 and ff.
2. By 'intra-brand' competition is meant that between the goods which are the subject of the restrictive agreement in question and other such goods that the supplying party produces. By 'inter-brand' competition is meant that between the goods which are the subject of the agreement and the competing goods of other producers.
3. To illustrate the former (*i.e.* the enhancement of inter-brand competition) Whish gives the instance of an exclusive distribution agreement leading to the intensification of effort by the distributor and a resultant increase in competition between the goods which he sells and the competing goods of other producers. As an illustration of the latter (*i.e.* the reduction of inter-brand competition) he instances an exclusive purchasing agreement, the upshot of which will be the increase in difficulty for competitors of the producer in question to supply competing goods and hence a diminution in competition between those goods and the brand of goods which are the subject of the agreement.
4. *Competition Law*, 3rd Edn. Butterworths, p. 544.
5. *Ibid.* p. 545.
6. *i.e.* between producers.
7. *i.e.* between distributors or retailers where the selective dealing involves a refusal to deal with significant numbers of them.
8. *Competition Law*, 3rd Edn. Butterworths, p. 546.
9. *Ibid.* p. 547.
10. *Ibid.*

11. Cm 2524 (1994). (Though freezer exclusivity, along with other perceived problems, would again become the subject of Commission scrutiny, with a reference to that body of the whole of the impulse ice-cream industry at the end of 1998 (See Office of Fair Trading Press Release No 54/98 22nd December 1998).)

    A few years previously, the Commission had also been concerned with series of vertical agreements emanating from oligopolistic suppliers in inquiries made into *Petrol* and *Beer*; (indeed their concern was not only with vertical agreements, but also with vertical integration). In the former case (*Supply of Petrol* Cm 972 (1990)), the Commission found a competitive wholesale market and believed that the public were harmed neither by the oil companies' ownership of garages nor the exclusive purchasing terms which those companies imposed on retailers. And by contrast, in the latter case, (*Supply of Beer* Cm 651 (1989)), the Commission found harm to the public in *inter alia* the way in which dominant brewers were protected from competition by the foreclosing of their 'tied' estates to competitors, (the 'tie' of exclusivity being effected by restrictive terms in leases and advantageous loans).
12. Cm 1808 (1992). It should be added that though inter-brand competition was found to exist, it was limited by a system then prevailing of voluntary export restraints.
13. – in March, 1999. (See Office of Fair Trading Press Release 8/99 17th March 1999.)
14. Cm 2380 (1993).
15. The inquiry was concerned with the supply in the UK for retail sale of perfumes, eaux de toilette, *etc.* to retail at a resale price exceeding £15 per 50ml.
16. *Domestic Electrical Goods I* Cm 3675 (1997) related to 'brown' goods, *i.e.* TVs, videos, hi-fi systems and camcorders; *Domestic Electrical Goods II* Cm 3676 (1997) related to 'white' goods, *i.e.* washing machines, tumble driers, dishwashers, fridges, *etc.*
17. – often, too, retailers would complain to suppliers about price cutting competitors.
18. The Restriction on Agreements and Conduct (Specified Domestic Electrical Goods) Order, 1998 (SI 1998 No 1271).
19. Permitted grounds for withholding relate to the nature or circumstances of an order for goods, and also (albeit within stringent bounds) to the criteria by reference to which a supplier chooses his dealers.
20. Cm 2242 (1993).
21. It is of interest to observe the attention given to vertical issues arising from situations other than those involving restrictive agreements. For instance, in 1996, the Director General being concerned that certain vertically integrated groups in the foreign package industry might be in a position to promote the groups' own holidays at the expense of those of non-integrated groups, referred to the Commission certain monopoly situations. The Commission

found that while certain practices were against the public interest, the current levels of concentration in the tour operator and travel agent markets meant that the integration had only slightly anti-competitive effect, and that there were not '...sufficient grounds for condemning vertical integration as a whole in the travel trade'. (*Foreign Package Holidays*, Cm 3813 1997, para. 1.10).

And rather more recently, the Commission was asked by the Director General to investigate certain discriminatory conduct believed to have been pursued by Birds Eye Wall's (BEW) in the course of the distribution of wrapped ice cream. It appeared that BEW (who supplied about 70 per cent of wrapped ice cream in the UK) supplied their dedicated distributors on more favourable terms than other wholesalers, and granted discounts to retailers solely on ice cream purchased from the dedicated distributors. Amongst the conclusions reached by the Commission were that the conduct had restricted competition between wholesalers, further, that given the dependence of other suppliers on wholesalers, it had distorted competition between manufacturers, and, yet further, that competition at retail level had in consequence been reduced. With no offsetting benefit to the public, the Commission believed that the reduction in competition operated against the public interest, and recommended that the discrimination should cease (*Birds Eye Wall's Ltd.* Cm 3971 1998). Undertakings were given by *Birds Eye Wall's* to the Secretary of State.

22. See 'A prohibition approach to anti-competitive agreements and abuse of dominant position: draft Bill', August 1997 DTI, para. 3.8.
23. *Ibid.*
24. *Ibid.* Of relevance here is a study commissioned by the Office of Fair Trading into vertical restraints, one of the aims being to identify the conditions in which '...detrimental effects are likely to dominate benign social welfare effects, and *vice versa*...'. The view was reached that the possession of market power at either or both manufacturing and retailing levels was '...a necessary condition for vertical restraints to have a public policy significance' ('Vertical Restraints and Competition Policy', Dobson & Waterson, Research Paper 12, Office of Fair Trading, 1996).
25. The (draft) Vertical Agreements (Competition Act 1998) (Exclusion) Order.
26. 'Competition Act 1998, Exclusion of Vertical Agreements' (DTI, 1999).
27. – or in respect of the marketing of services.
28. 'Green Paper on Vertical Restraints in EC Competition Policy', [1997] 4 CMLR 519.
29. *Ibid.* p. *i*. The existing European law and policy on vertical restraints is enormous in scope and complexity. Its *basic* components are as follows:–

(i) *Exclusive distribution*:– Since the classic case of *Consten and Grundig v Commission* [1966] ECR 299, [1966] CMLR 418, it has been clear that exclusive distribution agreements can be caught by Article 85(1) of the Treaty of Rome. If such an agreement is drawn so as to comply with Regulation 1983/83 it will benefit from the 'bloc' exemption which that

Regulation imports, but if it falls outside the Regulation then an individual exemption under Article 85(3) will have to be sought. Were the agreement to contain export bans or resale price maintenance conditions then, it is thought, that other than in the most exceptional circumstances, it would be denied any such individual escape.

(ii) *Exclusive purchasing*:– Exclusive purchasing agreements are likewise susceptible of being caught by Article 85(1). If they are appropriately drawn they may shelter under the umbrella of the 'bloc' exemption bestowed by Regulation 1984/83, but again, if an agreement should fall outside the provisions of this Regulation, it would have to be vetted for an exemption on an individual basis.

(iii) *Franchising*:– The leading case of *Pronuptia de Paris GmbH v Pronuptia de Paris Irmgard Schillgalis* [1986] ECR 353, [1986] 1 CMLR 414 made it plain that while restrictions in a franchising agreement designed to impose common standards and protect the franchisor's intellectual property rights did not come within Article 85(1) at all, restrictions involving territorial division or resale price maintenance would be caught thereby. There followed on this decision a series of cases, all of which led in due course to the provision, by Regulation, of another 'bloc exemption'. If an agreement falls within the terms of this Regulation (4087/88), then, once again, it gains protection.

(iv) *Selective distribution*:– The principles governing selective distribution systems basically emanate from case-law and administrative practice. The position is complex, but at its centre is the leading case of *Metro v Commission* (1) [1977] ECR 1875, [1978] 2 CMLR 44, from which it emerges that it is possible to pursue such a system without infringing Article 85(1) at all. According to the European Court of Justice such systems accord with Article 85(1) '...provided that resellers are chosen on the basis of objective criteria of a qualitative nature...and such conditions are laid down uniformly...and not applied in a discriminatory fashion'. To fall within the so called 'Metro doctrine', the goods have to be such as to make it legitimate for them to be re-sold only through restricted outlets, and the criteria used for limiting the resale outlets should be both 'qualitative' and applied non discriminatorily. If a system has features which cause it to fail to meet the 'Metro doctrine' (perhaps because of the extent of the burdens placed on resellers or a limit on the number of approved dealers) then it will be caught by Article 85(1), and exemption for it will need to be sought under Article 85(3).

30. – changes including '...concentration, reduction in numbers of traditional wholesalers, transformations in the retail sector and a tendency towards diversification and internationalisation' (See p. 13).
31. – with products 'pulled' rather than 'pushed' through the distribution system.
32. Under such systems, certainty and efficiency of supply is more important than the benefits accruing from engagement in parallel trade.

33. The Green Paper, p. *iii*, and pp. 13-16.
34. *Ibid.* p. *iii*.
35. *Ibid.*
36. *Ibid.* p. *iv*.
37. *Ibid.*
38. *Ibid*, see p. *ix*.
39. *Ibid.*
40. *Ibid.* p. *xi*.
41. 'Communication on the application of the Community competition rules to vertical restraints', OJ 1998 C 365/3 [1999] 4 CMLR 281.
42. – *i.e.* taking a 'black clause' rather than a 'white clause' approach.
43. Certain combinations of restraint are also conceived as 'hard-core'.
44. In material contained in information entitled 'Council gives green light for reform of the EU competition rules applicable to vertical restraints' [DN: 1P/99/286, (7th May 1999)] it was explained that the Commission would pursue a consultation process based on a market share threshold of 30 per cent.
45. It may be noted that agreements falling in 'bloc' exemptions do not have to be notified to qualify for exemption.
46. See Regulation 1216/99 – replacing the relevant provision in Regulation 17.
47. For a succinct explanation of the way in which the revolution in information technology has changed the entire character of the supply chain, see the Green Paper on Vertical Restraints at pp. 12-13.
48. See Office of Fair Trading Press Release No 33/98 (30th July 1998).
49. See Office of Fair Trading Press Release No PN 11/99 (8th April 1999).
50. Because it can be displayed in many forms. See 'Buying power - the exercise of market power by dominant buyers', Report of the Committee of Experts on Restrictive Business Practices, OECD, Paris 1981.

    The many possible practices through which buying power can find expression include the formal inducement of price discrimination, the taking of unreasonably extended credit, requests for some measure of exclusivity or 'tying', and requests for refusals to supply competitors selling below cost. Further, its exercise may be supported by 'de-listing', a practice involving the withdrawing from a distributor's shelves of the products of a supplier who fails to meet the distributor's terms.
51. – Dobson, Waterson & Chu (Office of Fair Trading, September 1998).
52. *Ibid.* para. 1.5.
53. *Ibid.* para. 7.6. The authors dealt at some length with the kind of *scenario* in which the powerful firm's negotiation of powerful discounts enables it to act in a predatory fashion when re-selling, thereby force small competitors to withdraw, gain market share, and, in consequence, reinforce both its power and competitive advantage. 'For the dominant retailer this can represent a virtuous circle…' of spiralling cost and market share advantage. 'But for suppliers and other retailers, they are equivalently caught in a vicious circle.' Suppliers are forced to give even greater discounts, and the viability of

competing retailers is undermined. It was concluded that the '...overall effect...on consumers is not certain, but they may ultimately lose out through reduced choice...as well as increased prices...'.

54. *Ibid.* para. 1.5.
55. – suggesting that retailers were '...increasingly able to retain the benefits from their increased buying power' (see para. 8.6).
56. (1997) OJ L 110/53.
57. The development of private brands was likewise perceived as a 'key element' in the growth of retailer power.
58. [1997] ECLR 75.
59. *Ibid.* at p. 77.
60. [1997] ECLR 492.
61. [1998] ECLR 4.
62. *Ibid.*
63. He pointed out that efforts by certain countries (*e.g.* as in Article 8 of the French *Ordonnance* of December 1st, 1986) to overcome the 'drawbacks' of competition law with measures to cope with abuses of economic dependence had run into difficulties.
64. [1998] ECLR 4.
65. *Ibid.* p. 5.
66. *Ibid.* p. 9.
67. [1997] OJ L 110/57.
68. 'The Retail Sector and Application of Antitrust Rules' [1997] 8 ECLR 492 at p. 495.
69. *Ibid.*
70. *Ibid.*
71. [1998] ECLR 473.
72. 'The regulation of networks can be defined as ...the legal rules...aimed at encouraging competition in activities in which having a network, which is of prime importance in order to have the link with users, is considered as such an important advantage and so dangerous for the balance of the economy, that it justifies compliance with specific rules' (*Ibid.* p. 474).
73. *Ibid.* p. 473.
74. See 'The Welfare Consequences of The Exercise of Buying Power', Dobson, Waterson & Chu (Office of Fair Trading 1998, para. 8.4).
75. [1997] ECLR 492.
76. *Ibid.*
77. (1997) OJ L 110/53.
78. Under Article 22.
79. See further 'The Lessons of the Kesko/Tuko Decision', Michael B. Hutchings, [1997] 2 ECLR 75.
80. HC 311 (1981) paras. 9.34-35.
81. *Silhouette International Schmied GmbH & Co. KG v Hartlauer Handelgesellschaft mbH* Case C-355/96, [1998] 2 CMLR 953.
82. 89/104/EEC of 21st December 1988 (OJ 1989 L 40, p. 1), Article 7.

83. 'Shades of Grey', *The Grocer*, 20th June 1998.
84. The following is a slightly fuller account of the case:– Silhouette International produced high quality, fashion spectacles in the higher price band, distributing them under the 'Silhouette' trademark, which was registered in Austria and elsewhere. In Austria, the company supplied its spectacles to specialist opticians, and the defendants, Hartlauer, who sold spectacles across Austria at low prices, were unable directly to obtain Silhouette's product. However, the latter company sold certain outdated models to a firm called Union Trading, with the intention that they be resold only in Bulgaria and the former Soviet Union, and while it was not clear exactly from whom, Hartlauer was able to purchase and import them into Austria. Silhouette objected to their resale in Austria by the defendants under the trademark.

    Under the principles of EC law, (to which effect is given by Article 7 of the Trade Marks Directive) if trade marked goods are sold in the Community by the owner of the mark (or with his consent) his trade mark rights are said to be 'exhausted'. This, the so called 'exhaustion principle' (which has been extended from the Community to include the European Economic Area), has the result that, other than exceptionally, if anywhere in the relevant area others use the mark in later dealings in these goods, the trade mark owner cannot oppose that use. In the particular circumstances though, Silhouette sought an order prohibiting Hartlauer from re-selling the spectacles under its trademark arguing that under the Directive their rights were exhausted only if the goods had been put on the market by them (or with their consent) in the European Economic Area, and that in this case the goods had first been marketed outside that area. Accordingly, Hartlauer contended, their rights remained and merited protection.

    One of two questions raised for European law by the Austrian Court was whether or not member States were permitted (or indeed required) by the Directive to provide for the exhaustion principle to apply not simply when goods had first been put on the market in the European Economic Area, but also where that had happened in a third country, *i.e.* to provide for a principle of international exhaustion.

    Advocate General Jacobs so construed the Directive that not only did it impose no obligation upon member States to provide in their law for the principle of international exhaustion, but, on the contrary, it precluded them from so doing, with the consequence that the rights of Silhouette were not exhausted, and the company could indeed ask for an order prohibiting Hartlauer from reselling their spectacles under its trade mark. A few months later, the judgement of the European Court of Justice was to similar effect, clearly stating that the national rules providing for the principle of international exhaustion are *contrary* to Article 7 of the relevant Directive. (See, on a related point: *Sebago Inc. and Another v GB-Unic SA* Case C-173/98, *The Times*, 7th July 1999.)

A postscript
~ in the 'millennium spirit'

Always on the move, our subject does not lend itself to any neat ending. Indeed, the last chapter alone raised issues and questions destined to beset competition policy for years to come. It was nevertheless thought appropriate to reflect briefly upon certain leading aspects of our major themes, doing so in the fashionable 'millennium spirit' of looking forward.

Although the passage of the Competition Bill attracted attention, for much of the time of writing this book the spotlight tended to be on the planning rather than the competition component. The great 'in or out of centre' debate rolled ever onwards, the associated, equally controversial, problem of 'food deserts' gained higher profile, and planning stayed firmly in the public eye. With the reference of superstores to the Competition Commission, however, the inter-related impact of the two régimes gained express recognition. Voicing a concern that prices might often simply be set to match those of competitors, the Director General explained that the need to ensure the existence of effective competition was made more imperative on account of the significant barriers to entry posed by the planning system.[1]

This overt acknowledgement of the joint relevance of the two régimes brought in its train questions which are fundamental in our context. First, is planning law capable of controlling a situation which has already spread so far? Here it is apt to note that in early 1999 the strength of the desire to sustain town centre viability was made plain. In a written answer, Planning Minister Richard Caborn sought to clarify the national planning guidance in PPG 6[2] by explaining that, in the sphere of new retail and leisure development, the establishment of need and the adoption of the sequential test should not only be taken into account at the plan preparation stage, but also in the handling of edge of centre and out of centre proposals which are not in accordance with an up-to-date development plan strategy.[3]

Such evident commitment aside, the next question is whether planning law should be expected to contain the situation? Necessarily, the planning régime has its inherent limitations as, likewise, does the competition régime,[4] and it is submitted that while the objectives and grasp of each remain separate and distinct, the resolution of the multi-faceted superstore issue lies beyond the reach of them both. Indeed, the point could not have been more succinctly put than by Tim Lang when he expressed himself unhopeful that the Commission, '...with its formal competition criteria, [would] be able to address the real social, environmental and health impact of the sector which is the real problem for consumers'.[5]

This allusion to the pivotal problem of fragmentation would have provided an appropriate note on which to draw to a close, were it not for the capacity of the retail sector ever to spring surprises – this time of course in the shape of the bid for Asda by the vast, American 'Wal-Mart'. While the offer made by this US giant[6] for the Leeds based chain was viewed by some in the dramatic light of the sector never being the same again, even when shorn of the accompanying excitement, it is apparent that such a move could well bring about fundamental changes in the UK's retail landscape. On the central issues of pricing and competition the Press opined that an arrival of this kind could have more impact than the investigation by the Competition Commission. 'Legislation', it was pointed out, was 'hardly a free-market solution, whereas Wal-Mart would instead apply the whip of competition'.[7]

With the visions of possible price wars there came also prophecies of consequential mergers (even to the extent of a 'rash of merger activity across Europe').[8] Indeed, a rich assortment of possible marriage ventures, both national and international, were mulled over. And in this context, it is interesting to note the observation made by *The Times* City Editor earlier in the year that the Competition Commission would '...almost certainly put a stop to any further strengthening of the big four by mergers...' and that this would '...open the way for foreign owned grocers to bid'.[9]

Again, alongside the pure 'competition' issues, the media referred to a perceived possibility that, given the Government's desire for lower prices, part of a welcoming hand to Wal-Mart could be a willingness generally to loosen the constraints on retailing imposed by the planning system.[10] Within a few days, however, any such notion was rejected, the Planning Minister making it clear that there was a firm commitment to the protection of town centres.[11]

The issues we have raised in truth go far beyond the bounds of planning and retail competition policy: they relate to the entire future of urban policy in this country. This issue was highlighted by the issue in June 1999 of the report of The Urban Task Force set up under Lord Rogers of Riverside[12] with the objective of improving the quality of life in English towns and cities while at the same time protecting the countryside against development. Though the issues raised by the report go far beyond the remit of our studies, it is interesting to note how many of the themes touched on relate to matters we have considered. The key proposals are that first of all there is a need to create sustainable towns and cities, followed by a commitment to making those urban areas work, particularly by the development of Urban Priority Areas where special regeneration measures will apply. This must be reinforced by making development of 'brownfield' sites more attractive than building on 'greenfield' land, and a priority must be to ensure that the planning system operates strategically and flexibly in securing urban regeneration working in partnership with local people. In addition there must be a commitment of sufficient public funds to bring about 'leverage' of private investment into regeneration projects. Once established this policy needs to be sustained as a political priority over a 25 year period.

Clearly the report is concerned with a whole range of matters from land for house building through to securing new urban transport initiatives, and the reduction of through traffic in towns and cities, all with the object of making them attractive and sustainable places to live. But that is what much of this book has been about also, and one of our themes has been that central retail regeneration depends rather less than might be supposed on restriction of off-centre development and rather more on the revivification of our towns and cities generally. There has been for a generation or more a circular process, most apparent in older industrial areas, of inner area decline matched by the outward movement of economic activities. This we have considered from the point of view of retailing, but parallel studies could have been made of manufacturing, distribution, and residential development. In one sense none of this is new for the traditional pattern of English urban development has been ever outwards, and fear of this was known in the 19th as well as in the early part of the 20th centuries. However, the scale of that process and the economic and social forces behind it, have, we believe, notably increased in magnitude of late, while at the same time there has been a growing realisation that in a small, overcrowded and already overdeveloped island this change is unsustainable.

If our existing urban areas are to be renewed an approach along the lines of the Rogers report seems inescapably necessary. It is not enough to rely on simply negative or restrictive legal controls, an almost revolutionary change in thinking must commence bringing together planning, competition, social, transport, and, most important of all, fiscal policies. To that extent it is true to say that it is the Treasury that holds the power to determine whether the Rogers report will lead anywhere. Taxation policy needs to be biased in favour of regeneration and against out of town development, though the working out of that change in detail lies beyond the compass of this work: it is enough, however, to state the principle here. One detailed point we would make is this. It is a false assumption to believe that relaxing planning controls will bring about an urban renewal by opening up a new range of choice for people *via* less restricted competition. The lesson we have sought to demonstrate in this book is that it was relaxing planning rules in favour of retail development in the '80s that has led to many of our current problems. Simply to have a virtual 'let it rip' policy on retail development will not revive urban areas, there must be both controls and incentives to channel development back into existing areas, and that development must not be solely of shopping outlets, but also of forms of housing which are attractive to a whole range of people built in styles that consume much less land than we have grown accustomed to of late, and this must be coupled with job creation not just in service industries, and the provision of high quality educational and leisure and health facilities.

Such a radical rethinking of urban policy, indeed land policy generally, must encompass both the public and private sectors, for nothing less would appear to be able to bring about renewal, and indeed such has been the approach adopted in other nations from whom we can learn much. This vision of renewal was briefly alluded to earlier in this book where it was argued that our towns and cities cannot be revived, rather they need to be re-invented.

Retail policy as an application of both competition and planning policy is but one strand in overall urban and social policy. However, we hope we have shown that the weakness of that policy, particularly over the last 25 years, has done much to foster a spirit of division in the nation between a clear majority who have been able to participate in new forms of retailing, and a sizeable minority who have not. A philosophy of social inclusiveness can tolerate that no more than a philosophy of sustainable development can tolerate the constant encroachment of new building on virgin sites while older sites are simply left untouched, derelict and underused. We believe that there is a growing acceptance of those points of view across all sectors of society, but we do not underestimate the gulfs which lie between the various schools of thought as to how best to solve the problems. But surely policy on retailing must be a core component of any effective urban renewal policy.

So, to conclude...while we have sought to draw out matters which might perhaps influence the road ahead, we acknowledge that, in the end, it remains an unknown pathway. It is one which we see strewn with the meeting of challenges, the fighting of battles, the dashing of hopes, and then, the dreaming of new dreams. In these perhaps lie the only real certainties – and it is on these certainties that retailing and the law can truly meet.

Notes

1. In the course of making the reference Mr Bridgeman observed that '...sites for new stores [were] dwindling and this [gave] the existing stores an advantage. Planning delays, site development costs and the ability of the largest stores to outbid smaller rivals add to the problem. This should not be seen as criticism of planning policy – it is simply to state the fact that there are significant barriers to entry...' (OFT Press Release PN 11/99, 8th April, 1998).
2. Planning Policy Guidance Note 6: Town Centres and Retail Development.
3. 11th February 1999. The advice adds that consideration of need and the sequential test should equally apply to extensions to edge of centre and out of centre retail and leisure developments.
4. Note, for instance, the Office of Fair Trading report on *Competition in the Supply of Petrol in the UK* (May 1998) in which, when addressing concerns that the loss of independent retailers could lead to areas with too sparse a coverage of outlets, the point was made that this was '...not a concern which competition legislation can address'. Desirous, however, of achieving a 'level playing field', the Office adverted to the pursuit of the question of adjusting the rating régime so that it became proportionate to turnover in the supply of petrol. (Explorations of the changing structure of the market, the possibility of anti-competitive behaviour and impact upon the public, led to findings by the Office of intense competition, no evidence of predatory, collusive or exclusionary behaviour, benefit to consumers, and no need for intervention.)
5. – being quoted in 'Planning to be at the heart of MMC investigation', *The Grocer*, 3rd April 1999.
6. Hailed as the 'biggest retailer in the world', Wal-Mart sells an enormous range of merchandise from clothing to cosmetics, and food to household goods. According to *The Times* on 15th June 1999, from its stores across America (the largest of which covers some 200,000 sq.ft) it achieves sales the equivalent of about a tenth of Britain's economic output. As earlier noted, the European Commission gave the concentration the 'green light' in July 1999, being of the view that the operation did not raise competition concerns. (See IP/99/561, Brussels 26th July 1999, 'Commission clears the merger between Wal-Mart (USA) and ASDA (UK)'.)
7. *The Times*, 15th June 1999. For the pricing (and other) changes apparently wrought following the purchase by Wal-Mart of hypermarkets in Germany see *The Grocer*, 19th June 1999.
8. *The Grocer*, 19th June 1999.
9. *The Times*, 26th March 1999. Writing on the Wal-Mart takeover in *The Sunday Times*, 25th July 1999, Dominic Rushe pointed out that other foreign retailers were '...thought to be hovering in the wings'. (See 'Store Wars'.)

10. *The Guardian*, 16th June 1999, was moved to observe that the '...government [was] expected to relax planning constraints to allow a wave of new hypermarkets to be built in the wake of this week's takeover...', and that such a reversal would be '...justified by lower prices...', with, furthermore, the savings outweighing environmental concerns.
11. *The Times*, 25th June 1999, reporting on advice given by the Planning Minister to the Commons.
12. 'Towards an Urban Renaissance' (the Rogers report), published by the Department of the Environment, Transport and the Regions, London 1999. (It is not only urban policy which is a current issue. The latest report from the National Federation of Women's Institutes shows that villages are suffering from the closure of shops as they cannot compete with the supermarkets. See 'Villages dying as shops and services close', *The Times*, 5th July 1999.)

Index

For Product Safety Concerns and Information please contact our EU representative GPSR@taylorandfrancis.com Taylor & Francis Verlag GmbH, Kaufingerstraße 24, 80331 München, Germany

Batch number: 10725991

Printed by Printforce, the Netherlands